D1710747

North Dakota's
Indian Heritage

Mary Jane Schneider

NORTH DAKOTA CENTENNIAL HERITAGE SERIES

The University of North Dakota Press
Grand Forks, North Dakota

North Dakota's Indian Heritage / Mary Jane
Schneider. -- Grand Forks, N.D.: University of
North Dakota Press.
(North Dakota Centennial Heritage Series)
Includes bibliography and index.

Photograph credits:

NDSHD -- North Dakota State Highway Department and North Dakota State Historical
Society.

UND -- Special Collections, Chester Fritz Library,
University of North Dakota, Robinson Collection.

AMNH -- Anthropology Papers of the American Museum of Natural History, 1907.

SHSND -- State Historical Society of North
Dakota.

CM -- Carnegie Museum of Man, Pittsburgh,
Pennsylvania.

ARBAE -- Annual Report of the Bureau of
American Ethnology. 1886, 1890.

SD -- W. H. Over Museum, State Historical
Society of South Dakota.

HM -- Harpers New Monthly Magazine, 1859,
1860.

NDH -- North Dakota History, 1908.

MA -- Marquette Archives, Marquette University, Milwaukee, Wisconsin.

TM -- Stella Davis and Irene Fox Davis, Turtle
Mountain Chippewa Historians.

BBAE -- Bureau of American Ethnology Bulletin 198

Copyright © 1990
Mary Jane Schneider
Library of Congress Catalog Card
Number 90-071221
ISBN 0-9608700-6-7

First Printing

Production Notes: Page layout, editing and design on IBM
PS/2 Model 70 (386) personal computer, utilizing Aldus
PageMaker 3.01 run on Microsoft Windows version 3.0. Final
output @ 1200 dpi obtained through Southern California
Printcorp, Pasadena. Printed by Friesen Printers, Altona,
Manitoba, Canada. Production coordinated by the University
of North Dakota Office of University Advancement, Grand
Forks, N.D., Randy Omdahl, designer. Typefaces used:
Palatino, Times Roman.

Contents

Acknowledgments

A Note on the North Dakota Centennial Heritage Series

Chapter 1
Past and Present: Images and Realities 1

Chapter 2
Where Did They Come From? 11

Chapter 3
Indian Life Before the Reservations 24

Chapter 4
International Relations: Indians and Hat-Wearers 47

Chapter 5
Fort Berthold Reservation 66

Chapter 6
Fort Totten Reservation 86

Chapter 7
Standing Rock Reservation 104

Chapter 8
Turtle Mountain Reservation 122

Chapter 9
A Long and Difficult Path 141

References Cited 145

Index 152

Acknowledgments

Many people have contributed in many ways to this book, which was born in the minds of a committee organized by Dr. James Davis. The committee wrote a grant proposal to the North Dakota Humanities Council for support of a book on North Dakota Indian history that would be a centennial project. Shortly after I began work on the book, Dennis Blue replaced Dr. Davis in the Department of Public Instruction. The first committee I met with included Terry Yellow Fat, Alma Wilkie, Bennet Yellow Bird, Myrna Demarce, and Jack Barden. Many people, when they learned I was working on the book, volunteered information, answered my questions, and reviewed parts of the manuscript. Others such as Dorothy Lentz, Theresa Martin, Irene Thomas Davis, Carol Davis, Leslie LaFountain, Viola Champagne, Bob Gipp, and an anonymous group of educators from Standing Rock, read large portions of the manuscript and gave me specific comments. I am grateful to all of these people for their help.

A Note on the North Dakota Centennial Heritage Series

Ten years before the celebration of North Dakota's centennial in 1989, the North Dakota Humanities Council, an affiliate of the National Endowment for the Humanities, established and funded the North Dakota Centennial Heritage Series to celebrate the centennial in a series of books about the state's culture and history. The first volume, *The North Dakota Political Tradition*, appeared in 1981 and *Plains Folk: North Dakota's Ethnic History* was published in 1986. In 1990 *Dakota: The Literary Heritage of the Northern Prairie State* and this volume, *North Dakota's Indian Heritage*, complete the series. Funding for this book came from the North Dakota Humanities Council, the University of North Dakota, and the North Dakota Centennial Commission which earmarked it as a centennial project for the Centennial Bookshelf. The people of North Dakota thank these agencies for their generous support.

D. Jerome Tweton
Centennial Heritage Series Coordinator

Chapter 1

Past and Present: Images and Realities

Indians have always existed in two worlds: the world of reality and an imaginary world created by non-Indians. Once, when I was attending an Indian powwow in Oklahoma, I witnessed an event that plainly demonstrated this difference. A group of Boy Scouts who had been practicing Indian dances to demonstrate at an international scouting jamboree in Japan was asked to give a special presentation at the powwow. I was horrified and embarrassed to see the boys start to hop and skip and whoop in imitation of movie Indians. For a short time the audience hid laughs behind broad smiles and turned heads; then a hundred Indian dancers stepped out on the floor and showed the boys how real Indians dance. A few Boy Scouts caught on and tried to dance in the proper style, but most did not. I never found out if the Boy Scouts changed their demonstration before they got to the jamboree, but I am fairly certain they did not, because even after 500 years of contact, Euro-Americans still believe in images that are as obviously wrong as the Boy Scouts' dance steps.

American Indians have caught people's imaginations more vividly and with greater strength than any other ethnic group, but most people have little factual knowledge of Indian culture and history and know even less about contemporary Native Americans. Wild West shows, romantic western novels, and Hollywood movies have created an American Indian image and sent it into the farthest corners of the world. No doubt the people who attended the scouting jamboree in Japan immediately recognized the Oklahoma Boy Scouts' Hollywood-style Indian dance. We may, like writer and educator Michael Dorris (Dorris 1987:98), be amazed to find stuffed toy monkeys wearing Sioux- style war bonnets and brandishing tomahawks in a souvenir shop in the remote Pacific island capital of Avarua, but we and the Cook Islanders have no difficulty recognizing the toys as Indians. Braids, beads, canoes, tipis, and totem poles, other components of the image, also bring instant recognition and have become so standardized that many Native Americans have found it neces-

Indian images used in advertising maintain stereotypes from earlier times.

sary to adopt one or more of these symbols in order to indicate their Indian identity.

The Hollywood image of the American Indian is so convincing that people act on the image. Like the Boy Scouts, many others, with their juxtaposition of the real with the image, have produced some grotesque situations. For example, during the casting of the television series, *Centennial*, Native American actresses were rejected for leading roles because "they didn't look Indian enough."

In addition to erroneous visual symbols of Indian identity, we have also been given a false idea of American Indian history. In order to tell a good story, writers have often depicted Indians either as murderous savages treacherously betraying Whites or as saintly innocents risking their lives to save Whites. The story of Pocahontas saving John Smith's life is a classic example of the "good Indian" approach and, because the story did not appear in Smith's books until after Pocahontas married John Rolfe and went to live in London, may be the first case of media hype. Under pressure from Native Americans the "savage" image has disappeared from television, but the "noble" Indian has been remodeled in the current television theme of Native American heroes risking their lives to save the environment or ancestral burial grounds from destruction by corrupt businessmen. The facts of Indian history and contemporary Indian culture have not been as attractive to screenwriters as the stereotypes.

The images are so compelling and the truth so complex that writers of our history books have been unable or unwilling to challenge the stereotypes. During the 1930's and 1940's, when movies were increasing in popularity, history textbooks were giving less and less attention to Indians until, by the 1950's, many American history textbooks made no mention of Indians at all (Fitzgerald 1979:92-93). The agitation for civil rights in the 1960's was eventually reflected in greater attention to minority history and culture, but American Indians were

In the late 1800's popular books like "Wild Life on the Plains and the Horrors of Indian Warfare" depicted Indians as murderous savages.

▼ Contemporary popular novels still tend to portray Indians as warlike.

still generalized as former inhabitants who had a minor role in early American history and then disappeared under the onslaught of disease and White culture. Totally lacking in these histories is any sense of Native American participation in the local, national, and international events of their day.

Although we might justify the inadequate treatment of Indians and other minorities in textbooks devoted to national issues by pointing out the difficulty of dealing specifically with so many different nations and peoples, we also find similar trends in state and local histories. The classic *History of North Dakota* by Elwyn B. Robinson (Robinson 1966) includes Indians as important elements in the early history of the state, but they gradually disappear as more and more White settlers move in. Robinson does mention the Standing Rock Sioux' participation in World War I but neglects to mention that the other tribes also sent men, bought Liberty bonds, and planted war gardens. Nor does he mention tribal participation in World War II or the Korean Conflict. Local centennial histories usually discuss the prehistory of the area, but make few additional references to Indian history. Recent local centennial celebrations usually ignored the Indian presence and began with "the first settlers."

If histories do not deal adequately with American Indians, can we look to other sources for information? Unfortunately the answer is no. Neither television news programs nor national news magazines provide much coverage of American Indians and, when they do, their producers are sometimes deceived by the stereotypes. Not too long ago, television news heralded a young man dressed in a war bonnet arriving in Israel for his bar mitzvah as an "hereditary chief of the Sioux." News magazines later reported that none of the Sioux tribes recognized the man as chief and pointed out that tribes no longer have such positions.

The truth is far more interesting and more complicated than movies, textbooks, or popular knowledge can tell. It is no understatement to say that our uniquely "American" culture comes not from our European forebears but from our Native American ancestors. Before European settlement, North America was inhabited by innumerable tribes and nations speaking distinct languages and living totally different life-styles, but sharing a similar conception of humans as integral parts of the natural world. The family was at the center of a series of concentric rings which related everyone to each other and to the plants and animals. Generally, all beings within these rings were equal to each other.

Like the American Indians, the European nations also varied in language and life-style but shared a common idea about man's place in the world. Based on an interpretation of Christian principles, human beings were part of a strictly organized, pyramidal social order. The king was God's representative on earth, and the class distinctions between rich and poor were part of God's plan. Some men were superior to others; all men were superior to women, and all humans were superior to animals and plants.

The story of how these two different perceptions met and influenced each other has usually been told from the point of view of the European colonists, yet there is another perspective. Although the European colonizers maintained some of their cultural beliefs, it was clear from the start that they would have to adapt to life on this continent and that the Indians were going to be their teachers. The Indians introduced the Europeans to new crops and new technologies. Corn and tobacco have been identified with Indian people by the advertising industry, but there were many other foods, maple sugar, cranberries, potatoes, tomatoes, beans, and avocados, that were unknown in Europe. Long pants, moccasins, parkas, canoes, kayaks, toboggans, and rubber balls were among Indian contributions to colonial technology.

One of the greatest contrasts was in social organization. The Europeans were overwhelmed by the discovery of people whose lives were not organized hierarchically. Some were unable to accept what they saw and described Indian cultures in European terms, and so the idea of Indian princesses and references to Indian kings crept into our mythology; others, however, studied the Indian concepts and reported them accurately to their European colleagues. Influenced by this new "anthropology," philosophers such as John Locke, Michel de Montaigne, and Jean Jacques Rousseau began to discuss ideas such as liberty, equality, and government by the people (Cohen 1952). One of the more dramatic results was Benjamin Franklin's use of the League of the Iroquois as a model for the 1754 Albany Plan of Union (Vogel 1972:48), the forerunner of the Articles of Confederation which held the Union together from 1781 to 1789.

One other "typically American" trait, team sports, can also be attributed to Indians. The

Many North Dakota businesses use Indian symbols to identify their products.

The North Dakota highway system uses the profile of Red Tomahawk, Standing Rock Sioux, to identify state road numbers.

Americans continue to enhance American life.

States, too, will find that much of their particular cultural identity can be traced to their first residents. Twenty-five state names are derived from Indian words, and most states have at least one city or natural landmark with an Indian name. More importantly, all the states, including Hawaii, have American Indian communities, but there may be little awareness of their presence. People who live on the east coast will travel all the way to the Dakotas or the Southwest to see Indian dances, even though there are similar powwows much closer to home.

Even states with recognizable Indian populations may fail to acknowledge the importance of Native Americans. In North Dakota city names such as Wahpeton, Mandan, and Devils Lake, and team names such as Redskins, Warriors, and Fighting Sioux may be intended as a tribute to Indian people, but names and symbols do not necessarily reflect an informed public. In fact, one could argue that if people were more knowledgeable about Indian history, there would be less use of stereotypical logos and derogatory depictions of North Dakota's tribal peoples.

Some idea of the magnitude of Indian contributions to North Dakota history and culture can be gained by trying to imagine North Dakota without any Indian influences: no names, no logos, no highway symbols, no trails, no forts, no powwows, no Sitting Bull, no Sacajawea, no Joseph Rolette, no Dakota flint corn, no Great Northern Bean, and significantly fewer parks, museums, books, artists, doctors, lawyers, architects, and educators. Without its Indian heritage, North Dakota would not be the same.

Not only has the Indian heritage resulted in a unique North Dakota culture, but the Indian history of North Dakota is different

athletic events of pre-Columbian Europe were usually individual contests that pitted men against one another, like archery contests or jousts, or against birds and animals, as in boar hunts. In America the newcomers found group or team sports such as lacrosse and shinny in which individuals acted as a unit and there was no individual winner.

The contributions of American Indians did not end with the adoption of the Declaration of Independence, with the establishment of reservations, or with the admission of New Mexico and Arizona, the forty-seventh and forty-eighth states, to the Union in 1910. There have been Indian Senators and Congressmen and an Indian Vice-President. In the years preceding the Second World War, refugee Surrealist artists Max Ernst, Kurt Seligmann, Echaurren Matta,

Yves Tanguy, and their friends became interested in Northwest Coast and other American Indian art. Ernst's interest eventually led him to spend several years in Sedona, Arizona, where he created works influenced by Southwestern art. Not so many years later, Jackson Pollock, traveling through the Southwest, watched Navajo sand painters drip colored sands through their fingers to create complex designs on the earth. Pollock later incorporated these and other ideas from American Indian artists into his innovative "drip" paintings and founded two new movements in American art: action and field painting. During World War II, Navajo men used their language to devise an unbreakable code for sending secret military information. The innumerable, usually unrecognized, contributions of Native

from that of any other state. From prehistoric times to the present the tribes developed lifestyles adapted to the particular environment of North Dakota. Many people are familiar with the history of the Sioux, more properly referred to as Lakota, in North Dakota, especially in relation to the military history of the state, but other Indians were equally important. On the Missouri River in western North Dakota, the Mandan and Hidatsa can be considered to be that region's oldest settlers. Along with the Arikara, these three tribes were important participants in the western fur trade. On the eastern front the Dakota and Yanktonai can claim to be the oldest residents, while the Chippewa were also vital contributors to the success of the eastern fur trade.

Each of these tribes, Arikara, Turtle Mountain Band of Chippewa, Hidatsa, Mandan, Dakota, Lakota, Yanktonai, and Yankton, spoke different languages and had different customs, ceremonies, and histories. These cultural differences provided opportunities for resource development that resulted in trade networks later utilized by Euro-Americans. Unfortunately, the differences also resulted in intertribal hostility that was sometimes exploited by fur traders and military men.

Another way in which North Dakota's history differs from other states is in the general lack of hostility between Indians and Whites. Despite the severe disruption of the tribal lifestyle by the presence of non-Indians, first by diseases such as smallpox, to which the Indians had no immunity, and then by reduction of hunting territory, the Indian tribes remained basically friendly to non-Indians. Sitting Bull and his followers may have publicly advocated killing all Whites, but in private they held

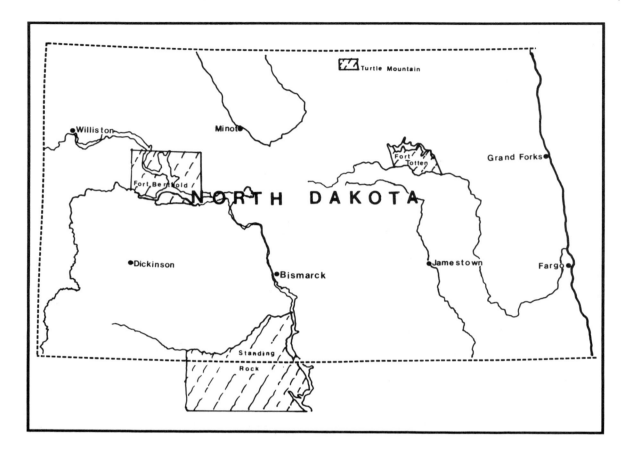

region around Devils Lake was recognized and they were allowed to remain in their traditional hunting territory which became part of the Fort Totten Reservation.

The history of Standing Rock Reservation is quite different from that of Fort Berthold and Fort Totten because Standing Rock was originally part of the Great Sioux Nation Reservation established by the Treaty of Fort Laramie in 1868. As a punishment for Sioux' participation in hostile activities, the Great Sioux Nation was broken up into six smaller reservations and members of various Lakota bands were forced onto these reservations. Today, Standing Rock is the home of descendants of many different Lakota bands, including Hunkpapa and Blackfeet, and some Yankton and Yanktonai.

Another method of creating reservations is illustrated by the history of the Turtle Mountain Reservation, which was established by an executive order signed by President Chester A. Arthur in 1882 after treaty making was officially ended by an act of Congress. The Turtle Mountain people are descended from Algonquian speaking Chippewa and Cree ancestors, some of whom married French, British, and Scottish immigrants and created a new culture and language, Métis or Michif.

The manner of establishing the reservations is significant because the treaties obligated the federal government to protect the rights of and to provide services to the tribes included in the treaties. These treaty agreements varied according to the relationship between the signatory tribes and the government. Tribes perceived by treaty makers as hostile were treated differently, often more generously, than tribes whose reservations were created to protect tribal claims. When the obligations defined in the treaties were not

strong friendships with many non-Indians (Miller 1965; Heski 1978). The so-called Indian "wars" that were fought in North Dakota were never the result of hostility by local tribes but were always begun in other areas, and the Whites who were killed by Indians were more often victims of inter-tribal feuding-style warfare than of open hostility toward Whites; such warfare can also be partially attributed to changes in territory caused by non-Indians moving westward.

Even the reservations in the state have different histories of establishment. A study of North Dakota's reservation history is a mini-history of United States federal Indian policy because each of the reservations was established at a different time, under different cir-

cumstances. Territory claimed by the Arikara, Mandan, and Hidatsa was first defined in the Treaty of Fort Laramie of 1851, but Fort Berthold Reservation was not established until 1870, following complaints from the three tribes about non-Indians using their land. Under pressure from non-Indians the reservation boundaries changed from time to time, but until the mid-1880's the Mandan, Hidatsa, and Arikara remained in their traditional earthlodge village of Like-a-Fishhook. A totally different situation resulted in the establishment of the Fort Totten Reservation in 1867 when Dakota from Minnesota who had not participated in the Dakota Conflict of 1862 sought a place to settle. At the same time, the claim of the Cuthead Band of Yanktonai to the

6

carried out properly, the tribes sued the government and won. Some of these suits, like the one involving the Black Hills, are still being negotiated. Because of the treaties, the federal government is still obligated to aid the tribes, and this support brings millions of dollars into North Dakota's economy. Indian people who work for the federal government spend their paychecks in North Dakota stores and pay taxes which help support state needs.

Even though they were established under different circumstances, the North Dakota reservations are similar in geography, economy, and recent history. Generally, because the reservations were originally created on land not highly desired by White settlers, they share some similarities of terrain and location. The four reservations are all located away from major urban areas. The Devils Lake Sioux Reservation is 90 miles west of Grand Forks.

Turtle Mountain Reservation is 150 miles from Grand Forks. Fort Berthold Reservation is 75 miles from Minot, and Standing Rock is 40 miles from Bismarck.

The more remote parts of these reservations are even farther from the cities mentioned above. The rural nature of these reservations has made it possible for Indian people to maintain their distinct cultures, but it has also meant lack of job opportunities. Indian people have found it necessary to travel to the urban areas for work, shopping, and medical and social opportunities. All four reservations have areas of great unspoiled beauty. Water resources are available on all the reservations, but these, too, can be considered a mixed blessing. For the Devils Lake Sioux, the Three Affiliated Tribes, and the Standing Rock Sioux the presence of significant bodies of water has resulted in legal disputes over water rights and uses, while the

number of lakes on the Turtle Mountain Reservation has reduced the amount of land available for other purposes.

The similar conditions found on reservations today depict all too clearly the impact of the federal government on tribal society. By the time most of the reservations in North Dakota were formalized, government control was well established, and decisions made in Washington, D.C., were carried out by agents appointed by the Secretary of the Interior. The orientation of the administration was to "civilize" the Indians by teaching them to farm, to live in houses, to wear White-style clothing, and to become Christian. In order to attain these goals, the agents prohibited many traditional activities, even those relating to hunting and religion. Traditional communities were disbanded and the inhabitants scattered on farmsteads. Children were forced to attend

The horse and tipi have given way to the pick-up and camper.

schools where they were taught English, vocational and domestic skills, and Christian beliefs. Modern scholars are still seeking to understand how different tribes adapted to these pressures to change. The apparent success of federal policies for assimilation is primarily on the surface and Indian customs, beliefs, and identity have survived.

Today's Indian people may choose to identify themselves in various ways. Many non-Indians have become accustomed to using the term Native American to refer to Indian people. Native American was suggested by Indian people who were searching for a term that would avoid some of the negative and stereotpical images associated with the word Indian, but it is not generally used by Indians to refer to themselves. One reason that Native American is not more widely used is that it is more inclusive than Indian. The federal government now includes Native Hawaiians as well as Eskimos and Aleuts in its definition of Native

Americans. Another reason is that most people are used to thinking of themselves as Indian, not as Native American. Tribal identities are still the most important. For a while scholars thought that tribal identities would merge into an Indian identity and then gradually disappear, but today this shows little sign of occurring. Even when a person's identity is traced to three or four tribes, he or she will include all of them. Recent federal policies have encouraged strong tribes and, as more and more Indian people return to their roots, there is a renewed interest in tribal traditions and histories.

North Dakota Reservations and Populations Today

People who closely study a North Dakota road map may note five reservations marked on the map, Fort Berthold, Standing Rock, Fort Totten, Turtle Mountain, and Sisseton, but on the basis of the location of their administrative

centers, only four of these are considered to be North Dakota reservations. The Sisseton Reservation extends into southeastern North Dakota, but the administrative center is in South Dakota and so, despite close historical and tribal ties with the people on the Fort Totten Reservation, Sisseton Reservation is considered to be in South Dakota. Conversely, although the largest part of Standing Rock Reservation is in South Dakota, it is considered to be a North Dakota reservation because the administrative center is in North Dakota.

Although the slightly more than 20,000 Indian people counted in the 1980 federal census are only a small proportion of the total North Dakota population, Indian people living in cities and on reservations represent North Dakota's largest ethnic minority. These Indian people are primarily from the tribes that have reservations in the state, but members of many other tribes also live in North Dakota. Some of these Indians may be married to other Indians, or they have found work and other opportunities in North Dakota. The Indian people in North Dakota are sharing in a trend toward urbanization that is occurring in other states, too. Reservation populations are growing at a rapid rate, but employment opportunities are not, and so many Indian people, especially the better educated and more highly skilled, are moving to cities where there are better chances for jobs. These people maintain close ties to the reservations and may participate in reservation events even though they live and work elsewhere. All the cities in North Dakota have Indian populations, but, unlike the national scene, where more Indian people live in urban areas than on reservations, most of North Dakota's Indian people still live on or near a reservation.

Reservation populations vary considerably and are difficult to characterize statistically

The reconstructed earthlodges at On a Slant Village, near Mandan, are an important tourist attraction.

8

The United Tribes Technical Education Center in Bismarck, North Dakota holds one of the region's largest powwows.

▼ Our lives are enriched by the works of North Dakota Indian writers and artists. Louise Erdrich, Turtle Mountain Chippewa, is nationally acclaimed for her work.

because two different groups can be considered. One group consists of enrolled members of the tribe or tribes for whom the reservation was established. Not all members of the tribe live on the reservation and so the tribal membership must be distinguished from the reservation population. The second group, the reservation population, includes those Indians living on or near the reservation and Indians from other tribes who live on the reservation for various reasons. In 1985 the Three Affiliated Tribes of Fort Berthold Reservation, the Arikara, Mandan, and Hidatsa, had a tribal enrollment of 6,897 (North Dakota Indian Affairs Commission 1985). In 1980 the national census (U.S. Bureau of the Census 1983) counted 5,577 Indians living on the Fort Berthold Reservation. What percentage of these were enrolled members of the Three Affiliated Tribes was not determined.

At Fort Totten a different situation exists. The Devils Lake Sioux tribal enrollment was 3,144 in 1985 (North Dakota Indian Affairs Commission 1985), while the 1980 national census (U.S. Bureau of the Census 1983) showed 3,313 Indians living on the reservation. We know, however, that some of the people living at Fort Totten were enrolled members of the Turtle Mountain Band of Chippewa whose families were given allotments at Fort Totten because there was not enough land at Turtle Mountain.

Standing Rock is a large reservation which had an Indian population of almost 9,000 people in 1980 (U.S. Bureau of the Census 1983). The tribal membership in 1985 was 9,642 (North Dakota Indian Affairs Commission 1985). Like the other reservations, Standing Rock has residents who are enrolled in other tribes, and many of its enrolled members live off the

reservation.

Turtle Mountain Reservation presents a unique situation in North Dakota. The reservation is too small for the large tribal enrollment of over 22,000 (North Dakota Indian Affairs Commission 1985), and so most of the population lives off the reservation, many in other parts of North Dakota or in Montana. The national census taken in 1980 (U.S. Bureau of the Census 1983) listed the resident Indian population of Turtle Mountain as 4,311. The North Dakota Indian Affairs Commission, however, considered the figure to be more than 9,000 because people living near the reservation are considered to be part of the Indian population even though they do not physically reside within the boundaries of the reservation. One group of Turtle Mountain Chippewa lives at Fort Totten; another group lives in the Trenton-Williston area, and a third lives near Havre, Montana.

Because the Indian population of North Dakota is the state's largest ethnic minority, it may appear large to many people, but the fact is that fifteen other states have larger Indian populations, and twelve states have more reservations than North Dakota (U.S. Bureau of the Census 1985). California is the state with the largest Indian population, most of it located in Los Angeles and other cities. In the northern Plains, South Dakota has nine reservations and an Indian population twice the size of North Dakota's; however, unlike North Dakota's culturally diverse Native American population, most of the Indian residents of South Dakota are former members of the Seven Council Fires or Sioux Nation, that is, either Lakota, Dakota, Yankton, or Yanktonai, and speak dialects of the same language.

Although North Dakota's diversity may make it difficult for people to learn about the state's Indian cultures, the opportunities for understanding are also enhanced. For instance, the non-agricultural life-style of the Lakota and Turtle Mountain Band of Chippewa can be constrasted and compared with the agricultural culture of the Arikara, Mandan, and Hidatsa. The calamitous impact of federal policies such as allotment is demonstrated by the realization that eight very different tribal societies located on four separate reservations suffered similar land losses and community disruptions. In modern times, the presence of different tribal communities creates opportunities for developing historical sites and tourism. The Knife River Villages National Park focuses on Hidatsa tribal life and history, while Fort Totten, one of the last complete military-square forts in the country, is closely associated with the reservation history of the Devils Lake Sioux. The Three Affiliated Tribes and the Turtle Mountain Band of Chippewa have opened heritage centers that depict the unique histories of the reservations and their people.

But the impact of Indian people on North Dakota is not only in the past. Indian artists and writers are winning national acclaim and recognition for North Dakota, while at home, Indian educators, social workers, nurses, doctors, lawyers, journalists, architects, and other professionals add to the quality of life for all of us.

Chapter 2

Where Did They Come From?

Introduction

"Where did they come from?" may be the oldest and most often asked question about American Indians. Just as the earliest European explorers found answers in the Bible and believed the Indians were descendants of the sons of Noah or one of the Lost Tribes of Israel (Huddleston 1967), Indian people sought explanations for their origins, migrations, and development in their religious beliefs. Today, scientists search for the answer in early Indian artifacts and the remains of camps. Early explorers and modern scientists are in agreement that Indians originated outside North America and migrated to this continent. In contrast, most Indian people believe that they were either created here or that they were sent here from an underworld or from a sky-world.

Indian Origin Traditions

Indian origin traditions are part of extensive oral histories that include descriptions of ceremonies, sacred bundles, and supernatural events which have sometimes been kept from outsiders. But some of the first non-Indian visitors to the northern Plains made brief, written reports that indicate the antiquity and strength of these traditions. In the 1830's George Catlin, an artist, and Prince Maximilian of Wied-Neuwied, a German scholar, asked Mandan people about their origins and were told that some Mandan were made by the Creator as part of the creation of the region around the Missouri River, while other Mandan came from under the earth and traveled many years before reaching their relatives on the Missouri.

Catlin summarized his findings in the following statement:

> I am not yet able to learn from these people whether they have any distinct theory of creation; as they seem to date nothing further back than their own existence as a people; saying (as I have before mentioned) that they were the first people created. . . or that they were created inside of the earth, as their tradition says; and that they did not make their appearance on its outer surface until after the Deluge (Catlin 1973:179).

Maximilian received more complete information from Dipauch, a Mandan, who described how Lone Man and First Creator made the land on either side of the Missouri:

> The lord of life then desired the first man to make the north bank of the Missouri, while he himself made the south-west bank, which is beautifully diversified with hills, valleys, forests, and thickets. The man, on the contrary, made the whole country flat, with a good deal of wood in the distance. They then met again, and when the lord of life had seen the work of the first man, he shook his head and said, 'You have not done this well: all is level, so that it will be impossible to surprise buffaloes or deer, and approach them unperceived. Men will not be able to live there. They will see each other in the plain at too great a distance, and will be unable to avoid each other, consequently they will destroy each other.'
>
> He then took the first man to the other side of the river, and said, 'See here, I have made springs and streams in a sufficient abundance, and hills and valleys, and added all kinds of animals and fine wood; here men will be able to live by the chase, and feed on the flesh of those animals' (Wied-Neuwied 1906, vol. 23:306-307).

One hundred years after Catlin and Maximilian, Alfred Bowers (Bowers 1950:353-361) collected similar traditions from the Mandan, who explained in great detail how the two creators also made medicine pipes, tobacco, human beings, and ceremonies. These human beings were successful and grew so well that

Lone Man had himself born into the tribe as a supernatural child with great powers. These ancient Mandan and their sacred child had many unusual experiences. One was the imprisonment of all the animals by Hoita, an evil half-supernatural-half-human being. Another event was a great flood which threatened to drown all the Mandan, but First Man saved them by building a sacred willow fence around the village. These experiences and others were celebrated in the ceremony of the Okipa and commemorated by the sacred cedar, a wood structure built in the center of each Mandan village.

The other origin tradition recorded by Catlin and Maximilian maintained that the Mandan originally lived below ground near the sea. Even before Catlin and Maximilian, William Clark, one of the leaders of the Lewis and Clark expedition that explored the Northwest, reported that the Mandan nation

> first came out of the ground where they had a great village. a grape vine grew down through the Earth to their village and they Saw light Some of their people assended by the grape vine upon the earth, and saw Buffalow and every kind of animal also Grapes plumbs, &c. (Reid 1947-48:343).

The Mandan decided to leave the underworld and climbed upward on the vine, but when half the men, women, and children had reached the surface, an overweight woman broke the vine. No one else could climb up, and some Mandan were left in the underworld. Prince Maximilian (Wied-Neuwied 1906, vol.23:312- 326), Catlin (Catlin 1973:179-180), and Bowers (Bowers 1950:157- 157) continue the narrative. Under the leadership of Good Furred Robe, those on the earth traveled about

until they came to the Missouri, where they found the other Mandan living. Good Furred Robe and his brother and sister helped the Mandan for many years before dying in a sacred manner. Even today the Mandan can point to places where their sacred helpers performed ceremonies, fought supernatural evil-doers, and instructed the Mandan in the rules of life.

The origin traditions of the Hidatsa are much less clearly recorded than those of the Mandan because the Hidatsa lived in three or more separate villages that had different traditions recorded by different reporters. Another difficulty arises from the fact that the reporters frequently obtained their information by asking the Mandan about the traditions of the Hidatsa, and the stories of the two tribes did not always agree. In his attempt to clarify the origin traditions of the Hidatsa, William Clark observed that each of the three villages of the Hidatsa claimed that its members had always lived on the Missouri, while the Mandan and other Hidatsa claimed that one or more of the villages had come from the East to settle on the Missouri (Thwaites 1906, vol. 6:90-91; Reid 1947-48:78; Jackson 1962:524-525). When Clark asked Big White, a Mandan leader, where the Hidatsa had come from, he answered that the Menitarras (Hidatsa) had come out of the water to the east (Thwaites 1904, vol.5:348; Reid 1947-48:343).

Some of the differences in origin traditions may also be the result of the close relationship between the Mandan and Hidatsa which developed after the great smallpox epidemic of 1837. In 1834, Maximilian recorded that the Hidatsa were created by First Man, but a scant one hundred years later the tradition had been changed to include Lone Man as a co-creator and, possibly, the idea of an emergence from an underworld (Bowers 1965:297). The brief report by Maximilian included the statement, "When the Manitaries were created by the first man they formed one nation with the Crows" (Wied-Neuwied 1906, vol.23:375); but when Alfred Bowers interviewed the Hidatsa, they had apparently merged Mandan and Hidatsa traditions into an origin sequence that explained that after First Creator and Lone Man had made the earth, they brought the people up from under the ground. These events took place on the Missouri River. The Hidatsa then left the Missouri and traveled around until they came to Devils Lake. Like the Mandan and other people, the Hidatsa had many experiences with supernatural beings who helped them learn how to live according to the Hidatsa way. Eventually the people separated into the Awaxawi, the River Crow, and the Hidatsa. Each of these groups had other adventures before returning to their origin spot on the Missouri. Once there, they found their relatives, the Awatixa, who claimed to have been created when Charred Body came to earth and established a village (Bowers 1965:298-299). The significance of the origin story is not, however, that there are inconsistencies or difficulty verifying it historically but that it teaches the Hidatsa about proper behavior and the conduct of ceremonies.

Like the Mandan and Hidatsa, the Arikara say that they came from the underworld where they lived in a dark, gloomy cave with animals and Mother Corn. In these ancient times, animals and people talked to each other and

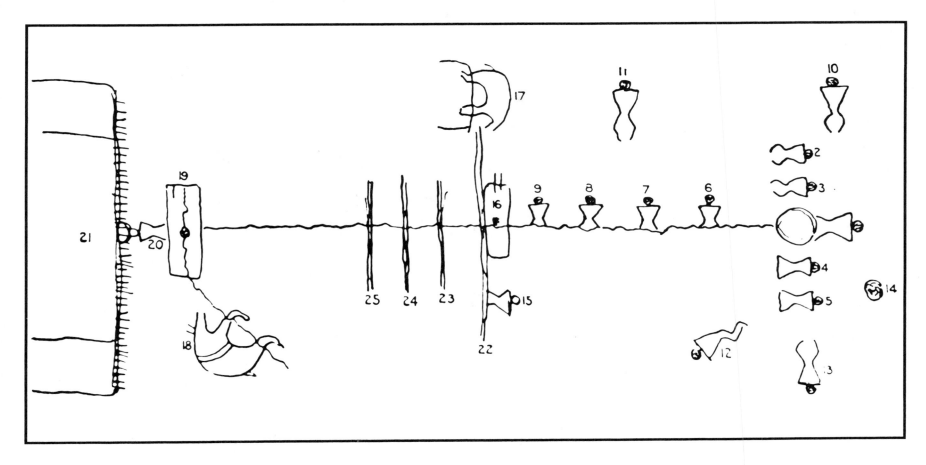

Sikassige, a Chippewa from White Earth, Minnesota, drew this picture of the origin tradition for W.J. Hoffman. The Great Spirit is the largest figure on the right, sitting on the world. The figures on either side of the world are the two men and two women he created. The rest of the figures are spiritual beings who helped in the creation. Line 22 marks the earth and the beginning of the Midewiwin ceremony. People who pass through the four stages of the ceremony live on earth in a sacred manner, as shown in 21. (ARBAE)

helped each other. The animals did not like to see the people living in darkness, so they decided to dig upwards to see what kind of land was above. The bears dug; then the badgers; then the moles, but all gave out before they reached the surface. The mice tried and succeeded in breaking through to the surface, but they came back with their noses worn sharp, and ever since mice have had pointed noses. After working their way through the hole made by the mice, the animals were able to help the people emerge, but it was such a difficult task that the animals were marked by their various efforts, and those marks are still visible today. Once upon the surface of the earth, people became confused and did not know which way to go. Mother Corn called upon the gods to help them, and the people headed toward the West. Eventually they came to a place where Mother Corn told them to stop and build a village while she went up into the heavens to find out more about how the people should live. When Mother Corn returned, she brought many rules and laws for the people to live by. She made a bundle with songs and ceremonies and taught the people to offer smoke to the different gods. Then Mother Corn guided the Arikara to a new place where she told them that she had to leave them and warned them to remember all that she had taught them and promised that, if they made a sacred bundle with corn in it in her memory, she would always care for them: "I shall hereafter come to you in dreams and tell you about these things that are in this bundle" (Dorsey 1904:12-30).

The Chippewa origin tradition is similar to those of other tribes; it maintains that the people were created under the ocean or on the shores of the Atlantic Ocean and were led to the West by a sacred shell known as the megis, or, as some say, by an otter. William Warren, a Chippewa historian who lived and wrote in the late 1800's, interviewed a Chippewa elder and recorded his version of the origin and migration of the tribe:

'My grandson,' said he, 'the megis I spoke of means the Me-da-we religion. Our forefathers, many strings of lives ago, lived on the shores of the Great Salt Water in the east. Here it was, that while congregated in a great town, and while they were suffering the ravages of sickness and death, the Great Spirit, at the intercession of Man-ab-o-sho, the great common uncle of An-ish-in-aub-ag, granted them this rite wherewith life is restored and prolonged. Our forefathers moved from the shores of the great water, and proceeded westward. The Me-da-we lodge was pulled down and it was not again erected, till our forefathers again took a stand on the shores of the great river near where Mo-ne-aung (Montreal) now stands.

'In the course of time this town was again deserted and our forefathers still proceeding westward, lit not their fires till they reached the shores of Lake Huron, where again the rites of the Me-da-we were practised.

'Again these rites were forgotten, and the Me-da-we lodge was not built till the Ojibways found themselves congregated at Bow-e-ting (outlet of Lake Superior), where it remained for many winters. Still the Ojibways moved westward and, for the last time the Me-da-we lodge was erected on the Island of La Pointe, and here, long before the pale face appeared among them, it was practised in its purest and most original form' (Warren 1974:80).

As an historian, Warren was more concerned with showing that the origin tradition had an historic base than he was with the sacred elements of Chippewa origins. Thus his brief description does not include many of the supernatural experiences that occurred on the westward journey, although he does say that the whole story compares in length and complexity with the Old Testament (Warren 1974:71).

Lakota stories of their origin were gathered, organized, and written down by a physician, James Walker, who lived with the Oglala at Pine Ridge for a number of years. Walker's collection illustrates clearly the complexity of the narratives, as well as how each narrative contributes to the explanation of some observation or custom. According to the Lakota, Inyan or the Rock existed before any other thing. Inyan then created the earth by taking a piece of himself and opening his veins to make water. Inyan gave so much of himself that he shrank and became hard and almost lifeless. Following the creation of the earth, various gods were created, and they lived on the earth like humans with human personalities and desires while the Lakota people lived in a lower world where they were visited by the gods from earth. Eventually the Ikce (real people) were tricked by Iktomi into leaving their underworld home to live on earth (Walker 1983:370-373).

The origin traditions of all these tribes are highly complex explanations that account for animals, human differences, linguistic variations, different customs, moral behaviors, and ceremonies, and warn of the end of the present

world. A Hidatsa man, Wolf Chief, told Alfred Bowers the Mandan version of the end of the world:

> Lone Man said to the Mandan, "I am going to leave you some day and go back home. When there is a change in the world I will be back again. The sign will be when the Missouri River changes its course and flows in the other direction. Then the big trees will grow in the opposite direction with the roots sticking up at the top. Then the antelopes will have no flesh on the lower part of their breasts. All that will be a sign that I will come back again (Bowers 1950:365).

Because the origin traditions place Indian people on this continent long before Europeans arrived, Indian people are reminded that they are the real settlers of the continent with a history that is separate from European history.

Archaeological Evidence for Indian Origins

A different answer to the question, "Where did Indians come from?" is provided by archaeologists and geologists. Archaeologists search for evidence left behind by ancient peoples, but the most revealing evidence of past life, such as plant, animal, and human remains, decays easily, making it difficult to find. Artifacts made of rock survive longer,

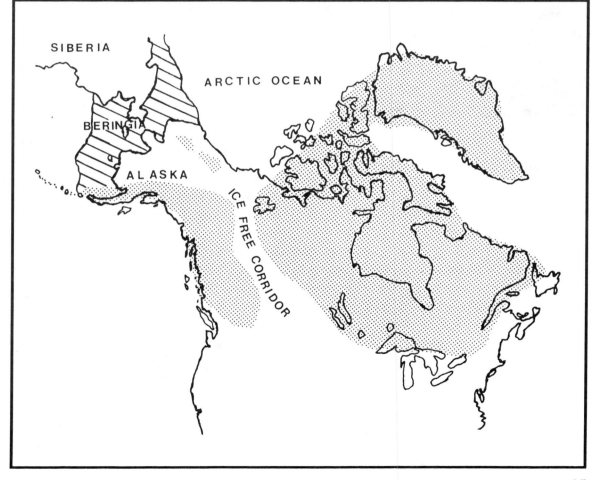

Thousands of years ago, glaciers covered the northern half of North America and lowered the ocean levels so much that Alaska and Siberia were connected. This land bridge, called Beringia, would have allowed men and animals to move from Asia into North America and vice versa, but most of the time the way to the interior was blocked by the glaciers. Twice, between 32,000 to 36,000 and 20,000 to 28,000 years ago, the glaciers melted enough to leave a corridor enabling the first humans to reach North America.

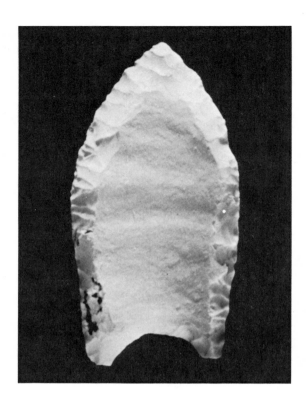

▲   *Folsom points like this one provide evidence for the presence of Paleo-Indians in North Dakota.*

but without other supporting materials, a single stone artifact cannot tell much about a previous way of life. Because they sometimes show where people sat to work or have traces of bones or seeds that can give some idea of what people ate, ancient campsites provide useful information for archaeologists. Sites where people killed and butchered bison are also important sources for information about hunting techniques and food preferences.

Determining the age of a site or artifact is a great problem for archaeologists. Without some idea of how old the evidence is, archaeologists have difficulty building a picture of the origins and life-style of prehistoric peoples. Most archaeologists have to date their sites by comparison to sites whose general age has been determined by some other means. Radiocarbon dating, the most widely used technique, can be done only on organic remains such as bone or wood. Stone and pottery and other objects that were never alive do not have radioactive carbons and so cannot be dated by this method. In addition, radiocarbon dating does not work too well on very recent or very old

materials. Other methods of dating are more difficult, more expensive, or limited to specific kinds of materials.

On the basis of currently available information, scientists have placed the origin of human beings in Africa approximately four million years ago (Leakey and Levin 1977:88). From their point of origin, these early humans spread into Europe and Asia, where adaptations to different environments resulted in the many different cultures and languages now known throughout the world. Sometime before 25,000 years ago, some of the people living in northeastern Siberia crossed from Asia into what is now Alaska.

The distance between Asia and Alaska is as short as 55 miles, and scientists have suggested several ways in which people could have traversed this passage. Even today, polar bears and other arctic animals move between the continents by crossing the polar ice cap in winter. It is possible that the people who became American Indians crossed the Bering Strait in boats or walked across the ice, but the woolly mammoth, giant moose, and other large

During the Archaic the buffalo became the most important resource for Plains Indians.

game animals must have moved from Asia into America by foot. Geologists have hypothesized that Asia and Alaska were once connected by a wide, grassy, tundra-like area, which they call Beringia, formed when the glaciers that covered Europe, Asia, and North America lowered the water level of the oceans. The animals seeking food and water in this area could have crossed into North America without knowing it. Following these game animals, small groups of hunters also crossed into America, eventually making their way to the tip of South America. The geological evidence

for the glaciers and the lowering of the sea level is well accepted, but the archaeological evidence for human beings entering the New World is the source of much disagreement because single artifacts or human remains have not provided dates that can be accepted unquestionably.

Evidence that is endorsed by almost all archaeologists shows that human beings were well-established in North America some 12,000 years ago. Highly distinctive stone points found embedded in mammoth bones are unquestionable evidence of the presence of human beings.

Evidence that is not so widely recognized suggests that the First Americans arrived from Asia around 30,000 years ago, bringing with them a bone-tool technology that has not survived. Some archaeologists, most notably the late Louis S. B. Leakey, believe there is sufficient evidence to support the idea that the first Americans were here 40,000 to 50,000 years ago. Leakey thought that similarities between some roughly cracked stones found in California and the ancient hand tools he had excavated in Africa demonstrated an early human presence in North America, but geologists have

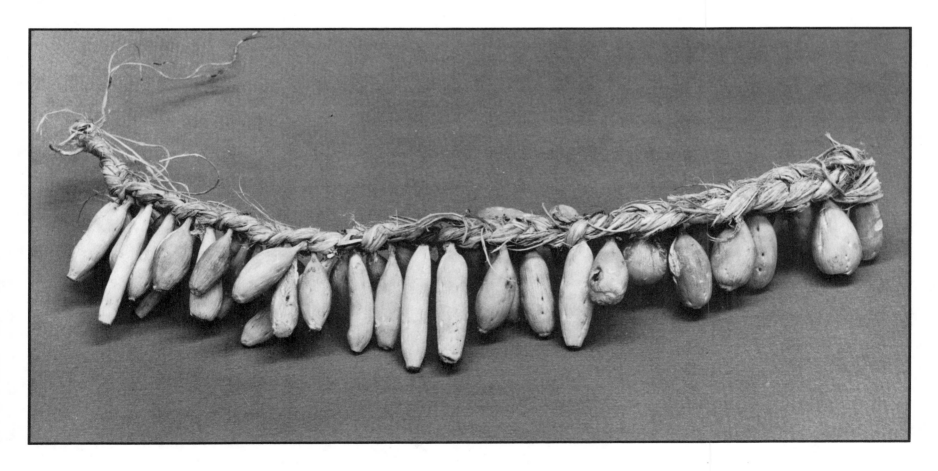

Archaic foragers learned to use local plant resources like the prairie turnip.

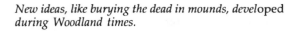

New ideas, like burying the dead in mounds, developed during Woodland times.

argued that there is no evidence that the stones were cracked by human hands, since natural processes can also shape stones to look as if they were purposefully made by humans (Canby 1979:351).

No one knows what these ancient American Indians looked like, but we can assume that they were similar in appearance and intelligence to modern brown-skinned humans. While some evidence suggests that these early people were users of bone tools, the earliest known stone artifacts (Clovis spear points) show that the first Americans were highly skilled stone-workers. Because we do not know who these people were or what language they spoke, archaeologists refer to them by names describing some cultural characteristic or referrring to the site where their remains have been found. The earliest Americans, hunters of game animals that are now extinct, are called Paleo-Indians. Because the Paleo- Indian life-style is found throughout North and South America, regional and temporal differences are noted by different names. The Clovis culture is named after the site in New Mexico where it was first recognized. The Folsom culture, Plano culture, and others represent different Paleo-Indian adaptations to the environment.

The first North Dakotans were Paleo-Indians who left behind Clovis, Folsom, and other ancient projectile points to mark their passage.

Pottery was another new idea introduced during the Woodland times.

Unfortunately, these points have not been found in conjunction with animal bones or other materials, and we do not know what the first North Dakotans preferred to eat or how they dressed or camped. From other parts of the country, however, we know that these people hunted mammoths, giant bison, horses, and camels. Stone scrapers suggest that these people also worked hides which they may have used for tents or turned into clothes. Later Paleo-In-

dians, creators of Folsom and Plano points, relied primarily on bison hunting, developing the surround and the drive-over-a-cliff hunting techniques that continued to be used by Plains Indians until the destruction of the bison herds in the late 1800's. These hunters also used plant foods and hunted deer and other animals (Claiborne 1973:55).

Following the Paleo-Indian period, which lasted until the extinction of the mammoths, mastodons, horses, camels, and giant bison, 8,000 or 9,000 years ago, is a way of life archaeologists call the Archaic. It is clear from the evidence that the Archaic was really an adjustment to changing animal populations and en-

vironments rather than the development of a new way of life. Archaic peoples developed new projectile point forms and a wider variety of stone tools, but continued their basic hunting techniques. The new stone tools, such as axes, drills, and gouges, suggest the processing and working of nuts and other plant foods and materials. Bone needles found at some sites may mean that these ancient peoples sewed hides into clothing.

In North Dakota the Archaic life-style is well represented by scattered finds of projectile points and other stone tools, but few Archaic period sites have been excavated. One such site, the Red Fox Site in southwestern North Dakota, had two fire hearths and a cache or storage pit located in a depression ten feet square and six inches deep. Excavators believe that this depression was the floor of a house (Syms 1970:134), one of the earliest known buildings in North Dakota. Other Archaic peoples apparently used tipis (Gregg 1985:105-109).

In some parts of the country the Archaic continued into recent times, but on the Plains and in the East, the Archaic transformed into the Woodland period as pottery making, the bow and arrow, extensive trade networks, and the growing of corn provided people with more elaborate life-styles. Such developments were slow to reach the Dakotas, and the Woodland period on the northern Plains is indicated more often by the presence of pottery and the use of burial mounds for the dead. Bison hunting continued to be the major subsistence economy. About 1,000 years ago earthlodge villages began to be built along the Missouri River (Lehmer 1971). The lodges in these villages were square or rectangular, not round like the later ones, but other features such as

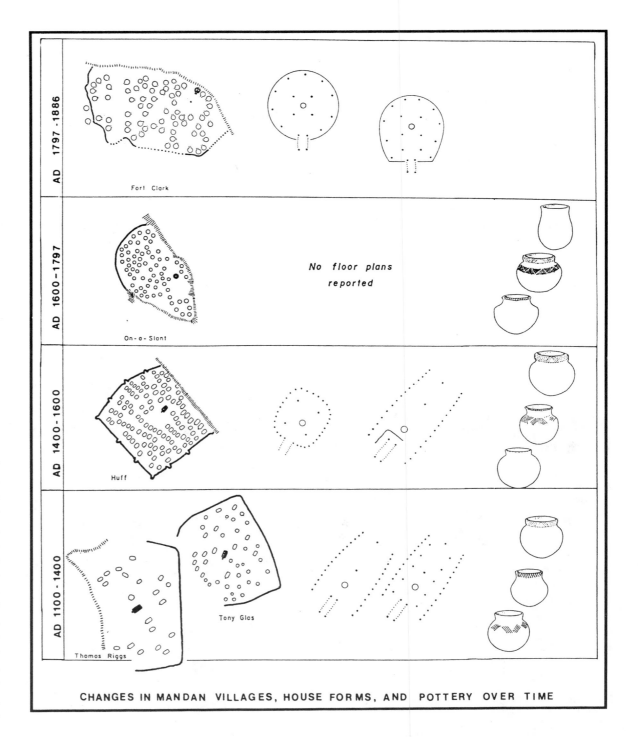

CHANGES IN MANDAN VILLAGES, HOUSE FORMS, AND POTTERY OVER TIME

the growing of corn and the use of scapula hoes and many bone and stone tools suggest similarities between this early Plains Village culture and the later Arikara, Mandan, and Hidatsa life-styles (Lehmer 1971:136). So far we have no way of connecting the Arikara, Mandan, and Hidatsa with these early village sites, but sufficient evidence indicates that the way of life of the earthlodge users was old and well-established before the Europeans arrived.

Other life-styles appeared during the Woodland period. In the James River Valley of eastern North Dakota, campsites used by bison hunters and small villages indicated by round house depressions remind us that there were different peoples living in the state (Good,et.al,1977). The round houses were not constructed like earthlodges and may have been similar to the bark- and hide-covered sapling structures used by the Chippewa and Dakota in later times. Rock circles indicate the continuing use of tipis for shelter, although they do not provide much other information about the inhabitants.

Several hundred years ago, the entry of metal trade goods, beads, guns, and other materials changed the way of life of the Woodland peoples once more. At first the trade goods passed from tribe to tribe without causing much disruption, but soon these goods were followed by epidemic diseases and then by non-Indian explorers and traders. The written reports of these non-Indians mark the beginning of the Historic period.

The Historic period is well known because there are numerous sites as well as written materials to describe the way of life of these people. Some of the sites that date from this period have been associated with known tribes. For instance, in eastern North Dakota the Biesterfeldt Site, which has round earthlodge houses arranged around a central plaza, has been linked with the Cheyenne on the basis of Cheyenne traditions of their having occupied such a site on the Sheyenne River (Wood 1971). On the Missouri River, Lewis and Clark (Stewart 1974) noted sites that had once been used by the Arikara, Mandan, and Hidatsa. Before Garrison Dam created Lake Sakakawea, many of these sites were excavated, and so we know a great deal about the history of the Mandan and Hidatsa. Sites in South Dakota have provided similar information about Arikara history.

Archaeology has added significant information to our knowledge of early North Dakota Indian cultures. First, there is no doubt that American Indians lived in North Dakota long before White men entered the state. Some early explorers and historians (Wilkins and Wilkins 1977:23) believed that survival was impossible without horses and guns, but modern evidence shows people hunting bison and living in tipis and earthlodges for generations before the introduction of horses and guns. Second, many of the typical Plains Indian customs and techniques, such as the buffalo drive, the use of tipis and earthlodges, the use of bows and arrows, and the importance of both corn growing and buffalo hunting, can be demonstrated archaeologically, indicating that these traditions have great antiquity. Third, the presence of different life-styles is also illustrated by the archaeological record. Although many people are disappointed to learn that it is usually not possible to relate ancient sites to modern-day tribes, the evidence supports the assumption that some of the later tribes, especially the Mandan and Hidatsa, were here at an

Circular stone rings, often occurring in groups, are believed to mark the locations of tipis. Numerous tipi rings throughout North Dakota indicate the importance of the structure in prehistoric times.

20

The Knife River villages once held many earthlodges. Today, only circular depressions show where the earthlodges once stood.

early time. Because of the changing North Dakota environment, many tribes probably moved in and out of the state, and definitive answers concerning ancient tribal origins must wait for more archaeological explanation.

Historic Movements into the State

The availability of written documents and oral histories makes the question of how and when the present-day North Dakota tribes entered the area less controversial and easier to answer than the one about ancient origins. Even the Mandan and Hidatsa origin traditions agree that some of the Hidatsa arrived on the Missouri not knowing how to grow corn and that the Crow were once part of the Hidatsa tribe. Arikara oral histories claim that the tribe once lived in Nebraska and South Dakota, a fact substantiated by archaeology and written records. Other records indicate that the Mandan and Hidatsa gradually moved up the Missouri River in the 1700's. Some evidence suggests that the Mandan lived along the Heart River until the smallpox epidemic of 1781 forced them to join the Hidatsa for protection against marauding Lakota and Yanktonai bands (Stewart 1974). The Hidatsa were living on the Knife when they were joined by the Mandan, who established villages near them. The epidemic of 1781 also caused the Arikara to move nearer the Mandan and Hidatsa, and by 1804, when Lewis and Clark arrived at the Mandan villages, the three tribes were well established on the Upper Missouri.

The Lakota, Dakota, Yankton, and Yanktonai were occupying and/or using the region between the Red River and the Missouri when they were first contacted by Europeans. Both Pierre Esprit Radisson in 1660 and Father Louis Hennepin in 1679 reported the presence of "prairie Sioux" (Meyer 1967:1-11). By this time, the Assiniboins, who had separated from the Yanktonais, were well established in the area between Devils Lake and Lake Winnipeg (Robinson 1904:25).

The entrance of the Chippewa into North Dakota has been associated with the fur trade, although it is probable that there were Chippewa in the area before the records begin. Harold Hickerson's study of fur-trade journals

21

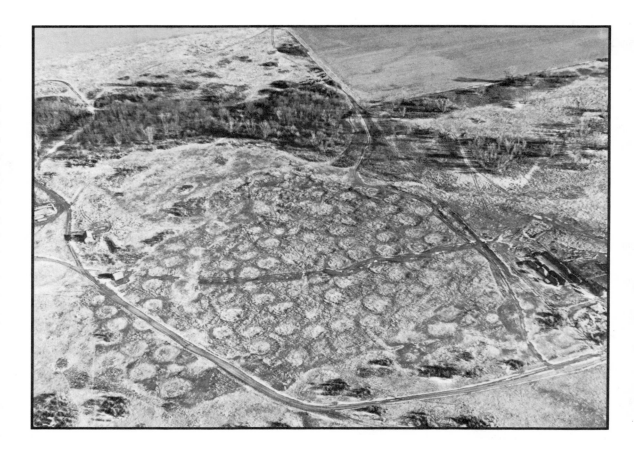

The Knife River Villages, now a national historic site, were visited by Lewis and Clark and other White explorers. (NDSHD)

and other early documents led him to conclude that the Chippewa entered the area north of the present-day Minnesota-Canada boundary before moving into Minnesota and westward into North Dakota (Hickerson 1956:290). In their westward movement, the Chippewa encountered Dakota and Yanktonai bands whose claim to the whole area was based on a continuing struggle with the Cree and Assiniboin peoples as far north as the Assiniboin River (Hickerson 1956:296). For safety, the Chippewa formed alliances with the Cree and Assiniboin. By 1789-1790, the Chippewa were penetrating into the Assiniboin River area and using the river as an entry to the Missouri River and Rocky Mountains. The earliest evidence for Chippewa in North Dakota comes from the journal of fur trader Charles Jean Baptiste Chaboillez (Hickerson 1959), who, in 1797, opened a trading post on the Red River near the modern town of Pembina. Two other trading posts were also established on the Red River at this time, and Chippewa were recruited to supply these posts with furs and meat. With the influx of Chippewa and fur traders, the Dakota withdrew to the Sheyenne River, which became an informal boundary between the Chippewa and Dakota, to be crossed at risk of one's life. Once established on the Red River, the Chippewa moved westward to the Turtle Mountains and the Missouri River. In 1832 George Catlin painted the portrait of Shacopay, "The Six," a Plains-Ojibwa headman "of that part of the Ojibbeway tribe who inhabit these northern regions," and other Plains Chippewa whom he met at Fort Union (Catlin 1973,vol.I:53-58). Catlin's paintings show people dressed in typical Plains Indian clothing decorated with quillwork rosettes and painted symbols of war exploits, an indication of how successfully these

Chippewa had adapted to the Plains way of life (Hassrick 1977:123,146,147).

The answer to the question, "Where did the Indians of North Dakota come from?" depends on various points of view. First, Indian people say they were created, along with the land, animals, food, life-styles, and ceremonies, by one or more creators who intended them to live on the earth where they were made. The second response to the question is made by scientists who say that human beings originated in Africa and migrated to the Western Hemisphere where they diversified into the different tribes of North, Central, and South America. A third answer is provided by oral and written histories which depict the movement of present-day North Dakota tribes into the region.

All three answers agree that the original inhabitants of the northern Plains were Indian people who established a way of life that was maintained until the Euro-American newcomers changed it irrevocably. The antiquity of Indian presence and the Indian ability to survive as buffalo hunters without horses or guns are not in doubt. Just as horses later enriched the lives of Plains Indian people, agricultural products made their lives a bit more secure and more settled, but neither agriculture nor horses were necessary for survival. Survival of the Indians in the pre- European years did necessitate a close personal relationship with the land and its resources.

22

Contributions to North Dakota History and Culture

The lengthy period during which Indian people adapted to the Plains brought about an awareness of the Plains as a fragile environment that had to be treated with love and respect. Humans had to live efficiently in order to maintain the delicate balance between the land and all living things. Understanding that prolonged use of a scarce resource could destroy it, the ancient Plains peoples diversified their subsistence base and lived in small groups that would not leave too great an impact on any one place. Indeed, they left so few traces of their coming and going that early scholars thought the Plains were empty until Indians obtained horses (Wilkins and Wilkins 1977:23), but their marks can be found in tipi rings, earthlodge remains, and in the names of the landforms and waterways which they knew so well. The Plains Indian conception of life as a circle in which humans were a connecting link was recently adopted by modern American citizens concerned about the impact of pollution from pesticides and industrial development on our environment.

With the exception of the James River, the major lakes and rivers in North Dakota carry names derived from Indian languages. Devils Lake was known to the Dakota and Yanktonai as Mni-wakan, sacred or mysterious water (Federal Writer's Project 1950:253). The Hidatsa also called it sacred water, Midihopa in their language (Matthews 1873:xvi). People still talk of the strange sounds that issue from the lake on still summer nights. The Sheyenne River takes its name from the tribe who once lived on its banks. Although Missouri is an Indian word meaning big muddy, the Missouri River was not called the Missouri by the North Dakota tribes. The Hidatsa called it Amati, which may mean "earth" or "boat," but also contains the word ati, which means lodge or home (Matthews 1873:144). To the Lakota, it was Mnishoshe, slow moving waters (Sneve 1973:31). The Heart River was so named by the Mandan because it "flowed out of the country of the `Middle Hole'" and corresponded to the heart of the human body (Williams 1966, vol.4:10). The real reason for the name Red River is not known, but historians have suggested the Chippewa named it for its color when it flows into Lake Winnipeg or because it glows red at sunrise and sunset or because of a great bloody battle that took place along it. Medicine Lodge Spring near Williston was used by Indian people long before a homesteader bottled and sold the water (Federal Writer's Project 1950:241). The Yellowstone River, called Yellow River by the Hidatsa (Matthews 1873:147), was known to the Lakota as Elk River (Buechel 1970:758).

Hills and buttes were also important to Indian people, and the names used for them today are often direct translations of their aboriginal designations. To both the Dakota and Yanktonai, Mini wakan chante, or Devils Heart, was the center of the region around Devils Lake (Nicollet 1976:186-187). Dogden Butte, Bear Den Hill, Hawksnest Hill, and Heart Butte were named by Indian people (Federal Writer's Project 1950:260,289). The Killdeer Mountains, known to the Lakota as Tah-kah-o-kuty or "place where they kill the deer," were an important source of meat and hides (Federal Writer's Project 1950:304).

Unusual geological features were identified and named by the first inhabitants of the Dakotas. The Standing Rock or Inyan Bosndata in Ransom County is an upsidedown conical rock (Nicollet 1976:202). Standing Rock Reservation takes its name from another standing rock; one in the shape of a woman which the Lakota carried with them until they settled on the reservation. This rock can be seen at Fort Yates (Howard 1976:32).

It is no accident that many of the places known and loved by Indian people are now local, state, or national parks, because the newcomers also sensed the mysterious, beautiful, or historic attractions of these places. Along the Missouri River some of the former villages of the Mandan, Hidatsa, and Arikara are maintained as state historic sites. Slant Village, south of Mandan, recreates an earthlodge village on the actual site of one which may have been visited by Lewis and Clark. The National Park Service acquired the site of the Mandan and Hidatsa villages visited by Lewis and Clark, Catlin, and Maximilian and created the Knife River Villages National Park, now a growing tourist attraction. Extensive archaeological investigations at the Knife River Villages are contributing new details about the Indian history and culture of the area.

Although Indian names and historic sites are significant contributions to state history, the next chapters will show that the White debt to Indian people is even greater than these.

Chapter 3

Indian Life Before The Reservations

Introduction

Some authors depict the life of Indian people before they were settled on reservations as one of pestilence, poverty, and/or unceasing warfare (Robinson 1966:103-104), but the truth is that, while Indian life was hard, it was also satisfying. Based upon a strong extended family that shared necessities and participated in ceremonies, pre-reservation Indian life was organized and integrated to protect, nurture, and help individuals to survive the hardships. Each tribe accomplished these measures in different ways, and so it is not safe to generalize too much or to assume that even closely related tribes had the same practices or customs. For instance, the Sun Dance was held by many Plains Indian tribes, but each tribe had a different name for the ceremony and conducted it according to its own tribal beliefs.

Establishing an approximate date for the

Earthlodges provided room for several related families and all their possessions, including valuable hunting horses. (UND)

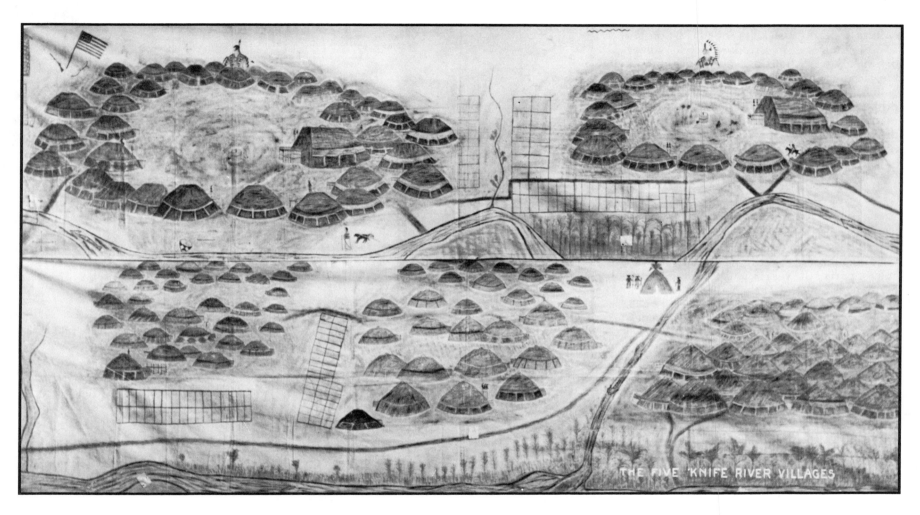

THE FIVE KNIFE RIVER VILLAGES

description of pre-reservation life-styles is difficult because the tribes currently living in North Dakota did not all arrive at the same time. In addition, we need to recognize that Indian life was indirectly influenced by White trade goods at an early date and that later pre-reservation cultures were more directly affected by the presence of military men, traders, missionaries, and other non-Indians. The Mandan and Hidatsa visited by Prince Maximilian in 1832 were changed so drastically by the smallpox epidemic of 1837 that a description of their life-style in 1860 would be quite different from one based upon Maximilian's observations (Bowers 1965:4,24).

Another difficulty occurs when we describe the traditional life of a group in terms that make it appear unchanging and static. Indian cultures differed seasonally and annually and changed over time. A visitor to a Hidatsa village in May would find people busy with planting and ceremonies; returning in July during the large summer hunt when many people were away from the village or during August harvest, our visitor would have a different idea about village life.

The quality of information concerning the tribes also varies. We know quite a bit about pre-reservation Hidatsa culture because early visitors, traders, missionaries, and military men recorded detailed information, but we know much less about the Arikara and other tribes. One way to deal with the variability of information is to approach pre-reservation tribal culture topically instead of tribally. By organizing the material into topics such as village organization and housing, subsistence, family life, social organization, government, religious beliefs, and major ceremonies, we reduce the problems of culture change and lack of information while illustrating the similarities and differences among the tribes without being repetitive.

Pre-Reservation Life Around 1860

Villages and housing

Many people make the mistake of thinking that all Indians lived in tipis, but most Indians, including those inhabiting North Dakota, lived at least part of the year in villages composed of permanent houses. The stability of these villages, their location near major waterways, and their participation in extensive trade networks attracted non-Indian traders who often became residents.

The villages of the Arikara, Hidatsa, Mandan, and Yanktonai were composed of large dome-shaped houses, called earthlodges, that sheltered many members of a family. The Mandan arranged their houses around an open plaza, but none of the villages were laid out with streets, and visitors often got lost. The earthlodges were constructed of logs covered with earth. A tunnel-like entryway led into the spacious interior of the lodge. The fireplace was the center of family life where meals were cooked and served, visitors were entertained, and elders were cared for (Brackenridge 1906:115). Hide-curtained beds and platform storage areas were located next to the walls where the roof sloped (Wilson 1934:387). Among the Mandan and Hidatsa, the people who lived in an earthlodge were related women and their husbands and children, and it was common among all the tribes for three or four generations to occupy a single lodge (Bowers 1950:26; 1965:138).

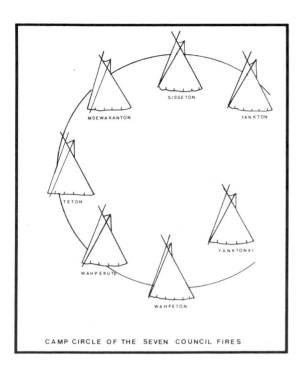

CAMP CIRCLE OF THE SEVEN COUNCIL FIRES

SISSETON
MDEWAKANTON
YANKTON
TETON
YANKTONAI
WAHPEKUTE
WAHPETON

▲ *Usually tipi camps were arranged according to the terrain, but when special ceremonies were held, tipis were set up in a circle in which each tribe or band had its assigned place.*

When the Chippewa moved into the Red River Valley they adopted the tipi. (SHSND)

The village plan was complicated by the presence of other structures. Outside the door of each earthlodge was a large raised wood platform for drying and storing food. During hot days, the drying stage also served as a shelter for women who sat in its shade to work. Many of the men had sacred symbols raised on one or more tall poles placed in front of the earthlodge. Dog kennels and frames for working hides were also located near each earthlodge.

The large earthlodges were used primarily during the spring and fall while crops were being planted or harvested. During the winter smaller earthlodge villages were built along the river in protected areas near water and firewood (Boller 1972:187-194). These lodges were not so sturdily constructed as the larger earthlodges, since it was expected that they would be washed away in the spring floods. During the summer, when the Arikara, Mandan, Hidatsa, and Yanktonai were traveling or hunting away from the village, they used tipis of hides and poles similar to those of the Lakota (Bowers 1950:89; Bowers 1965:53; Denig 1961:48).

When they were living in Minnesota, each of the four major groups of the Dakota, the Santee, Wahpeton, Sisseton, and Mdewakanton, had its own territory which was further divided into many villages named according to their location or for their leader. One of the villages of the Wahpeton was called "Village at the dam or rapids" and one of the Sisseton villages was called "Village at the north island" (Dorsey 1897:216). These named villages, composed of large bark-covered gabled houses, were used only in the summer; tipis were used

INDIANISCHE BISONJAGD.   INDIENS CHASSANT LE BISON.

INDIANS HUNTING THE BISON

Karl Bodmer, a Swiss artist who accompanied Prince Maximilian on his trip up the Missouri, made this picture of a buffalo hunt. (SHSND)

28

▲ *Corn, squash, beans and sunflowers grown by the Arikara, Mandan and Hidatsa were important foods and trade products.*

on hunting trips, and during the winter, and by those who could not afford a proper house (Pond 1986:37-39). Occupied by two or more families, the large houses could have a single door or one at each end, depending upon the number of occupants. A central fireplace provided heat and light, and wide hide-covered benches arranged along the walls served as sitting and sleeping places. Rev. Samuel William Pond, who spent twenty years as a missionary to the Mdewakanton, reported that the houses were waterproof and very comfortable (Pond 1986:39).

Although well-established villages with permanent houses were common in Minnesota and the Dakotas, all the tribes were familiar with the tipi and used it for temporary housing or on hunting trips. For the Lakota, however, the tipi was used year-round. The Lakota are famous for their handsome and functional tipis. The tipi camps of the Lakota were usually small because they were occupied by a group of related families, called a tiospaye. For special occasions, the camp was arranged in a circle with each family having an assigned place, but for most of the year families set up their tipis in patterns suitable to the terrain and

their personal choices. When camp circles were used, the tipis were arranged in a large ring with an opening at one end. It must have been an impressive sight with each band in its appointed place in the circle and all the tipis facing toward the center. An extra-large tipi was sometimes erected to serve as a council or meeting place (Hassrick 1964:13,23-24).

Tipis, designed for mobility, efficiency, and comfort, were simple structures composed of covers sewn from buffalo hides and of poles made from tall straight lodge-pole pine trees found in the foothills of the Rocky Mountains. Setting up or dismantling a tipi could be done very quickly. The conical shape meant that only a small amount of wood was used for heating. The lower edges could be raised in summer to keep the interior cool and sealed down with rocks and logs in the winter to keep heat inside (Hassrick 1964:184-185). Harmonious living in the restricted space of a tipi required organization and a strict etiquette. Men sat on the right side of the fireplace, while women sat on the left. The rear of the tent was the place of honor where visitors sat and religious objects were kept. No one was permitted to pass between the fireplace and

Mandan women cooked buffalo stew and corn soup in hand-made pots like this one. (CM)

someone sitting in the tipi. Tipi furnishings were simple, but comfortable. Hides served as beds. Woven willow backrests made sitting comfortable. Untanned hides were made into envelopes and bags for storing food, clothes, and sacred items (Hassrick 1964:186).

Like the other tribes, the people who eventually came to be known as the Turtle Mountain Band of Chippewa lived in small groups of related families that were smaller in the winter months and larger during the summer when families met for fishing and ceremonies. The Turtle Mountain Band of Chippewa also used houses that were adapted to the seasons and the environment. In Minnesota, the Chippewa built four different styles of bark houses. The domed style, generally called a wigwam, was the most common form and was used throughout the year. A peaked lodge, a house-like lodge, and a tipi-like style were used when convenient. Three or four generations occupied a winter wigwam, with the youngest members living in the center of the lodge so that they had to pass by the elders whenever they entered or left the house. The beds were made of cedar boughs covered with woven rush mats on which skins were placed at night. During the day the bedding was rolled up and used as seats (Densmore 1929:22-29).

When the Chippewa and Cree moved from their forest homes to the prairies, they adopted the hide-covered tipi and camp life-style of the other Plains tribes (Howard 1977:40). Other forms of housing continued to be used for special occasions (Howard 1977:41). The fur traders taught the Chippewa to build log cabins for winter use, and these became the permanent homes of Chippewa Métis during the times they were not hunting. Then they used tipis.

Subsistence

What some non-Indian geographers referred to as "the great American desert" was actually a region with a wide variety of animal and plant resources that were used by the native peoples. Two basic subsistence options for Plains dwellers were hunting and farming. Some scholars thought that the tribes who practiced agriculture were less dependent on the buffalo than the other tribes (Lowie 1954:21), but archaeological investigations of the prehistoric Missouri River villages demonstrated that the buffalo were a basic resource for all the tribes, even for those who grew corn, squash, and beans. The Dakota and other woodland tribes hunted buffalo along the eastern margin of the prairie.

It may be that buffalo made life easier for Plains Indians by providing a large supply of meat that could be obtained with less effort than bagging a deer or an antelope. The thick, furry buffalo hide could be used for robes or tanned for clothes and tipi covers. In addition, the buffalo provided bones for tools, sinew for sewing, hair for stuffing saddle pads and pillows, paunch and heart covering for containers, and horns for spoons and ladles (Denig 1961:13-14). Deer, elk, antelope, and smaller animals were also important sources of food, especially when the buffalo were scarce.

Buffalo hunting involved the tribes-people in two ways. For most of the year, small groups of men and their families could hunt buffalo whenever food or other materials were needed. During the summer and fall, however, buffalo hunting was a major enterprise of the whole tribe and was conducted under rigorous military and religious control. Because these tribal hunts provided food and hides to ensure the survival of the tribe through the winter, individuals were expected to put the tribal welfare before personal needs. The tribal hunts employed the whole village except those too old or too infirm to travel easily. Before the hunt, sacred religious ceremonies were held to guarantee good hunting and the safety of the people (Bowers 1950:88). For the Lakota, this ceremony was the Sun Dance. During the hunt, the military police kept strict control so that nothing would frighten the buffalo away or do harm to the group. Any man who went out to hunt before the command was given was subject to severe punishment (Lowie 1954:111). These large hunts used the surround or the drive techniques designed to kill as many buffalo as could be processed efficiently and quickly (Lowie 1954:14-19). Following the hunt, the men butchered the

Lakota children were welcomed with decorated cradles made by their aunts. (SHSND)

buffalo and carried the chunks of meat to the camp where it was sliced and hung to dry by the women. Men and women worked diligently because getting the meat prepared for winter use before it could spoil was a major concern.

Plant foods, both wild and domestic, were also important components of the diet. Although some early students (Robinson 1904:29) of Plains Indian culture thought that vegetables were not important, we know that Plains

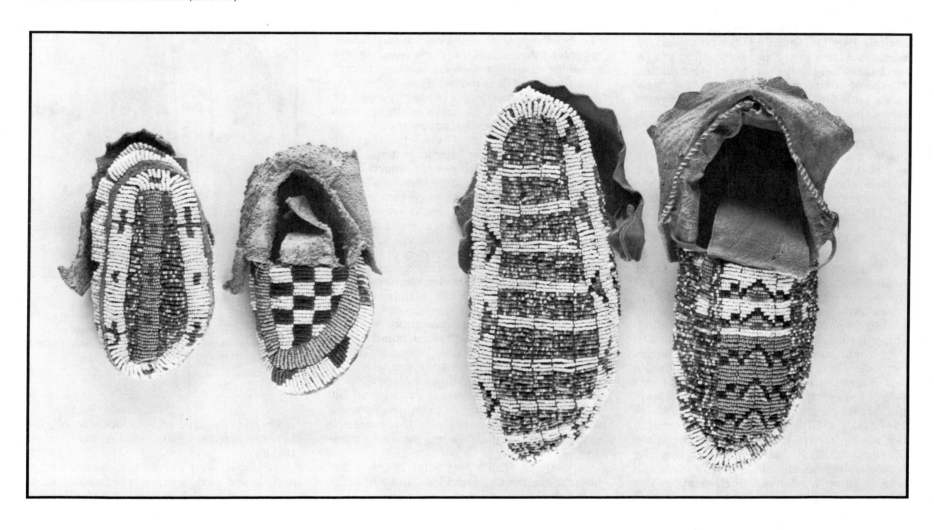

Indians utilized many different plants (Gilmore 1919). The wild turnip or prairie turnip was one of the most important plant foods because it could be eaten in a variety of ways, fresh or dried, and when dried, the turnip would not spoil (Denig 1961:11). For the Chippewa and Dakota in Minnesota, wild rice served much the same purpose as the prairie turnip. In fact, the Dakota called the wild turnip by a name very similar to the one used for wild rice because they regarded it as a plant with similar qualities. Other important wild food plants were the wild potato, ground beans, and nuts, fruits, and berries of all kinds. Maple and boxelder trees provided sap that could be made into sugar syrup for sweetening foods, and many plants were steeped for teas.

In addition to their utilization of wild plant foods, the Arikara, Hidatsa, Mandan, and some Yanktonai and Dakota grew corn, squash, beans, and sunflowers in small garden plots near their villages. These gardens were cleared, planted, cared for, and harvested by the women, highly skilled agriculturalists who developed nine kinds of corn, five kinds of beans, and several varieties of squash (Wilson 1917:56,84). In good years, the women would raise a large enough crop to supply the family and yet have enough left over to trade with tribes such as the Lakota, Plains Cree, Assiniboin, and Plains Chippewa, who did not garden. Since the crops belonged to the women, they determined how much to trade and were known

31

throughout the Plains as astute traders.

With no salt, little sugar, and no alcoholic beverages, the diet of the early Plains Indians was healthy and nutritious. White men (Brackenridge 1906:116; Boller 1972) who visited the northern Plains in the pre-reservation era recorded a variety of dishes served at mealtimes. The most common preparation was a stew made with buffalo meat and whatever vegetables, prairie turnips, corn, squash, beans, were available to the cook. Roast buffalo ribs were a special treat as were cakes or puddings made from berries. Some visitors, however, reported times of starvation when either the buffalo failed or the crops were insufficient to last through the winter (Wied-Neuwied 1906 vol.24:58-63).

Family life

The environment was an important factor in food, housing, and village organization, but the family was the most important determinant of how people lived and acted. The family was so important that terms of close relationship were extended to distant relatives and to people who would not be considered relatives by modern Euro-American standards. A Lakota man might call all of his cousins on his father's side "brother" and treat them as if they were his brothers (Walker 1914:104; Hassrick 1944:344). A Hidatsa woman considered all her mother's sisters to be her mothers, too (Bowers 1965:81). The result of extending family relationships was to make everyone in the village or camp a relative. Such relationships filled several needs. First, since everyone was related, everyone cared about everyone else. Second, people behaved toward each other in ways established by their kinship. A man was expected to treat his brothers differently from his cousins. Men and women who called each other brother and sister could not marry. Grandmothers and grandfathers were expected to give special loving attention to anyone they called grandchild, and grandchildren took good care of anyone they called grandmother or grandfather. The result of these extended family relationships was that village life was warm and caring with little need for rules and

32

regulations.

Some tribes extended family relationships even further through membership in a clan. In a clan system children were born into the clan of one of the parents. The Mandan and Hidatsa organized themselves into clans based on relationships to related women, and the children took the clan of their mother (Bowers 1965:64). In a patrilineal clan system like the Chippewa's, the children took the clan of their father (Densmore 1929:10). The advantage of clans is that they continue to exist even when the original relationships have been forgotten. Think how it would be if all people named Smith considered themselves to be members of the Smith clan. Even if they no longer remembered the ancestral links, they would know whenever they met someone named Smith that they would be treated like close relatives. Clans had names that reflected some aspect of their history, and the same names were found in other villages or camps so that clan members knew they would be treated like members of the family whenever they visited another village. Clans also managed important properties such as houses, gardens, and sacred bundles, and when a clan member died, the clan would decide who would inherit the property, and there would be no fighting over ownership. Because the property would enhance all the clan, the members worked together to acquire sacred bundles or ceremonies that were too expensive or complex for one person to manage.

A strong family was vital to the tribes because the family provided child and elder care, education, and moral and physical support. Families also sponsored religious ceremonies that extended spiritual protection to the whole tribe. As soon as a child was born, the family welcomed it with gifts and prayers (Hassrick 1964:272; Bowers 1950:58-60). One of the sorrows of tribal life was that many infants died shortly after birth, and so families paid special attention to youngsters. Names that were thought to be strong and health-giving were bestowed on children, and if a child seemed not to thrive, a different name would be tried. A Hidatsa woman recalled that she was originally named Good Way, but

Visions painted on shields protected the men during dangerous activities. The owner of this shield was protected by a thunder-horse. The wavy lines indicate supernatural power.(AMNH)

when she appeared to be a sickly infant, her father renamed her Buffalo Bird Woman (Wilson 1971:8).

Children were nursed until they were two or three and were never spanked or slapped or whipped (Hassrick 1964:275-276). Children who misbehaved were talked to, scared by stories, or had water thrown on them. As soon as a boy could walk, he was given a little bow and arrow and began his education as a hunter and warrior. A boy's first kill, no matter how small, was celebrated so that he would be encouraged to continue. As soon as a girl was strong enough, she began to help her mothers and other women, developing the skills that would make her a good wife and mother. Even girls four or five years old were considered old enough to take care of younger brothers and sisters while their mother went about her chores.

People of all ages participated in games of skill, like this archery contest painted by George Catlin, and gambling games. (UND)

One of the most important events in the life of a boy was seeking spiritual guidance. Plains Indians believed that numerous unseen forces in the universe were stronger than humans. If a human presented himself in a sacred manner, humbly and pitifully, one of these forces might consent to provide protection for him. All of the tribes practiced various ways of seeking this spiritual protection, but generally an individual spent several days praying in a remote spot without food and water (Hassrick 1964:226-254; Bowers 1950:63-66). Some form of self-mutilation might also be carried out, especially if the individual had not been successful in an earlier quest. On his first vision quest, Goodbird, a Hidatsa boy, suspended himself by thongs through his shoulder muscles (Wilson 1985:58). The results of a vision quest were variable. Usually the spiritual protector gave the seeker a song, prayer, symbol, or some other evidence of his protection, and sometimes a man would

33

be told to avoid certain things that would offend the protector. The most powerful protectors often gave the most specific instructions about how they wished to be treated and how the man should act. In return, such powerful protectors gave the man certain abilities that would make him a successful hunter and warrior.

Once a boy had achieved a spiritual protector, he was ready to learn to be a warrior. On his first war party, a boy would be expected to act as an attendant to the warriors and not to take part in any dangerous activities, although most young men were eager to prove themselves and frequently got involved in action. It was an honor for a young man to be considered a good "worker" and no shame if he did not participate in fighting, but it was also an honor to return home with a success story (Hassrick 1964:279-280; Bowers 1965:137-138).

When a young woman was able to demonstrate skill in woman's work, she was considered ready for marriage. Because learning to be a hunter and warrior took longer, a man was usually older than the woman he chose to marry. The preferred form of marriage in all the tribes was by gift exchange, sometimes known as "bride-price," whereby the parents of the young man would give gifts to the young woman's family, but this practice created a misunderstanding in the minds of visitors and traders who often reported that Indian men bought their wives like slaves. What these observers failed to note was that these gifts indicated that the young woman was held in high regard by her prospective family. Plentiful and expensive gifts also demonstrated the groom's willingness and ability to support his wife. If the match was satisfactory, the bride's family would consent to the marriage (Hassrick 1964:117-118;Wilson 1979:278-284). During the marriage ceremony, the bride's family would give the groom's family many expensive gifts to match the earlier ones, showing that they, too, were pleased by the marriage. The Mandan, Hidatsa, and Arikara considered it appropriate for the newlyweds to move into the earthlodge of the wife's family, although other arrangements would be made if the earthlodge was full (Bowers 1965:139,140). The wealthi-

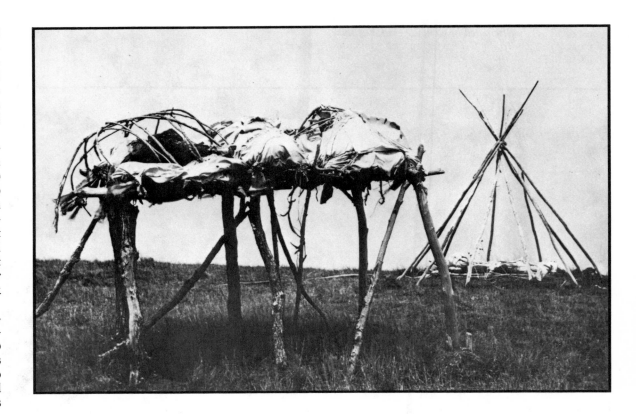

▲ *Most plains tribes buried their dead by placing them on platforms in trees or on scaffolds. (SHSND)*

▼ *Stone hammers were given to young Hidatsa men when they joined their first society, called the Stone Hammer Society. (SHSND)*

34

est families arranged to exchange gifts as a mark of approval for the union, but in most marriages the young man simply moved in with his girlfriend or vice versa, and this constituted public notice of the new relationship. Young men preferred this manner of marriage because it saved them the cost of the gifts, and it was simpler.

In all Plains Indian societies, divorce was achieved by the unhappy partner moving out. Children usually went with their mother, but older children could choose where they wanted to live. Luther Standing Bear recalled that his mother, who was from a different Lakota band, went home to visit, and that it was a few days before anyone realized that she was not planning to return. Sometime later his uncle came and took him to his mother, and he stayed with her until his father came and got him (Standing Bear 1985:28).

A mistaken notion, apparently fostered by movies like *Centennial*, is that elderly Indian people were mistreated and often left to die alone on the Plains, but the evidence is quite different. People did not live as long as they do today, and those few individuals who reached old age were important to the tribe because they had experiences and knowledge to pass on. Grandparents and grandchildren were especially close, and the grandparents were responsible for teaching the youngsters what they had learned. Even when people became quite feeble, the family continued to care for them. Brackenridge (1906:122) reported seeing a very old man carried out of the house each morning and gently placed in the sunshine. The Lakota placed their elderly on the travois and let them ride from camp to camp. The myth of mistreating the elderly may have started because in some rare occurrences food was scarce, and grandparents may have asked that their food be given to their grandchildren, or a person who felt that he was a burden to his family might ask to be left behind when the camp moved, but such situations were uncommon.

Plains Indian men painted their war exploits on shirts, robes, tipi covers, and household furnishing. Black Fox, Arikara, made this record of some of his battles. (SHSND)

When death came, the family mourned the loss of their loved one. Among most of the Plains tribes, the dead were treated with great respect. The relatives dressed the deceased in the finest clothing and then wrapped the body in robes. Infant and adult bodies might be placed in trees, but adult bodies were usually placed on scaffolds erected in a cemetery area near the village or camp (Hassrick 1964:295-296; Bowers 1964:170). The Chippewa buried their dead in the ground and covered the graves with a wood or bark structure that resembled a house. Food for the departed would be placed at the entrance of the little house (Densmore 1929:75-77). As part of the mourning, women would cut their hair, and both men and women might slash their arms and legs when a close relative died.

The Minnesota Chippewa, Lakota, and Dakota had a ceremony called "Keeping the Soul" which permitted special recognition of the deceased for a year. A lock of hair from the deceased was done up in a bundle and treated like a living person for a whole year. During that time it was recognized that the family was in mourning, and everyone in the village would take care of them. When the year was over, a ceremony was held to bury the bundle and return the mourners to their place in the tribe.

Social organization

Success as a warrior was a requirement for admission into membership in the men's military societies. Young men could join a beginners' society before they went to war, but without demonstrating their bravery as warriors they would not be invited to become members of other societies and would never be respected as leaders. These men's societies encouraged their members to achieve success in warfare, celebrated their members' success, mourned the loss of members, sponsored ceremonies, and provided leadership. Some military societies acted as police forces during the tribal hunts and important ceremonies. The Hidatsa Black Mouth Society also conducted village cleanups (Bowers 1965:184-194). A man who obtained membership in the highest society was considered to be wise in warfare and could be asked to lead the village during times of danger. If such a man also showed wisdom of other kinds, he might also lead his family during peace times.

The names and number of societies varied from tribe to tribe, but most northern Plains tribes had at least six men's societies; and Foolish or Crazy Dog Societies, Buffalo Societies, and Raven Societies appear to have existed in all the tribes. Membership requirements differed from tribe to tribe, but all followed the custom of one society "buying out" another. Membership in a society was considered a "right" that could be bought and sold.

SCALPTANZ DER MÖNNITARRIS.	DANSE DU SCALP DES INDIENS MEUNITARRIS.

Women's societies generally reflected women's interests. Karl Bodmer showed Hidatsa women celebrating the successful return of their sons and husbands by dancing with the scalps of their defeated enemies. (SHSND)

37

When all the members of a society agreed to sell their rights to the members of a lower society and the younger society had collected sufficient goods, a ceremonial transfer took place in which the young men were taught the songs, dances, and rules and given the ceremonial regalia of the society. The sellers used the goods they obtained to purchase the rights of another society. Eventually, old men sold their society membership and retired.

Among the Mandan and Hidatsa, membership in the societies was generally based upon age, and members were expected to progress from one society to another in a logical order. Pre-teen boys first joined the Stone Hammer Society. After a few years, they would sell their membership rights to younger men and use the proceeds to purchase the next higher society. The parents helped the young boys, but purchasing the more advanced societies became more expensive, and only the best hunters and warriors would become members (Lowie 1913).

The societies of the Arikara, Dakota, and Lakota were based solely upon achievement (Lowie 1954:111), although, for obvious reasons, age generally correlated with achieve-

▲ *Lewis and Clark gave out small, medium and large medals to identify the three levels of chiefs they made. (SHSND)*

▼ *The group now known as Sioux had three major linguistic and cultural divisions: the Lakota, the Waciyena, and the Dakota. Each of these was further divided into tribes. These tribal divisions were, and still are, the primary social and political units.*

ment. Men were invited to join the various societies, and the clubs competed to acquire the most famous warriors and hunters.

Women also had societies, but their functions were more ceremonial than social. Among the Mandan and Hidatsa, women belonged to the Skunk Women Society, Enemy Women Society, Goose Society, Old Women Society, Gun Society, River Women Society, Cheyenne Women Society, and the White Buffalo Calf Society (Lowie 1913). Lakota women had fewer established societies and more often formed groups based upon shared skills and experiences (DeMallie 1983:241).

Government

In contrast to the process depicted by Hollywood film makers, decisions were not normally made by chiefs and councils. In daily life the oldest or wisest man in a family was the major decision maker. He had little influence over other families, and if he did not make decisions that were acceptable to his family, the members would ignore him and follow someone else's advice. When important issues affected a large number of people, the heads of the families would form a council and meet to discuss the alternative actions they could take, but no voting or coercion took place (Walker

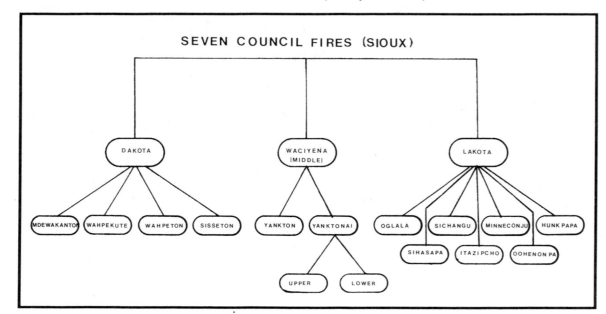

1982:23-30). Once the choices had been discussed and everyone had been heard, the group came to an agreement concerning the most suitable action and informed their families of the decision. If there were too many objections, the council would have to meet again and arrive at a different solution. This form of decision-making is called consensus and works in small groups where harmony and equality are important concerns.

Men generally did not actively seek leadership because of the grave responsibilities involved. A man who was asked to lead the tribal hunt was totally responsible for its success or failure. If the hunt failed, and someone died or there was insufficient meat for the winter, the leader would be blamed for accepting a job which he could not complete successfully. Among the Lakota, outstanding men were selected by the council to carry out its decisions. Called "shirt wearers" because they wore specially decorated shirts, these men were the executives responsible for the safety and livelihood of their people. The shirts were fringed with hair that represented the people of the tribe for whom these shirt wearers were responsible (Hassrick 1964:26-27). Although leadership appeared to be hereditary because a son often achieved the same position as his father, it is more likely that the son saw how his father executed his duties and was better prepared to assume such responsibilities.

The idea of permanent chiefs and councils was introduced by fur traders and explorers who wanted to identify men to represent the tribe in political and business dealings. On their trip up the Missouri in 1804, Lewis and Clark (Prucha 1971:18-19) created a number of chiefs of different ranks by presenting medals in three sizes and other gifts. These chiefs represented bands, tribes, or villages, depending upon the situation; and subsequent negotiations with these men solidified their

39

George Bushotter, a Brule Lakota, drew this picture of men participating in the sun dance. (ARBAE)

▼ *Long and elaborate ceremonies were held in the Arikara sacred earthlodge. (SD)*

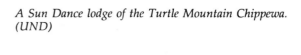

A Sun Dance lodge of the Turtle Mountain Chippewa. (UND)

▼ *The Oscar H. Will seed company specialized in crops native to North Dakota. Will got corn, beans and other seeds from Indians at Fort Berthold Reservation.*

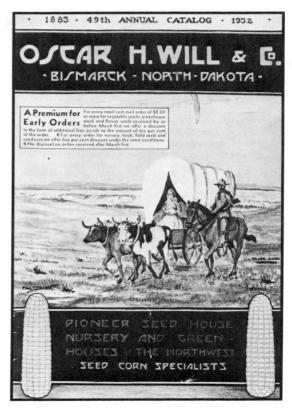

positions and made the groups into permanently recognized units. The chiefs and councils continued to be primarily political entities whose major task was to represent their people to outsiders. Internally, the chiefs and councils were expected to be good examples for their people, but they had little decision-making responsibilities and no coercive power.

Before the tribes came under the control of the Indian agents, a simple legal system maintained correct behavior. There were no laws or judges. Each tribe had a basic moral code that was understood by all. When someone violated the code, the family was responsible for punishing the offender. If others were injured, then the victim's family might also participate in the punishment, but generally justice was a private affair. Only during times when the welfare of the whole group was at stake was there a more generalized legal system. During the major tribal hunts and important ceremo-

nies, one of the military societies was in charge of making sure that everyone obeyed the laws. When the laws were violated, punishment was immediately carried out by the military society, and depending upon the severity of the crime, punishment could be as extreme as death. But as soon as the hunt, ceremony, or other special circumstance was over, the military society lost its power to punish anyone (Lowie 1954:123-127).

Religion

Religious beliefs and ceremonies are the most difficult for outsiders to understand and have been an area of great misunderstanding between Indians and non-Indians. Non-Indians who witnessed the Sun Dance focused on the self-mutilation and thought that the young men were proving their bravery (Catlin 1973,I:157). Instead, these young men were

This Chippewa song record was used by participants in the Midewiwin ceremony. (SHSND)

givers of life, could cause death if there was too much or too little, and so Plains Indians conducted elaborate ceremonies to keep all the spiritual manifestations in harmony.

Each tribe had different names for the Supreme Being or God and the various manifestations, although most tribes concentrated upon the manifestations and paid little attention to the Supreme Being - another point of confusion for non-Indians who assumed the Indians were worshipping natural phenomena. The Lakota and Dakota referred to their Supreme Being as Wakan Tanka or Great Mystery (Mysterious Power), although they most often addressed the Taku Wakan or powerful spirits (Walker 1980:95;Pond 1986:217;Lynd1864:152). The Hidatsa and Mandan called their Supreme Being First Creator in recognition of his role in creating the spirits, the world, the ceremonies, and the People (Bowers 1950:109;1965:282). Gitche Manitou was the name of the Chippewa Supreme Being, but, as in the other tribes, this term was rarely used except in the most sacred circumstances (Warren 1974:64).

Ceremonies were extremely important to Indian people because they assured the continued protection of the spirits. Myriad spirits and the need to maintain harmony between humans and the spiritual world created numerous ceremonies, some unique to a certain tribe and others more widespread. Even the ceremonies held by most of the tribes were conducted differently by each tribe, just as different Christian churches conduct some ceremonies differently. The ceremonies were related to two basic needs of the people: food and health. On the Plains, ceremonies relating to agriculture and buffalo hunting were vitally important, since failure of either of these resources was disastrous, but people were also concerned with maintaining physical and psychological health. In the woodland homes of the Dakota and Chippewa, ceremonies relating to health took priority, although ceremonies for hunting were also significant. Since

sacrificing themselves to bring harmony and good fortune to the others. The Plains Indian concept of a single god with innumerable manifestations and powers is difficult for Christians to comprehend. Christians may believe that only God can make a tree, but Indian people believed that a tree was a form of God and therefore had power to help or harm humans. Such beliefs emphasized the idea that humans were related to all the other elements of the universe, especially animals, and everything had to be treated with care. If a tree could injure, then a person had to treat trees with respect. Even sun and water, the

Prince Maximilian and Karl Bodmer spent the winter at Fort Clark, where Bodmer made this picture of Indians crossing the ice to the Mandan village of Mih-tutta-hang-kush. (SHSND)

43

many health problems were believed to be caused by angry spirits, complex, lengthy ceremonies were performed to keep the spirits happy.

The Lakota are best known for the Sun Dance, an intense and deeply moving ritual in which young men tortured themselves to bring spiritual benefits to the rest of the people. The Lakota considered seven ceremonies to be of great importance to them: the Sweat Lodge, the Vision Quest, the Sun Dance, Making of Relatives, Ghost Keeping, Young Woman's Puberty Ceremony, and Throwing the Ball (Black Elk 1971). Each of these sacred ceremonies was conducted by a religious leader who studied for many years before practicing his knowledge. Depending upon particular spiritual needs, other ceremonies were also available to individuals and to families.

The major Arikara, Mandan, and Hidatsa ceremonies focused upon agriculture, helping the crops to grow well, and upon buffalo hunting (Bowers 1950:107-108). These ceremonies took place at different times of the year and concerned different people. Women were greatly involved in the agricultural ceremonies while men participated most actively in the buffalo hunting ceremonies. Since all the ceremonies involved the survival of the tribe, they were conducted under extremely sacred conditions. During the winter buffalo calling ceremony, absolute silence was demanded for the village, and a person breaking the rule was severely punished. Dogs were killed if they barked. All three tribes also had ceremonies which symbolized the origin story, depicted the creation of animals, and represented adventures of the sacred heroes. During these elaborate ceremonies, men also demonstrated their abilities to cure.

In addition to the Sun Dance, the Dakota and Yanktonai had another major ceremony, the Medicine Lodge, which taught people ways to treat illnesses and cured the sick through their participation in the ceremony (Pond 1986:222-228; Gillette 1906). The Chippewa

Marie McLaughlin, wife of Indian agent James McLaughlin, made this collection at Standing Rock. (SHSND)

also performed a similar ceremony, which they called the Midewiwin, but those who moved to the Plains replaced it with the Sun Dance (Howard 1977:153-162).

Through many generations, the northern Plains Indians developed technical, social, and religious traditions that enabled them to survive the challenge of short, hot summers and long, cold winters. Hard work, extended families, and personal religious experiences brought joy and security to the Indian people.

Contributions to North Dakota history and culture

By breeding varieties of corn, squash, and beans that would mature quickly in the Dakota sun, the Arikara, Mandan, and Hidatsa created a resource for other Indians, as well as an important economic resource for the state. Obtaining seeds from Son of a Star, an Hidatsa from Fort Berthold, Oscar H. Will marketed the Great Northern Bean around the world.

Will's seed catalogs also sold Hidatsa red beans, Arikara yellow beans, Mandan white flour corn, and early Mandan squash obtained from Fort Berthold. Edward Heinemeyer, a farmer who settled on the Missouri in 1882, bred Heinemeyer Flint corn. Both activities were important elements in the state's early economy (Wilkins and Wilkins 1977:26; Robinson 1966:194).

The agricultural resources and the permanent villages resulted in the establishment of Indian trade centers that not only became focal points for non-Indian traders but also later attracted military establishments, missionaries, educators, and government agents. Initially these villages attracted artists such as Karl Bodmer, George Catlin, Seth Eastman, Peter Rindisbacher, and Paul Kane, whose paintings and sketches enrich our lives today. Gradually these villages and many other Indian settlements grew into modern North Dakota communities known as Grand Forks, New Town, Fort Yates, Pembina, Walhalla, and Belcourt.

From this period of tribal history grew the great museum collections in the state. As the Euro-American settlers and historians saw Indian culture changing, they began to write histories, take photographs, and collect objects as examples of Indian tribal traditions. Orin G. Libby, one of the state's leading historians, collected Indian artifacts and oral histories from all of the reservations in North Dakota and, in 1905, started the State Historical Society as a repository for these and other materials. Usher L. Burdick used the Dakota language he learned as a boy growing up near Fort Totten Reservation to interview Indian leaders and build an important collection on Indian history and culture that is now located in the State Historical Society. Smaller collections exemplifying tribal life are found in county historical societies around the state.

The tribal cultures captured the imaginations of people all over the world, and foreign visitors frequently come to the state to study

Usher L. Burdick collected this dress and many other wonderful Indian items which are now in the North Dakota State Historical Society. (SHSND)

45

the collections and report their research. Anthropologists and others interested in ancient tribal cultures have written numerous books and papers describing various aspects of North Dakota Indian life. A similar interest in tribal cultures brought about the preservation of Slant Village, once occupied by the Mandan, and the establishment of Knife River Villages National Park. Both parks inform tourists and local residents about North Dakota history.

The tribal cultures of North Dakota have made important economic contributions to the state through trade, agricultural development, and tourism.

Chapter 4

International Relations: Indians and Hat-Wearers

Introduction

When Northern Plains Indians first met British, Spanish, and French traders, they observed that all these light-skinned strangers wore hats, and, not knowing what else to call them, they referred to the Europeans as "hat-wearers" and described them in sign language by drawing their hands across their brows to indicate the brim of a hat (Ewers 1979). But even before the hat-wearers reached the tribes of the Dakotas, their presence had been felt. Trade items, especially metal knives and glass beads, and smallpox and other diseases, passed from tribe to tribe along well-established trade routes. Although Plains Indians were unaware of the cause, European colonization of the coasts was pushing eastern tribes westward and, like tumbling dominoes, these eastern tribes pressed against the western tribes and forced them into struggles for land and resources that had previously been plentiful for all. But these shadowy presences to the east were only the fuse for an explosion that would change Indian life beyond even the wildest prophecies.

Long before the White men appeared on the Plains, the tribes had established international policies that permitted peaceful trading and visiting among tribes that were usually hostile to one another. Some tribes were generally known as constant friends or allies. The Dakota and Lakota recognized this relationship in their name -- kota, koda, or kola -- which means friends and allies. Mandan and Hidatsa were generally peaceful toward each other, and Cree and Assiniboin cooperated in many ventures (Ewers 1975:404-406). Tribes not in a permanent alliance or known to be allied with an unfriendly tribe were always considered potential enemies and not to be trusted, except under limited conditions. Such conditions were in effect in 1806 when Alexander Henry (Coues 1965, vol.I:367-397) accompanied a group of Mandan and Hidatsa to an alliance-making conference with their long-time enemies, the Cheyenne. Both sides were very nervous and cautious, setting up guards and keeping a constant alert for signs of attack. When a group of Assiniboin arrived at the meeting place, the Cheyenne wanted to attack them but were

Indian records, called winter counts, depict White men in different ways, but always wearing hats.

▼ Non-Indian traders introduced new foods, metal tools and utensils, cotton and wool cloth, and glass beads. (SHSND)

prevented by the Mandan/Hidatsa. The suspicion among the tribes was so intense, though, that the conference disbanded before an agreement was reached.

Anyone who came openly to a camp or village usually received complete hospitality, consisting of food, a place to stay, a horse, and even a woman to mend a man's clothes and warm him at night. Henry reported that his host loaned him "the services of his young wife" for the duration of the Cheyenne treaty-making excursion, but Henry abandoned her in the crowd (Coues 1965, vol.I:367). Because this hospitality was extended to large groups of people, bands of Yanktonai, Lakota, and other often hostile tribes were able to visit the Mandan and Hidatsa villages without fear of attack. Anyone not approaching in an open manner or not under protection of hospitality was regarded as an enemy and subject to at-

▲ *Meriwether Lewis, the appointed leader of the expedition to explore the Louisiana Purchase, died three years after his incredible journey to the Pacific Ocean. (SHSND)*

▲ *After his trip up the Missouri and across the Rockies, William Clark was made Governor of Missouri, a position which included dealing with the Indians of the territory he had recently explored. (SHSND)*

tack. The guarantee of hospitality usually ended at the village limits, and visitors were liable to be attacked by their hosts or, just as likely, would attack anyone who followed them from the village.

Indians and Hat-Wearers Meet

From the Red River to the Missouri, Indian hospitality and friendship characterized the earliest Indian contacts with the hat-wearers. The first recorded White men to enter North Dakota were Pierre Gaultier de Varennes, Sieur de la Vérendrye, and his sons who, accompanied by Assiniboin and Cree, made a journey to the Mandan villages on the Missouri. When La Vérendrye met the Mandan on the morning of

November 28, 1738, the chief expressed friendship for the French (La Vérendrye 1927:320), and later the Mandan demonstrated their friendship by carrying La Vérendrye to their village (La Vérendrye 1927:326).

There is a documentary gap of some forty or fifty years before other explorers and traders are known to have visited the Mandan and Hidatsa villages, but British, Spanish, and Canadians found the same hospitality that La Vérendrye reported. Some of the traders, especially those from Canada, such as Rene Jusseaume, Joseph Garreau, Menard, Toussaint Charbonneau, and others married Indian women and became residents of the villages (Wood and Thiessen 1985:43-47).

Even more significant is the fact that the

Arikara, who later had a reputation for hostility toward Whites, had traders living with them in 1795 (Wood and Thiessen 1986:27). The friendly attitudes of the Arikara changed when they learned the traders were also supplying their enemies with guns and ammunition. These activities removed the traders from the category of allies and made them liable to attack whenever they were met outside the village. Non-Indian failure to understand the reasons for Arikara hostility resulted in the Pryor-Chouteau trading party of 1807 being prevented from reaching the Upper Missouri and established the Arikara's reputation as hostile (Nichols 1984). Their bad reputation notwithstanding, in 1811 the Arikara greeted Henry Brackenridge "with kindness, placed mats and skins for us to sit on, and after smoking the pipe, offered us something to eat" (Brackenridge 1906:117). Another member of the party, John Bradbury, reported the same cordial treatment (Bradbury 1904:129-135).

Even when the number of White visitors and residents increased dramatically, the hospitality of the Mandan and Hidatsa was unstinting. Meriwether Lewis, William Clark, and their men spent the winter of 1804-1805 in a fort near the Mandan and Hidatsa villages (Reid 1947-48: 76-194). Throughout the winter the men were provided with food, either in exchange for metal weapons or as gifts, and invited to attend ceremonies in the Indian villages (Reid 1947-48:117,161,167). When Alexander Henry and Charles Chaboillez visited the villages in 1806, they, too, were well received. Henry refers to their "kind" and "obliging" hosts (Coues 1965:329,332). Bradbury and Brackenridge left the Arikara village and paid a short trip to the Mandan where they were welcomed by Big White, who spoke some English, and other tribal leaders (Brackenridge 1906:162-164). The detailed and colorful descriptions of George Catlin (Catlin 1973) and Prince Maximilian of Wied-Neuwied (Wied-Neuwied 1906), who visited the Upper Missouri in 1832-34, have made them the best known of the numerous visitors, but the many others who preceded and followed them also found a warm reception from the Missouri River tribes.

▼ In 1806, Big White, who had been named a Mandan chief by Lewis and Clark, accompanied the explorers when they returned to Washington, D.C. After meeting President Jefferson, Big White visited Philadelphia where his portrait was painted by Charles Balthasar Julien Fevret de Saint-Memin. (SHSND)

SHA-HA-KA.
A MANDAN CHIEF.

PEMBINA FORT.

Events on the Red River quickly took a different direction, as agricultural settlement followed only a few short years after the fur traders entered the area, but the same policy of hospitality was extended to the fur traders. Charles Chaboillez established a fur trading post near Pembina in 1797. David Thompson, another trader, was in the area at approximately the same time. Only a few years later, Alexander Henry built his trading center at Pembina and located other posts in the northern Red River Valley. The Chippewa, Cree, Assiniboin, and other Indians associated with these eastern Dakota trading posts not only trapped furs for the post but also worked as hunters, messengers, and other employees.

One of the ways in which events on the Red River differed from those on the Missouri was in the outcome of marriages between Indians and non-Indians. On the Missouri, the men who married Indian wives generally settled down to live in the villages, and their children remained there. In eastern Canada the sons of Canadian fur traders who married Indian women entered the fur trade and moved westward with the trade. Some of the men employed by Chaboillez and Henry were the offspring of such marriages; following the custom, Charles Chaboillez, David Thompson, and Alexander Henry took Indian wives (Coues 1965, vol.I:304,163). Some of the offspring of these mixed marriages did not consider themselves either Indian or White and began to identify themselves as a "new nation of métis" (Giraud 1947) and to assert this identity in various ways. Many of these Métis were freemen; that is, independent trappers, voyageurs, and clerks who were not bound to Hudson's Bay trading company and would work for the company that offered the best benefits, highest pay, and most convenient conditions.

Wanatan and his son assisted the exploring expedition through the Red River valley led by Stephan Long in 1823.

White visitors were also well received by the Yankton and Yanktonai. In 1800 Robert Dickson, a British trader, married a sister of Red Thunder, the Yankton headman, and set up a trading post at Lake Traverse where he spent many years. Dickson later gained notoriety during the War of 1812 when he tried to incite the Indians of the area to join the British, but after the war Dickson returned to Lake Traverse (Robinson 1966:52,56-57). In its exploration of the Red River Valley, Stephen Long's expedition of 1823 encountered Wanatan, the headman, and his band of Yanktonai, who were camped near the Columbia Fur Company's trading post at Lake Traverse (Keating 1959,vol.I:448-458). Wanatan invited the expedition into his council tent and fed them a special feast. Later, remarking that the best dancers were absent from the camp, Wanatan complied with a request for a dance demonstration. When the expedition prepared to leave Lake Traverse, they were alarmed by reports of a large number of Yanktonai camped on the Sheyenne River and asked Wanatan to accompany them. Wanatan agreed, but, learning that the reports were false and that Wanatan's band needed to go buffalo hunting, the expedition leaders released him from his agreement (Keating 1959,vol.II:2-3). However, the expedition later caught up with Wanatan's camp and were again feasted, and this time Wanatan took some of the expedition with him on a buffalo hunt (Keating 1959,vol.II:6).

The Lakota on the Missouri also welcomed traders who were loyal to them, and marriages were made between traders and Lakota Indian women. In 1804, Lewis and Clark met Old Dorion, who had been living with the Sioux for more than twenty years (Thwaites 1904-06,vol.I:46-47). When the expedition reached the Brule tribe's camp near the mouth of the James River, the members found that Dorion's son was trading there (Thwaites 1904-06, vol.I:128). The expedition's initial meeting with the Teton (probably members of the Oglala band) was less cordial (Thwaites 1904-06,vol.I:164-165), but the next day the expedition was well received, and Clark described being carried into the camp on an elegantly painted buffalo robe (Thwaites 1904-06, vol.I:167).

When tribes on the Missouri and Red rivers departed from their standards of hospitality and generosity toward hat-wearers, the cause was either a misunderstanding on the part of the White men or an outgrowth of competition for increasingly scarce resources. The difficulty which Lewis and Clark had on their first meeting with the Tetons was apparently caused by the Captains' giving the Indian men some liquor (Thwaites 1904-06,vol.I:164-165). Other difficulties were caused by traders working for competing companies who were not above inciting their friends to attack the other company's posts (Nichols 1984). Overtrapping quickly resulted in declines in the fur trade that constantly forced traders to expand their territories. In the Red River Valley a complicating factor was the establishment in 1811 of an agricultural colony by Scottish immigrants under the direction of Lord Selkirk. When competition between Hudson's Bay and other trading companies became intense, and the traders felt threatened by Scottish and Swiss immigrants seeking to establish farms, the traders aroused the Métis, who, in June 1816, attacked the settlement and killed some of Selkirk's people (Robinson 1966:64). The attack focused attention on the Métis' grievances and resulted in an agreement between the Métis and the immigrant settlers. Later Lord Selkirk bought a strip of land running from the mouth of the Red River to Grand Forks from the Cree and Chippewa for his settlers. Feeling more secure in his attempt to develop the agricultural settlement of the area, Lord Selkirk asked for religious assistance to help maintain the peace between Métis and agriculturalists. In response to Lord Selkirk's request, in 1818 Father Sévère Dumoulin, a young Catholic missionary, was sent to Pembina where he built the first chapel and school in North Dakota (Robinson 1966:68;70). Most of his parishioners were Métis, and this activity began the long relationship between the Métis and the Catholic Church.

Indians Adapt to the Presence of the Hat-Wearers

Between 1835 and 1861, when Dakota Territory was formed, major changes occurred in all the Indian cultures of the northern Plains. Increasing White settlement of Minnesota and eastern North Dakota forced the Métis and Chippewa into new economic ventures. Both groups became buffalo hunters, but the Chippewa, who previously had kept a foothold in Minnesota, now fully adopted the life of nomadic Plainsmen (Hickerson 1956) and selected the Turtle Mountain area as their home base, while the Métis chose a way of life that alternated between the life of a hunter and the life of a townsman. Fort Garry (later Winnipeg) and Pembina became the Métis' home communities from which they left on summer and fall

The first treaty of cession affecting North Dakota lands was made by Lord Selkirk with the Chippewa and Cree. In exchange for annual payments of tobacco and cash, the leaders, whose clan signs are shown on the map, ceded lands on each side of the Red and Assiniboine Rivers.

buffalo hunts.

During their travels on the Missouri, Prince Maximilian (Wied-Neuwied 1906,vol.23:190-191) and George Catlin (Catlin 1973, vol.I:53-58) found Chippewa at Fort Union. Catlin reported that these Chippewa had no knowledge of their relationship to Chippewa living further east and no recollection of a separation from them (Catlin 1973,vol.I:53). Catlin painted several portraits of Plains Chippewas, including one of the chief, another of one of the chief's wives, and one of a young woman, Kay-a-Gis-Gis (Hassrick 1977:123,146,147). Although the Long expedition did not report any Chippewa living at Pembina, it received a description of the territory claimed by the Chippewa and learned that it stretched from Sault Ste. Marie to the Souris River, a tacit indication of the presence of Plains Chippewa to the west of the Red River (Keating 1959:148).

When the expedition under the command of Brevet Major Samuel Woods reached Pembina in 1849, it found both Chippewa and Métis living there, but all were away hunting buffalo (Woods 1850:23). Woods learned that the Pembina Chippewa's primary hunting range was the Turtle Mountains where they could find furs and game (Woods 1850:25). He reported a population of 500 to 600 Chippewa, and since they had no permanent chiefs, he appointed three men to represent them: Green Feather as first chief, and End of the Current and Long Legs as second chiefs (Woods 1850:24). Woods also received news of a confrontation between Chippewa and Sioux buffalo hunters in which both sides lost men.

Under the pressure of agricultural settlement and the failure of the fur trade, the Métis became a powerful force in the area. Acting as traders and hunters, and spending part of their time in the settlements, they became intermediaries between Indians and White settlers, adopting the customs of both whenever it was

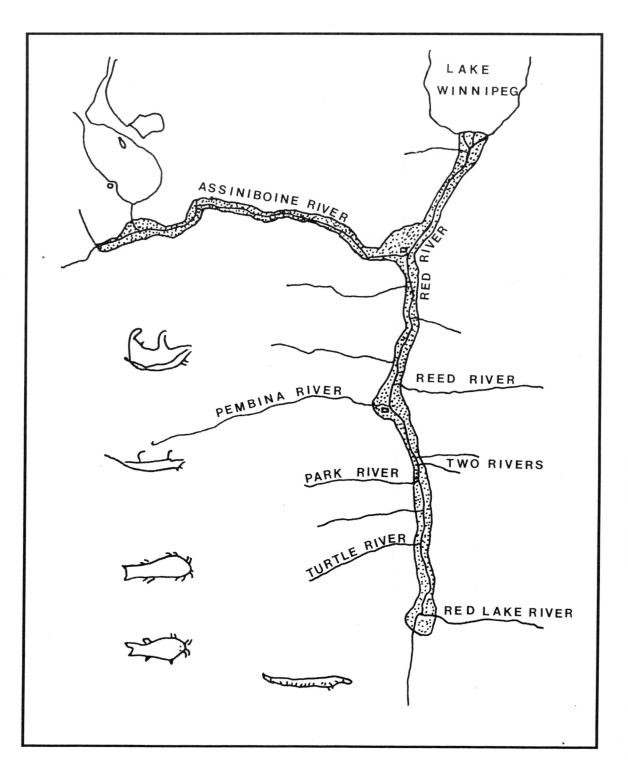

CAPTAINS OF TRAINS.

to their benefit and yet maintaining themselves as a distinctive cultural entity. When Stephen Long's expedition of 1823 arrived at Pembina, it consisted of 60 log cabins occupied mainly by Metis, who were away hunting buffalo. William H. Keating, a journalist with the Long expedition, described Métis dress as a mixture of Indian and White clothing which included a calico or muslin shirt, "moccasins and leather leggings fastened round the leg by garters ornamented with beads, etc." (Keating 1959,vol.II:40). Keating also noted that the

Métis hunters and carters were vital elements in the settlement and commercial development of the Red River valley. (HM)

Métis cultivated small fields of wheat, barley, maize, potatoes, and similar crops.

Woods's expedition of 1849 found over 1000 Métis living at Pembina (Woods 1850:27). He described the Métis in greater detail than he did the Chippewa, noting that the Métis built log cabins but used tipis while hunting buffalo (Woods 1850:28). Unlike the Chippewa, the Métis had a formal government organization consisting of a council of five men. Woods told the Métis to select men to be a permanent council, and the next day the Métis presented him with a list of nine men, headed by Mr. Wilky [sic.] (Woods 1850:28). Woods also obtained a description of a Métis buffalo hunt from Father George Antoine Belcourt, the Catholic missionary to the Chippewa and Métis. By supplying buffalo meat and pemmican to

JEAN BATTISTE WILKIE.

▲ *For many years, Jean Baptiste Wilkie, shown here in a sketch made in St. Joseph in 1860, was head of the Métis council. (HM)*

Hudson's Bay Company and to the agriculturalists, the Métis at Pembina provided crucial economic support and became vital elements in the successful occupancy of the Red River Valley by European settlers. The Metis also became involved in the transportation of goods and mail between St. Paul and Winnipeg (Robinson 1966:66). The population of Pembina continued to increase, although the church and most of the people moved fifty miles west to St. Joseph in 1853, and in 1870 St. Joseph and Pembina had a population of more than 800 "civilized Indians" or Métis (Walker 1872:106).

While the Chippewa and Métis were adjusting to agricultural development of the Red River Valley, the Missouri River tribes were facing other impacts of White presence. Although the Mandan had been decimated by smallpox and other epidemics that preceded the traders and visitors, the epidemic of 1837 that followed White contact was the most devastating, especially for the Mandan. Figures

Like-a-Fishhook Village photographed around 1870 by S.J.Morrow was an important trading center on the Missouri River. (SHSND)

55

vary, but there is general agreement that more than two thirds of the Mandan died. The Hidatsa suffered only slightly less than the Mandan (Meyer 1977:95-96). The loss of warriors was accompanied by increasing depredations by the Yanktonai and other Sioux tribes, causing the Mandan and Hidatsa to abandon their villages on the Knife River and move up the Missouri. Around 1845 the Hidatsa built a new village, named Like-a-Fishhook, on a hooked bend in the Missouri River, where some of the Mandan soon joined them. Other Mandan apparently remained near Fort Clark until 1857, when an agent reported them living in the village (Smith 1972:7). In 1866 the Arikara also moved into Like-a-Fishhook (Smith 1972:28). The large population made the village an important commercial center where steamboats docked, visitors arrived, and traders settled down. From 1858 to 1862 Henry Boller worked for the Opposition traders who had a post called Fort Atkinson at Like-a-Fishhook. They were called the Opposition because they were in direct competition with the American Fur Company post called Fort Berthold (Boller 1972:33). When Dakota Territory was formed in 1861, Like-A-Fishhook, with a Mandan-Hidatsa population of over 1,000 (Smith 1972:28), was the second or third largest community in the region and remained so for many years.

Life in Like-a-Fishhook was a continuation of earlier village styles with the added convenience of guns, metal tools and utensils, imported foods, fabricated clothing, and other trade goods. People continued to build earthlodges, to hunt buffalo, and to practice the traditional ceremonies (Boller 1972). Boller accompanied a group of Hidatsa to their winter village in the bottomlands near the river and described the villages and activities of the people with whom he lived (Boller 1972). Another source of information about life in Like-a- Fishhook is found in the biography of Buffalo Bird Woman (Wilson 1971), whose life spanned the beginning and end of the village.

Between 1863 and 1904, the Indian tribes of North Dakota gradually gave up most of their land.

By mid-century, all the Indians, while continuing traditional patterns of social and religious organization, had been affected by the presence of White people and had joined into the trading enterprise. Because the traders were much more interested in commerce than in political organization or missionizing, they made little attempt to change the Indian lifestyle. The formal establishment of Dakota Territory, however, brought many more settlers into the area and precipitated the eventual establishment of reservations and the institution of governmental controls.

The beginnings of territorial status came in 1857 and 1858 when Sioux Falls and Yankton were established. Before that, however, the Indian claims to the area had to be terminated. In 1858 the Yankton accepted a treaty in which they ceded 15 million acres for $1,600,000 and reserved for themselves a tract of 400,000 acres which became the Yankton Reservation (Robinson 1966:127;Schell 1975:71). Not all the Yankton were in agreement over the treaty, and White occupation of the ceded lands was delayed until July 1859, but rapid expansion of the southern part of the territory followed (Schell 1975:72). White settlement of the northern part of the region was considerably slower. Although Pembina sent delegates, called the "Moccasin Democrats" (Robinson 1966:128), to the Dakota Legislature, the delegation had few people to represent; in fact Pembina was not represented in the legislature between 1864 and 1867, when Pembina County was again established (Robinson 1966:128). At this time, surveying for townships along the Red River

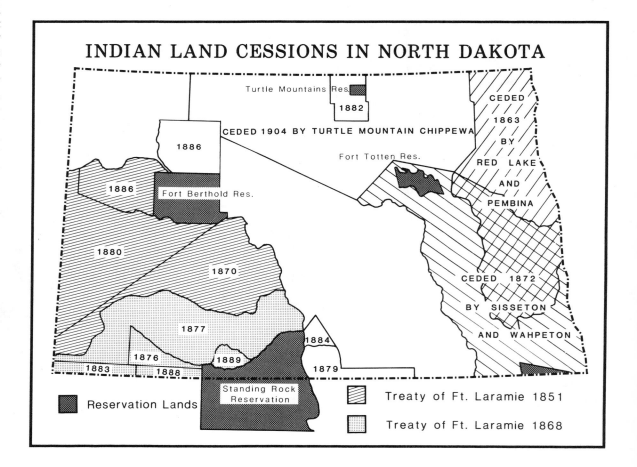

56

THE SIOUX WAR—CAVALRY CHARGE OF SULLY'S BRIGADE AT THE BATTLE OF WHITE STONE HILL, SEPTEMBER 3, 1863.—SKETCHED BY AN OFFICER ENGAGED.

began. By 1869, scattered farmsteads along the Red River and small communities around stage stops had sprung up, but it was not until 1871 that speculation about the railroad created interest in developing major communities. The railroad from St. Paul reached Fargo, then a tent city, in 1872 and Bismarck in 1873. From that point on, White settlement of Dakota Territory advanced rapidly (Robinson 1966:129).

International Tensions

Many of the more drastic changes in Dakota Territory were the result of events occurring in Minnesota, an early center of agricultural and industrial development. At first the Minnesota Dakota struggled through the treaty-making process to reserve some of their ancestral lands for themselves, but when their at-

The so-called Battle of Whitestone Hill, shown here in a drawing made at the time, was a massacre of innocent Indian buffalo hunters. (SHSND)

tempts failed, some of the Dakota turned to violence. Rather than join either side in the outbreak, a great many Dakota fled into Canada and into Dakota Territory. The Dakota Conflict of 1862 led to the only Army action against Indians in what is now North Dakota. In order to bring the fleeing Dakota under control, Generals Henry Hastings Sibley and Alfred Sully ranged through Dakota Territory, going wherever their scouts told them there were Indians. The records are unclear, but most scholars agree that the few times the Army located and engaged the Indians, they were not marauding Dakota, but innocent buffalo hunters. In the battle of Whitestone Hill, Sully's troopers killed 150 Indian men, women, and children, burned their lodges, shot the horses, and destroyed the dried buffalo meat (Robinson 1966:100-101). The presence of women and children and the buffalo meat suggests that these were buffalo hunters, and records of the Sully expedition indicate these were not even Dakota, but were either Yanktonai or Hunkpatina (Jacobson 1980:12). The Dakota Conflict resulted in the eviction of the Dakota from Minnesota, the westward displacement of a portion of the Yanktonai, the establishment of the first reservations in Dakota Territory, and the construction of a dozen military forts (Robinson 1966:101- 102).

58

As a punishment for the Conflict, most of the Minnesota Sioux were removed from Minnesota and sent to reservations in Dakota Territory. In 1863 Congress passed "An Act for the Removal of the Sisseton, Wahpeton, Medwakanton, and Wahpakoota Bands of Sioux or Dakota Indians, and for the disposition of their lands in Minnesota and Dakota" (Meyer 1967:140), which dispossessed all the Minnesota Sioux and required their relocation elsewhere. Crow Creek Reservation, on the Missouri River in eastern South Dakota, was established in 1863 for the Santee, but most of the Sisseton and Wahpeton who had remained in Dakota Territory were not included. In 1867 a

separate treaty agreement was made with the Sisseton, Wahpeton, and Cuthead band of Yanktonai for a reservation in eastern Dakota (Meyer 1967:199). The Sisseton and Wahpeton who settled on the southern part of the reservation that later became the Sisseton-Wahpeton Reservation were farmers led by Gabriel Renville. Other Sisseton and Wahpeton continued to hunt buffalo beyond the jurisdiction of Indian agents, but eventually they settled near Devils Lake in the northern section of the reservation. Some of the Dakota who had fled to Canada refused to return, and today their descendents still live on reserves in Canada.

Under the 1867 treaty establishing the Devils

Indian agents administered federal policies directed toward assimilation. This photograph showing the agent's office at Fort Yates was taken in 1906. (SHSND)

Army action against the Sioux, yet several forts were constructed in the territory of the "hostile" Lakota (Schell 1975:88-89). Later, Fort Yates became the agency center for the Standing Rock Sioux Reservation.

Although the forts were established to keep the peace, they were rarely attacked, and the soldiers suffered more from boredom than from battle fatigue (Mattison 1954:31-32). Indian people worked for the military as scouts, mail carriers, hunters, and interpreters. Indian attacks were still directed primarily against other Indians, but White people associated with specific tribes were victimized by their associates' enemies. White men living in Like-a-Fishhook village were targets for Sioux attacks. The gravest incident occurred in 1863 when a group of Sioux attacked a wagon train of emigrants led by Captain James L. Fisk. Fisk had successfully conducted other trains and was convinced that he was safe, but after leaving Fort Rice, he was attacked. The train successfully defended itself until aid was sent from the fort, but between six and twelve soldiers and civilians were killed. The number of Indians killed was not recorded (Collections of the State Historical Society of North Dakota 1908:34-85). Reports of hostile Indians continued to attract military attention. In 1864 a group composed of Sioux from many different bands was attacked by General Sully in the Killdeer Mountains. Official reports claim that Sully found as many as 5,000 warriors, but Doane Robinson interviewed survivors of the battle who said there were no more than 1,600 men (Robinson 1904:334). Sully believed that he was attacking an army, but Robinson's sources told him that the Indians had fled to the Killdeer Mountains for safety since they believed that Sully's goal was to kill every Indian in Dakota Territory (Robinson 1904:334). No doubt, the deaths of men on both sides contributed to the continuing hostility between Indians and Whites in the area.

Other demonstrations of hostility were often

Lake Reservation, no agency would be provided until 500 Indians had taken up residence there. During the four years that the "wild" Sioux debated settling at Devils Lake, those who did move to the reservation were looked after by the commanding officer at Fort Totten, and Fort Totten gradually assumed the function of tribal agency (Meyer 1967:220). The head chief of the Sissetons at Devils Lake in 1869 was Tiyowashte (Good House also called Good Fish). The Yanktonai at Devils Lake were led by Wanatan. Other Yanktonai settled on their traditional hunting lands on the Missouri River (Letters Received, Standing Rock Agency, August 1880, National Archives Record Group 75), while some ended up at Crow Creek Reservation, and later moved to Fort Peck Reservation in Montana.

Despite the general lack of hostility on the part of the Indian tribes, the decade immediately following 1861 was marked by a military presence that culminated in there being more than one soldier for every male Indian (Robinson 1966:176). Forts were built on the Missouri and Red rivers, at Devils Lake, and on the James River (Robinson 1966:176). These forts were often constructed in areas where Indians gathered, and the modern association of forts and reservations is no accident. Fort Totten was established in 1867 as a military deterrent against the Dakota and Yanktonai. Fort Stevenson was organized in 1868 to protect the Mandan, Hidatsa, and Arikara from depredations of the western Sioux and Yanktonai. The Treaty of Fort Laramie of 1868 was a peace treaty designed to avoid the necessity for any

59

CHARLES PACKINEAU
INTERPRETER
DIED---1875

PETER BEAUCHAMP, SR.
INTERPRETER
DIED---1878

HOWARD MANDAN
(SCARED FACE)
1847-1881

PETER BEAUCHAMP, JR.
1846-1892

DANCE FLAG
1834--1912

SON-OF-THE-STAR
1813--------1881

BLACK-FOX
1843-1896

BAD GUN
(CHARGING EAGLE)
1829-1909

BULL-HEAD
1828-1898

In 1874, this delegation of Mandan, Hidatsa and Arikara went to Oklahoma and then to Washington, D.C. to investigate the government's proposal that the tribe move to Oklahoma where farming would be easier. (SHSND)

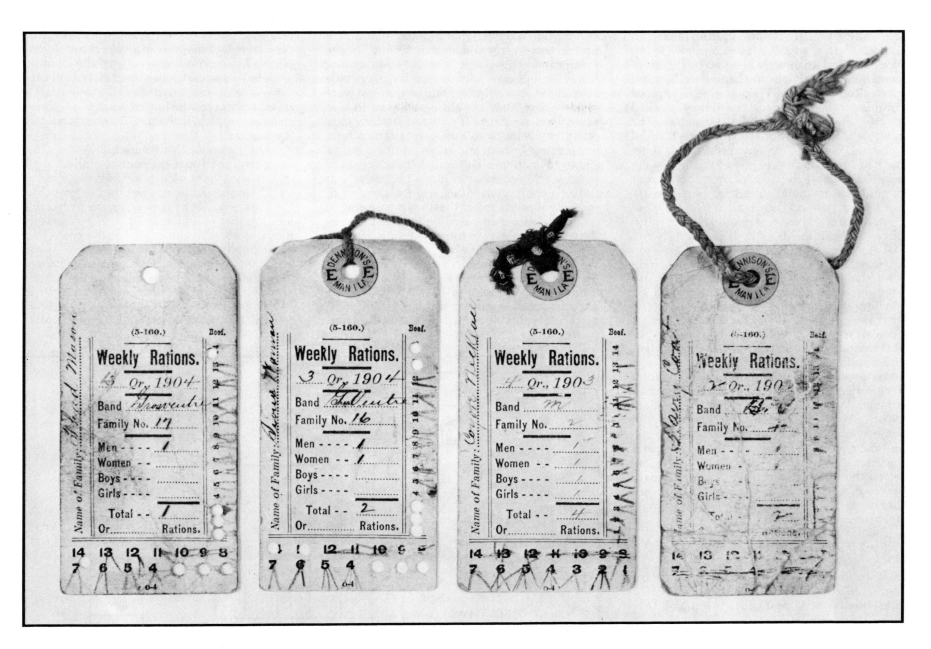

Because the tribes gave up land from which they gained their livelihood, the government agreed to provide food, clothing, education and medicine in exchange for the lands. Indian agents had to keep accurate records of the provisions distributed to each family. One way of doing this was by means of tickets which could be punched or marked off each week. (SHSND)

the result of failed communications between Indians and hat-wearers. The Chippewa living along the Red River were angered by the introduction of steamboats that frightened fish and game (Robinson 1966:115), yet the Chippewa complaints went unheeded until they attacked a cart train and threatened a steamboat. The result was the Treaty of 1853 in which the Red Lake and Pembina Chippewa ceded lands along the Red River. Formerly peaceful Lakota were angered when wagon trains of emigrants, hordes of gold seekers, and soldiers trespassed without punishment on their lands.

The forts and the reservation system introduced the rudiments of civilization to North Dakota. Reservations meant agents, missionaries, schools, and increased communication with the outside world. The military also brought an element of civilization, and by quelling the fears of Whites contributed to an increasing number of White settlers. Conditions were such that the missionaries, agents, and military men began to bring their wives and families with them. Sarah Canfield, who accompanied her husband to his command at Fort Berthold, described life at the post as a combination of luxury and deprivation (Canfield 1953). To entertain each other and maintain some semblance of a normal life, the officers and their wives held dances, card parties, and theatricals (Mattison 1954:39). Contacts between the military and Indians were limited, however, and the effort to change Indian culture came, not from the Army, but from missionaries, educators, and agents.

Federal Policies Affecting Indians

Ever since the first European colonists encountered American Indians there has been a question of how to deal with the Indians. One assumption has been that Indians should give up their own ways and learn to be just like the Europeans. This policy is called assimilationism. The opposite idea is that Indian people have their own cultures, and since they were already here, they should be allowed to preserve their languages and customs, taking only what they want from Euro-American culture. Supporting Indian and other ethnic groups' rights to maintain cultural distinctiveness is usually referred to as cultural pluralism, but Indian people more often use the concept of sovereignty and explain that they have a unique federal relationship based on treaties between the tribes and the government. Using either an assimilationist or pluralist approach, Congress determines how Indians are to be treated by the federal government's representatives, the officers of the Bureau of Indian Affairs. The assimilationist approach has been most common, and missionaries, bureaucrats, educators, and policy-makers have tried for centuries to turn Indians into Euro-Americans. Indian people have persistently resisted the attempts at assimilation and maintained their right to be treated as sovereign citizens. From time to time, support for the Indian point-of-view was strong enough to influence Congressional policy-makers.

Once assigned to reservations, the tribes were brought under the control of the Bureau of Indian Affairs, which sent agents to carry out the policies determined by Congress and the President. For many years the overriding attitude was assimilationist with policies and instructions to agents aimed at the goal of assimilating Indians into the general non-Indian population. Treaties and agreements carried guarantees to build houses and provide clothes, schools, medical services, and other aid to Indian people, but all of these were directed toward the ultimate goal of turning Indian

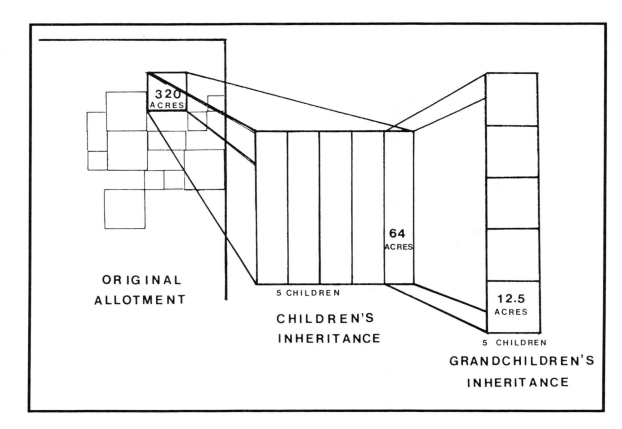

The problem of fractionated heirship. Under the Allotment Act of 1887, reservations were divided into 320, 160 and 80 acre plots and assigned to individual Indian owners. Children inherited equal shares of their parent's allotments. If a man had five children, each would inherit 1/5 of his 320 acres, or 64 acres. If one of these children had five children, each one would inherit 12.5 acres.

Sakakawea, who led Lewis and Clark up the Missouri River and across the Rockies, is the most famous Indian woman in America. (SHSND)

people into White people. Agents, instructed to prohibit customs which seemed to prevent adoption of White ways, banned religious ceremonies and dances. Any Indian person caught attending a native religious ceremony or dance was jailed and fined. In the schools, children were severely punished for speaking their native language and forced to speak English.

The first major Congressional policy to af-fect all the North Dakota tribes equally was the General Allotment Act of 1887, which directed that all the reservations in the country were to be divided into small parcels of land to be given to each Indian living on the reservation (Prucha 1975:171-174). Any land not allotted to Indians was to be sold and the proceeds used to support Indian education and medical needs and to purchase farm equipment and other items considered necessary by the agent. The allotted lands were to be kept in trust by the federal government for either twenty-five years or until the owner showed that he or she was a competent landowner.

The Allotment Act opened all the reserva-tions in North Dakota to settlement by non-Indians, and today most reservation lands are actually owned by Whites. The Allotment Act also required that the children of allottees share equally in an allotment, and one of the great problems on modern reservations is that par-cels of land are claimed by so many heirs that no one can use the land efficiently. The process of settling the heirs' legal claims is lengthy and difficult and much Indian land is simply leased to non-Indian ranchers and farmers. Share claimants, however, may be so numerous that the portions of lease payments each receives are too small to provide support.

Allotment and the general belief that Indi-ans must adopt non-Indian ways continued until 1934, when John Collier, the new Com-missioner of Indian Affairs, took a different ap-proach. Collier supported Indian sovereignty and believed that reservation lands belonged to Indian people whose culture should be pre-served. In 1934 Congress formalized Collier's ideas by passing the Indian Reorganization Act (Prucha 1975:222-225). The Act had four major provisions: to stop the sale of reservation lands, to strengthen tribal governments, to establish a more secure economic status for the tribes, and to encourage Indian religion, language, and culture. Tribes were given the right to vote on accepting the Indian Reorganization Act. Tribes that voted yes were allowed to establish consti-tutional forms of government, to incorporate themselves, and to borrow money to buy back land or to establish businesses. In North Da-kota only the people at Fort Berthold voted to

accept the Act, adopted a constitutional form of government, and incorporated into the Three Affiliated Tribes, the only North Dakota tribe to be so organized. The other North Dakota tribes eventually adopted constitutions and are now governed by councils of representa-tives elected from districts on the reservation.

The goal of the Indian Reorganization Act, to improve conditions for Indian people by making them more self-sufficient, made little noticeable change, and Indians remained the most impoverished, worst educated, and least healthy ethnic group in America.

Concerns about the Indians' conditions re-sulted in a return to the idea of assimilation. In 1953 Congress passed House Concurrent Reso-lution 108, often called Termination, which was designed to encourage independence from the Bureau of Indian Affairs by eventually doing away with all reservations (Prucha 1975:233). Treaties were to be legally ended. All reservation lands were to be sold. All special federal programs for Indian people were to be closed down, and Indians would be just like all other American citizens. Hearings were held on each tribe to be terminated and oppo-nents pointed out that the idea was contradic-tory to everything contained in the treaties, but, across the country, many tribes were ter-minated. The Turtle Mountain Chippewa and Three Affiliated Tribes were considered ready to begin the process, but no North Dakota tribes were terminated.

Congress signaled a return to Indian sov-ereignty in 1975 when it passed the Self-Deter-mination and Education Act. Under Self-De-termination, a tribe is permitted to contract with the Bureau of Indian Affairs for the funds to manage programs previously administered by the Bureau. Instead of decisions being made in Washington, D.C., or by non-Indians, Self-Determination allows each tribe to decide for itself how programs will be operated and funds allocated. Today most tribes operate schools, construction programs, road maintenance, and social service programs partially under con-tract and partially under the Bureau of Indian Affairs administration.

Because history shows that federal Indian policies change drastically every twenty or

Indian scouts camped at Fort Rice around 1870. (SHSND)

thirty years, there is growing concern about the future. Will there be a return to the ideas of assimilation and attempts to force Indians to give up their last remaining lands? One cause for concern is the increasing demand for energy resources found on many reservations. Another reason is the apparent lack of popular support for multicultural and bilingual programs that maintain ethnic differences. Even though there are many people who speak English as a second language, North Dakota recently passed a law stating that English is the official state language. What will this mean to those trying to retain a native language? No matter what the future holds, one fact is clear: Indian people will survive and continue to be an important element in the future of North Dakota.

Contributions to North Dakota History

A significant proportion of North Dakota's cultural identity comes from the period of Indian-White contact. The famous explorations of La Vérendrye, Lewis and Clark, Catlin, Prince Maximilian, and others were made possible by Indian good-will. The fur traders also relied on Indian hospitality and the experiences of Indian traders and entrepreneurs. It is no accident that the earliest fur trading posts were built on the Missouri River where the Mandan, Hidatsa, and Arikara had well-established trading centers. Indian people worked for the traders as trappers, hunters, soldiers, and interpreters. Fort Union, a major trading post on the Upper Missouri, currently under reconstruction by the National Park Service, is already attracting international attention to North Dakota.

During the period of White settlement, Indians continued to aid the newcomers. The Plains Chippewa and Métis hunters saved the Selkirk farmers from starvation by selling them buffalo meat and pemmican. It was also Métis willingness to make the trek from Winnipeg to St. Paul by Red River carts that made St. Paul a commercial center.

Indian people also worked as scouts, mail carriers, interpreters, and in various other capacities for the military. Many Indian men, like the Arikara who scouted for General Custer, were recognized by the Army for their bravery.

A number of military forts in North Dakota recall this phase of the state's history. The contributions of some of these men are commemorated in the names of Renville, Bottineau, and Rolette counties.

The first schools and churches were estab-

▼ *Poor Wolf, born in an earthlodge in 1822, moved to Like-a-Fishhook Village and then to an allotment, became a staunch Christian, and died several years after the first automobiles reached the reservation. (SHSND)*

lished for Indian people. Father Dumoulin established a Catholic mission at Pembina in 1818, and by the later 1840's there were several Catholic priests working in what is now North Dakota. Protestant missions began somewhat later and, at first, were less successful than the Catholic. In 1870 Agent H.L. Clifford opened a day school at Fort Berthold and the Grey Nuns began a Catholic school at Fort Totten in 1874.

The establishment of the reservations brought federal funds into the area in the form of agency employee salaries, purchasing and delivery of goods for distribution to Indians, and Indian cash accounts. These funds were deposited in local banks and used to pay the businessmen who sold services and products to the agency. When Indians earned money by working for the agency, by selling wood to the steamboats, and by selling their crops, they became consumers of local goods and services.

The strongest representatives of this period, however, are the Indian men and women whose contributions left indelible marks upon the state's development: Sakakawea, the woman who led Lewis and Clark to the Pacific Ocean; Gall, John Grass, Son-of-a-Star, Poor Wolf, and Mrs. Galpin, along with many other leaders who tried to help their people adapt to the changes being brought to them by the agents and missionaries; Crow-Flies-High, who defied the government agents to prove that Indians could survive away from the reservation; Cuthbert Grant, Antoine Gingras, Jean Baptiste Wilkie, and Pierre Bottineau, traders and politicians; and Louis Riel and Sitting Bull, who led their people in the last struggles for Indian dominance.

Despite the enduring stereotypes and myths about Indian-White hostility, relationships between North Dakota Indians and non-Indians have been more cordial than in other states. The hospitality that Indian tribes extended to

▼ *Many tribal leaders struggled to help their people adjust to life on the reservations, but some, like Sitting Bull, fought against the reservation system. (SHSND)*

explorers, traders, visitors, missionaries, and others continues today. Visitors are encouraged to attend powwows and rodeos, and non-Indians living on reservations share church, school, and the work place with Native Americans.

Chapter 5

Fort Berthold Reservation

Standing sturdily astride the ice-blue waters of Lake Sakakawea, in west-central North Dakota, is Fort Berthold Reservation, the home of the Mandan, Arikara, and Hidatsa tribes, now known legally as the Three Affiliated Tribes. Since 1862, when the Arikara joined the Mandan and Hidatsa in Like-A-Fishhook Village, the three tribes have shared a common political history, but each tribe also has a separate identity and maintains its distinctive language, customs, and beliefs.

The establishment of Fort Berthold Reservation illustrates a point in the treaty-making process when the federal government paid little attention to peaceful tribes. In the 1851 Treaty of Fort Laramie, an area extending from east of the Missouri River to beyond the Yellowstone River in Montana, more than twelve million acres, was set aside for the Arikara, Mandan, and Hidatsa tribes (Meyer 1977:114). A treaty made in July 1866 ceding some land and setting reservation boundaries was never ratified and no other agreements concerning a reservation were attempted until 1870, when agents became concerned about non-Indian settlers on Indian land (Meyer 1977:112). A search by the Office of Indian Affairs disclosed

that reservation boundaries had never been defined, and so an executive order signed by President Ulysses Grant in 1870 legally set aside over eight million acres as the Fort Berthold Reservation (U.S. Department of the Interior 1912,I:131-133). The reservation took its name from one of the trading posts at Like-A-Fishhook Village. Frederick Billings, President of the Northern Pacific Railroad, succeeded in 1880 in getting another executive order which reduced the reservation to less than three million acres. Although an Army investigator from Fort Stevenson reported the tribes were using the area for hunting and winter villages, Billings' argument that the Three Tribes were not making any use of the westernmost portion of their land was accepted (National Archives, Letters Received by the Office of Indian Affairs, Fort Berthold, D. Huston to Adj. General, Feb. 2, 1880; F. Billings to Genl. A. Terry, Jan. 15, 1880; U.S. Department of the Interior 1912,I:133-134).

Not all members of the Three Tribes were happy with the idea of a reservation, and these people, led by Crow-Flies-High, followed the traditional method of illustrating disagreement with their leaders by leaving the reservation.

Between 1870 and 1894 this band of "Huskies," as they were sometimes called, lived in the vicinity of Fort Buford where they were able to survive as hunters, wood cutters, and military assistants (Meyer 1977:138-141). When the extinction of game made hunting more difficult and the pacification of the Sioux made the fort less supportive of its Indian adherents, the Crow-Flies-High band was persuaded to return to the reservation.

By 1880 the presence of agents, missionaries, schools, and other elements of non-Indian life had greatly affected the Mandan, Hidatsa, and Arikara tribes. The Three Tribes were still living in Like-a-Fishhook Village, but log cabins had replaced many of the earth lodges; cloth had replaced hide for clothing; guns were used for hunting; beef, chickens, and imported canned foods supplemented traditional foods, and English was spoken by some younger people (Smith 1972). The village was crowded; wood resources were exhausted; the buffalo were gone, and enemy tribes were no longer a threat. The Bureau of Indian Affairs agents, who believed that breaking up the social and ceremonial activities would force the tribespeople to become more like the non-Indians around them,

Before it was abandoned in 1886, Like-a-Fishhook village was crowded with earthlodges, log cabins and drying racks. (SD)

▼   *Crow Flies High and other Mandan and Hidatsa who were unhappy with reservation life left Like-a-Fishhook Village and lived near Fort Buford. (SHSND)*

or, as the agents put it, "civilized," began encouraging families to leave the village to settle on small farmsteads scattered around the reservation. Settlement outside Like-a-Fishhook began in 1882 when twenty families moved twenty miles upriver to Elbowoods, where land had been broken for them (Annual Report of the Commissioner of Indian Affairs 1882:23-24). Other families followed, and by 1888 Like-a- Fishhook was deserted except for a few elders who refused to leave. As groups of related families chose to settle in areas where they had wintered or hunted, small communities sprang up that were recognized as the homes of various tribal or familial groups. Hidatsa families related to Small Ankle settled west of the Missouri near Independence.

Mandans led by Bad Gun and Crows Heart also settled on the west side of the Missouri. The Arikara stayed on the east side where their settlement became known as Nishu (Case 1976:199). Despite his conservative attitudes toward White culture, Crow-Flies-High's summer village off the reservation was a settlement of log cabins very similar to the ones built by other Mandan, Hidatsa, and Arikara (Malouf 1963).

Adjusting to life away from Like-a-Fishhook Village was not easy. Crops did not grow as easily as the agents had anticipated and men had to hunt to provide sufficient food for their families (Wilson 1985:55-57). Friends were separated by long distances. Ceremonies could no longer be held so easily because of the travel

▲ *Men dressed for a dance. (UND)*

▲ *When they abandoned Like-a-Fishhook in 1886, followers of traditional Indian religion took their medicine poles and set them up on their allotments. (SHSND)*

▲ *Most of the Three Tribespeople built log cabins on their allotments, but Charging Enemy and a few others built the more familiar earthlodges. (SHSND)*

(opposite page, top)   When Indian dances were prohibited by the agents, the Indians received permission to celebrate the Fourth of July with a powwow. (SHSND)

(opposite page, bottom)   The Congregational mission school opened at Elbowoods in 1876. (SHSND)

Native Americans
Celebrate Independence Day at Elbow Woods

"By Request of the Mandan Indians.

"when i was at Washingto the grate father tolde mea that he would give mea plenty to eat and it maid my hart good but when i cam back he giv meas nothing and my children died of like flyes, i know that the grate father giv us plenty but the agent dont giv it to us, he givs us the guts of the beaf and we dont like it. he dont giv us half a nuff to eat. When I sean the grate father he said i would not habt to work. We ar not strong and cant do hard work. the grat father gave us plenty but tha burnt it all up. This agent has maid us poor when his brother went a way he taken plenty of our money and then his wife and then he went and taken the balance, the grate father tolde mea that this man was good but when we came back we found it wors than it ever was. the grate father tolde us that the white man wouldn't chopping our wood but tha have not. when i was at Washington i wanted the agent to buy the stuf so I could see it but he would not. the grate father tolde mea that he would giv mea rations every six days but he did not. we looked hard for it he left. the grate father sed he would giv mea lots of henry. guns and neadle guns but he has not giv us but a few. when i shok hands with the grate father my hart was good. i have always been the white mans frend, i have treated them as my own peopel the grate father told us that we was good and tolde us to "phair" and we would have plenty. the grate father tolde us if this agent did not do right to send him of, but he went of himself. the grate father told us when we got a good man to keep him but we hav not got one yet.

Yours Exspetvasll
the Bold egle
the rushing War eagle.
Scared face
Members of the Mandan tribe."

▲   *Wolf Chief wore a calico shirt and wool blanket when he posed for this photograph. (SHSND)*

People living on the reservation often complained that the government was not living up to the treaty agreement. (NDH)

▲ *Despite pressure from missionaries and agents for burial in the ground, a few Indians continued to use the scaffold burial. (SHSND)*

▼ *The Catholic mission was established by Father Francis Craft at Elbowoods in 1889. (MA)*

time and the necessity to care for crops and farm animals. Agents often complained that attendance at ceremonies caused Indians to neglect their chores. Social events and ceremonies were severely restricted. The treaties had guaranteed that the Three Tribes would be provided with food, clothing, farm tools, stock, and other necessities until they could support themselves, but there was never quite enough to cover all of the needs because the federal government considered providing these items an unnecessary expense and sought by various means to reduce the cost (Meyer 1977:154).

Paul Hanna, a student at the University of North Dakota, asked Mandan and Hidatsa elders to compare their life in Like-A-Fishhook with life on the reservation and found that many people still wept when they recalled their former way of life (Hanna 1953:57-58). Hanna quotes a man who had been through the Sun Dance:

> 'I think that times were good when I was a boy. We seemed to have everything we wanted, then. There was plenty of meat; there was always plenty of every thing. It seems like after the buffalo were gone that things were never like they were before. We were wandering without knowing where we were going. The agent said that, from then on, we would live like white people. We would have all of the things we wanted. We would never have to worry again for food or anything. I know this is not true '(Hanna 1953:58-59).

The old man went on to explain that in the old days food was shared, but that under the new ways people were more competitive and not everyone had what he needed to survive. Others, however, expressed the idea that although the new way was difficult, at least now there was peace (Hanna 1953:67).

One way of reducing the cost of treaty provisions was to sell reservation land and use the proceeds to purchase rations, annuities, and other benefits. In 1886 the Mandan, Hidatsa, and Arikara and the Office of Indian Affairs reached an agreement to sell two thirds of the reservation land and use the proceeds to pay for homes, education, and other needs. In addition, the remaining reservation land was to be allotted to individual Indian owners, according to the provisions of the General

71

Poor Wolf adopted non-Indian ways. His daughters, Otter and Miriam, were educated at Santee School in Nebraska. (SHSND)

Allotment Act, except that unallotted lands were not to be sold but held in trust for the Three Tribes. The decision of 1886 was not ratified by Congress until 1891, and by that time the need to sell off so much land had diminished to the point that in 1892 an executive order signed by President Benjamin Harrison restored township 147 north, range 87 west, approximately 23,000 acres, to the reservation (U.S. Department of the Interior 1912,I:134).

At Fort Berthold allotment began in 1894, a few years after the General Allotment Act was passed by Congress. Close to 1,000 allotments were made. Heads of families received 160 acres. Other people over eighteen years old were given 80 acres, and all children received 40 acres (Meyer 1977:138). Family members selected their allotments close together so that their combined tract would be as large as possible, but people were not always able to get the allotments they wanted, which meant that families often ended up with a single 160 acre tract that they lived on and other land in other parts of the reservation. Crow-Flies- High demanded that his people be allowed to take their allotments together, but his request was refused, and his followers were scattered around the reservation (Meyer 1977:142). By retaining unallotted lands in trust, the tribe was able to make provisions for children born after the original allotment, but these allotments rarely touched the family tracts.

The agreement of 1886 stated that unallotted lands would be kept in trust as a reservation, but there was constant pressure from White landowners and officials of the Office of Indian Affairs to sell the land. By 1901 there were no more funds to support tribal needs, and the agents believed that selling land was the only way to obtain more money. The Indian people were vehemently opposed to selling the land and challenged James McLaughlin, special agent organizing the sale, over the government's right to break its promise, but

McLaughlin was persuasive and persistent, and the tribes eventually agreed to the sale (Meyer 1977:161). However, the agreement was never ratified by Congress. In 1910 a new agreement was approved by Congress and signed by tribal leaders. This revised agreement made most of the lands east of the Missouri available for sale (Meyer 1977:164).

Indian life on the reservation continued to be an accommodation to White culture that permitted traditional values and attitudes to be retained. Outwardly the members of the Three Affiliated Tribes dressed and lived much like the White farmers and ranchers in their

area, but languages, religious beliefs, and kinship continued the traditional patterns of thought and behavior. When necessary, traditional Indian customs were grafted onto non-Indian practices. For instance, the agents prohibited Indian dances and Give-Away Ceremonies, but Fourth of July celebrations were approved. In this way the Fourth of July became a time for dances, while Christmas became a time for Give-Aways because the agents permitted gift-giving at Christmas (Wilson 1985:71-72).

Some Arikara, Hidatsa, and Mandan people gave up more of the traditional life-style than others did. One of the reasons for greater

*Veterans of World War I were honored participants at
Memorial Day and other celebrations. (MA)*

adoption of non-Indian customs is found in education. The first school was established in 1870 by Agent H. L. Clifford, but it was short-lived. Another school, opened by Agent Lyman B. Sperry in 1873, continued to operate in various guises until 1883, when it was replaced by Fort Stevenson Boarding School (Annual Report of the Commissioner of Indian Affairs 1884:80). A mission school was founded in 1876 by Charles L. Hall, a Congregational missionary. In his school, Hall and his wife taught reading, writing, geography, Christianity, and domestic skills. Attendance at school was encouraged by feasts and special events,

but progress was slow at first. By 1895 a variety of educational opportunities were available to the children of Fort Berthold. The Congregational mission school was both a day school and a boarding school. Browning, a new boarding and day school at the agency, had replaced Fort Stevenson Boarding School; two day schools, one at Independence and one at Armstrong, had been opened to serve pupils in the more remote parts of the reservation (Annual Report of the Commissioner of Indian Affairs 1895:232). A Catholic boarding school which opened in 1892 attracted less than two dozen children (Schier 1938:75). All the schools

offered a mixture of basic education and vocational skills and continued to attract students by providing meals, clothes, and other benefits.

Students also had the opportunity to attend boarding schools off the reservation. Genoa Boarding School in Genoa, Nebraska; Carlisle Institute in Carlisle, Pennsylvania; and Hampton Institute in Hampton, Virginia, were federally supported boarding schools that recruited students from various tribes. Other boarding schools, such as Santee at Santee, Nebraska, were operated by missionary societies. Agent Abram J. Gifford reported in 1884 (Annual

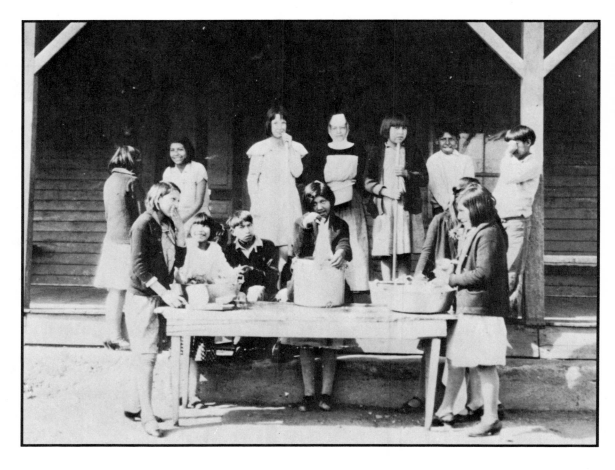

Report of the Commissioner of Indian Affairs 1884:80) that five reservation youngsters were attending off-reservation boarding schools. Underlying these boarding schools was the idea of removing Indian children from their parents' traditional orientation and training them as non-Indians. These students spent summers with White families and obtained experience working in non-Indian occupations (Howe 1892). The effects of these educational experiences were mixed. Some students returned to their reservations and found jobs as teachers and government employees. Charles W. Hoffman, an educated Arikara, returned to the reservation as a teacher and in 1908 was named agency superintendent, the first Indian to be named to such a position on his own reservation (Meyer 1977:154,179). Peter Beauchamp's story is similar to Hoffman's. After being educated at Hampton Institute, Beauchamp was hired as a school teacher at Shell Creek. Later he served as an interpreter, a tribal judge, and as a member of the tribal council (Case 1976:46-48). After completing her schooling at Hampton Institute, Annie Dawson taught in schools in Massachusetts and Nebraska before becoming a field matron, an early form of the county home extension agent on the reservation (Howe 1892:4). Others returned to a more traditionally Indian way of life (Howe 1892).

Following the opening of the reservation in 1910, interaction between Indians and non-Indians became much more extensive. By this time most of the Indians were living on farmsteads composed of a one or two room log house, a log corral, and a stable, and were engaged in trying to make a living as farmers and ranchers (Wilson 1985:59-64). Representatives of the federal government still found it necessary to consider ways to encourage Indian agriculture (National Archives, Central Files 1907-39, Fort Berthold, C. Davis, July 25, 1911, No.68170). By 1915 the towns of Plaza, Parshall, Van Hook, and Sanish were well-established commercial centers that introduced

74

Indian people to a wider variety of goods and opportunities than they had had previously. Now, instead of a few stores with little competition, there were choices for consumers, and stores vied to get Indian business (Meyer 1977:174). Newspapers and radios brought the events of the world closer. On June 12, 1909, the agency superintendent recorded in his daily log that "Mr. [W. Glenn] Sloan came back from Garrison with his new auto [and] the telephone from here to Shell Creek is completed" (Superintendent's Day Book, 1907-1912, Fort Berthold, National Archives, Kansas City, Record Group 75). Sears Roebuck and Montgomery Ward mail order catalogs also brought the outside world closer to the reservation.

In 1916, when James McLaughlin and his competency committee visited the homes of men and women who had applied for fee patents (title) to their allotments, they found that some reservation residents, despite drought, rust, and other problems, had become successful farmers. Tom Smith was not only cultivating 400 acres with modern farm equipment but also operating a small store. The committee cited his ownership of an automobile, piano, and victrola as evidence of his adoption of White culture and ability to manage his own business affairs (Copies of fee patent applications, 1916, McLaughlin Papers). However, few people actually received title to their land, and later studies of reservation conditions demonstrate that these successful farmers were exceptional men and that most of the Arikara, Hidatsa, and Mandan were not so fortunate.

World War I involved the reservation resi-

In 1934, Four Bears Bridge replaced the ferry across the Missouri River and connected the east and west sides of the reservation. (SHSND)

dents as soldiers and as fund-raisers to support the war effort. Because they were not citizens of the United States there was some doubt about their potential role in the military, but many Indian men enlisted and served courageously on all fronts. At home the reservation residents contributed more than their fair share to the Liberty bonds campaign, and abroad men from the reservation were decorated for their bravery. Tom Rogers, Jr., also known as Charges Alone and Windy Grass, was recognized as one of the bravest soldiers (Word Carrier 1925). World War I also gave Indian people an opportunity to participate in "victory" dances with less disapproval from the superintendent of the agency than usual. Entertainment, however, was generally restricted to "White" activities, such as circuses and county fairs.

While the Indian people at Fort Berthold were trying to adjust to education, farming, and the technological changes occurring around them, the government was working on the Indian Reorganization Act. At Fort Berthold the Act came too late to preserve reservation lands, but the tribes voted to accept the Act and, under its provisions, officially designated themselves as The Three Affiliated Tribes and drew up a tribal constitution that provided for a tribal council of ten elected representatives (Meyer 1977:195-196). In addition, a charter of incorporation was written and the Three Affiliated Tribes Business Council was formed. The Council played an important role in the negotiations surrounding the building of Garrison Dam and the inundation of Indian land.

The construction of Garrison Dam caused an even greater change in the life-styles of the Arikara, Mandan, and Hidatsa than the movement away from Like-a-Fishhook. The idea for dams along the Missouri River was ancient, but not until 1944 was a plan approved that would flood the reservation (Lawson 1982:45). The proposed dam would cause the Missouri River to back up and create a great lake that would cover all the communities of the Mandan, Hidatsa, and Arikara, established along the bottomlands and tablelands where farming was best. White communities and farms would also have to be relocated. Opposition to the dam was immediate and powerful as Whites and Indians joined in protest. Various plans for exchanging lands to be inundated for other lands were rejected, and finally in 1947 Congress passed Public Law 296, which provided for a cash settlement of more than five million dollars to be awarded if the Three Affilated Tribes could negotiate a satisfactory contract. These funds were to settle claims, cover the cost of relocating houses, roads, and cemeteries, and provide for improvements necessitated by the inundation (Meyer 1977:216-219; Lawson 1982:60-61). Having accepted the grim fact that the dam was a certainty, the Three Tribes agreed to an additional sum of seven million dollars.

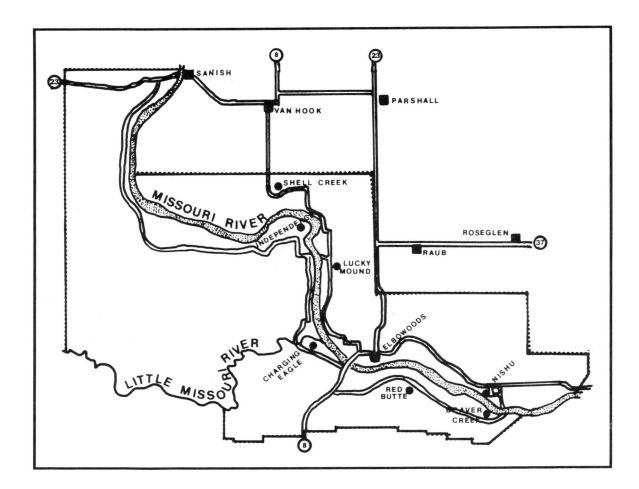

Before the dam was constructed, the reservation was visited by social scientists to make a record of the life-style of reservation residents and to determine how the Three Tribes could adjust to the changes. An early survey conducted by Gordon Macgregor found that people wanted to be resettled in communities composed of the same people with whom they currently associated, and most of the people intended to continue their same manner of earning a living (Macgregor 1949:53-55). As Macgregor pointed out, neither goal was likely to be realized without considerable difficulty. In his visits of 1951 and 1952-1953, Edward S. Bruner interviewed Mandan/Hidatsa living in the Independence area and found that a high percentage had retained some elements of traditional culture. Almost all spoke Hidatsa in preference to English and earned a living in much the same manner as they had when living in Like-a-Fishhook Village. Bruner wrote:

> Fuel is provided by wood from the timber, and from indigenous lignite outcroppings. Over half the families live in log cabins, which they erect themselves from timber found in the wooded bottoms. The food staples of corn and potatoes are obtained in part from small garden plots, now jointly worked by the men and women of the household. The meat supply depends largely upon the man's ability as a hunter of deer and small game. Abundant wild fruits and berries are gathered during the appropriate seasons and are pre served for use during the winter months (Bruner 1956:612).

▲ *Until the establishment of Lake Sakakawea, Indian communities were located in the fertile bottomlands along the Missouri and Little Missouri Rivers.*

Before Garrison Dam, families lived on small farmsteads, like this one at Nishu, grouped into communities of relatives. (MA)

The formation of Lake Sakakawea forced Mr. and Mrs. Byron Wilde to give up their land, including their first home, near Like-a-Fishhook Village. (SHSND)

inhabitants whose homes were covered by water. One new community, New Town, replaced the old agency town of Elbowoods as the administrative center of the reservation even though it was thought not be on the reservation. Other new towns were Mandaree, White Shield, and Twin Buttes. These new towns were different in composition from the former kinship-based settlements and did not maintain the hope expressed to Macgregor that the old communities and life-style would be continued.

The Reservation at the End of the Twentieth Century

Today Fort Berthold Reservation is very different from when it was first established. No longer reaching to the Yellowstone and now divided by the waters of Lake Sakakawea, it is less than one million acres in size. In 1970 the northeastern segment of land that was opened for sale in 1910, including New Town and Parshall, was declared to be part of the reservation, but the heart of the reservation continues to be west of the reservoir where a new tribal office building, museum, and health center are located.

Modern Indian life is a kaleidoscope of Indian and non-Indian patterns and ideas. There are as many individual combinations of Indian and non-Indian life-styles, attitudes, and behaviors as there are people, but researchers (Corfman 1979) have identified four basic orientations which they have termed traditional, bicultural, marginal, and transitional that are useful for explaining some of the differences, as well as some of the issues concerning modern reservation life.

The traditional orientation is strongly supportive of Indian values and negatively oriented toward White culture. Traditional people speak their native language, participate in Indian religion and ceremonies, and avoid non-Indians as much as possible. Because these people

This manner of living generally maintained the former male and female divisions of labor; the men were hunters, athletes, soldiers, and cowboys while the women were housekeepers and gardeners. Bruner also found the traditional values toward sharing, the extended kinship system, and sacred medicine bundles still in use by most of the residents of Independence (Bruner 1956:606). This and other surveys indicate that the people were ill-prepared for the disruption of their lives.

No money or land could adequately compensate the Three Tribes for the losses incurred by the building of Garrison Dam. When the families left Like-a-Fishhook village, they chose a time to leave, selected their new locations, and settled together as families. Now there was no choice! People took land wherever it

was available, sometimes many miles away from other relatives. Now they would be moving away from the river, away from the land they knew best, away from everything that was secure, into an almost unknown environment. The best farmlands on the east side of the river were primarily owned by non-Indians. The only place left was the rocky, wild land on the west side - an area more suited to stock grazing than agriculture. Instead of the snug protection of the hills bordering the Missouri, the tribespeople found themselves living on the barren, windy hill-tops. Where once the Missouri River had served to tie people together, a huge lake now separated them into five segments. The lake covered 150,000 acres of land and further reduced the reservation land base. New communities had to be built to house the

▲ *An important part of each Indian community was the community center where meetings, ceremonies, and dances were held. This building at Nishu reflected the sacred earthlodge that was once the center of each Arikara village.* (SHSND)

Homes, Bureau of Indian Affairs buildings, churches, and stores were all moved from the bottomlands to new communities high above the water.

Berthold had four or more years of college, twice as many graduates as any other North Dakota reservation.

Researchers define those people who have negative attitudes toward both Indian and White cultures as marginals. These marginal people find life very difficult because they have few goals and little hope or interest in the future. Poorly educated marginals are unable to find jobs and constitute a large number of the reservation unemployed. Unemployment only adds to the problems faced by marginal people.

The presence of these different orientations is an integral part of contemporary reservation life. Traditional people are storehouses of culture that make it possible for bicultural people to exist. The traditional people maintain the language and ceremonies and can teach the others. The bicultural people make a bridge between the traditional and the transitional. One difficulty, of course, is that these different points of view may result in disagreements over the direction the tribe should take. If there are different tribes represented, as there are at Fort Berthold, then these disagreements are exacerbated by tribal ties, and if there are limited funds, competition between tribes and different view points can be intense and disruptive. Adding to the difficulties are the great social, psychological, and health needs of marginal people which focus attention and funds away from more positive goals.

One of the most disruptive factors is the difficult economic situation. When the reservations were originally established, it was assumed that the Indian people would be able to support themselves as small, independent farmers, but when this proved to be unworkable in North Dakota, ranching activities were added to farming. Allotment was intended to make certain that each family had enough land for subsistence farming, but it did not work out this way, and many families found themselves without land and without sufficient income from farming/ranching to provide an adequate

have great pride in their own ways and find little to value in non-Indian culture, they are reservoirs of Indian culture and identity and serve as models for other Indian people. Traditionalism is an attitude that does not lend itself easily to counting, but one indication may be the ability to speak the native language. The 1980 census reported that 17.5 percent of the Indian people at Fort Berthold spoke a language other than English (U.S. Bureau of the Census 1980:36- 262). At Fort Berthold traditional people live in the rural areas, Arikara around White Shield, Mandan around Twin Buttes, and Hidatsa around Mandaree.

The transitional orientation is the exact opposite of the traditional approach because it takes a negative attitude toward Indian culture and stresses assimilation to White culture as much as possible. People with a transitional perspective believe that, while Indian ways were once useful, they are no longer appropriate. Because the Indian boarding schools stressed this assimilationist point of view, it was once

popular among well- educated Indian people, but it is no longer common. Indian people with a transitional attitude do not speak an Indian language, do not attend Indian events, and do not readily identify themselves as Indian. For obvious reasons, people with this point of view may choose to marry non-Indians and leave the reservation entirely.

Bicultural Indian people speak of living in two worlds because they have a positive regard for both Indian and non-Indian cultures and have integrated both life-styles. These people are supportive of Indian language and participate in Indian ceremonies, but they also want the same educational and employment opportunities as non-Indians. Bicultural people are the best educated and are often found working for the tribe as administrators and educators. One basic measure of biculturalism at Fort Berthold may be the relatively high percentage of college graduates. The 1980 census (U.S. Bureau of the Census 1980:36- 262) reported that eight percent of the people at Fort

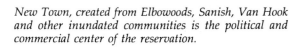
▲ *The rising waters of Lake Sakakawea cover the trees by the river and move toward Elbowoods, the reservation administrative center. (SHSND)*

New Town, created from Elbowoods, Sanish, Van Hook and other inundated communities is the political and commercial center of the reservation.

80

standard of living. These conditions still exist today.

A few Indian people have made a success at agriculture by leasing or buying land and making use of all the opportunities open to North Dakota farmer/ranchers, but most Indian people rely on income from salaries and wages. The 1980 federal census reported that while 84 percent of the Indian people at Fort Berthold had an earned income (U.S. Bureau of the Census 1983:236-238) only four percent was from farming. This figure may be compared to the 86 percent earned income reported for other North Dakota residents, of which 20 percent is from farming (U.S. Bureau of the Census 1983:56). Fort Berthold Indians also earn less from their farming efforts than the White farmers on the reservation (U.S. Bureau of the Census 1983:236-238).

Like those who have income from farming, Indians who have income from salaries and other sources earn considerably less than non-Indians. A relatively high percentage of Indian people at Fort Berthold also receive public assistance to compensate for low incomes. The average family income for Fort Berthold Indians was $12,122 (U.S. Bureau of the Census 1986:529), while North Dakota White families had an average income of $20,648 (U.S. Bureau of the Census 1983:56).

Because the reservations are located in rural areas, it has been difficult to attract industries of sufficient size to employ significant numbers of Indian people. Major employment opportunities are with federal, state, local, and tribal governments. At Fort Berthold, 64 percent of the workers are employed by the tribal or federal government. This includes people who teach in reservation schools, as well as those who are public administrators. The higher paying jobs, whether in government or private industry, require higher education, and the presence of more college graduates may mean that more Indian people will be eligible for these jobs. However, for those who lack sufficient education, many of the jobs are seasonal or depend upon federal or state funds and may end when the project is finished. The effect is to create great disparities in income which can cause hard feelings.

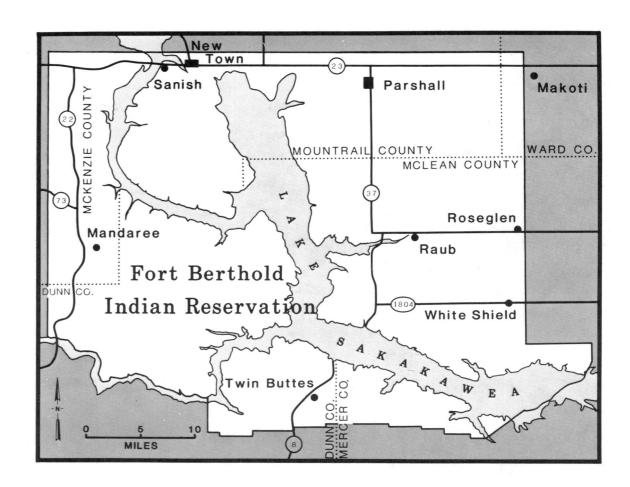

▲   *The reservation today. (Map)*

▼   *Four Bears Bridge, moved from Elbowoods, now crosses the reservoir just west of New Town.*

▲ *Indian children living near Mandaree attend this modern school.*

▼ *Every summer, the Indian communities sponsor powwows which attract many dancers and visitors.*

Because of the different economic situations and orientations toward Indian and non-Indian values, many different life-styles exist on the reservation. Although the reservation has few incorporated communities, some, like White Shield, Mandaree, and Twin Buttes, are identified as being Indian while others are considered non-Indian towns because the Indian residents do not involve themselves in the social or political life of these communities. Traditional people most often live in the Indian communities or in the more remote areas of the reservation, while the people who work in tribal or federal government offices live in New Town, the largest town on the reservation.

For most people, modern comfortable housing has replaced the older log and frame houses. Some of the newer homes were replacements for homes lost to Garrison Dam, but many more are the result of tribal building programs. These houses are found in Indian, non-Indian, and rural areas. Some of the more traditional people cling to the older home style because they believe it is more appropriate, and low incomes may cause some residents to live in inadequate housing.

Indian life on the reservation is much like non-Indian life, oriented around work, school, church, and group activities. Depending on where they live, Indian children attend either tribally operated, Bureau of Indian Affairs (BIA) supported schools or public, state supported schools. The major difference is that Indian children attending public schools are usually in a minority, while in the tribal/BIA schools they are in the majority. All of these schools attempt to provide some Indian cultural orientation. In addition to their academic offerings, all of the schools have the usual sports, dramatic, and extra-curricular activities. Teams with Indian players have been state champions in several major sports.

Religion is as varied as other aspects of Indian life. Indian people with traditional value orientations still follow many of the tribal religious beliefs and practices. Although the Sun Dance and other major tribal ceremonies are no longer performed on the reservation, people may attend such ceremonies on other reserva-

▲ *Families use the powwow for naming ceremonies, honoring and memorial ceremonies.*

▼ *Twin Buttes, North Dakota, the smallest, most rural reservation community has modern ranch-style housing.*

tions. The sweat lodge, vision quest, and other traditional practices are still observed and the few remaining sacred bundles are highly respected. There is also a branch of the Native American Church on the reservation. The major Christian religions are represented by churches and missions. Believing that all ways of worshipping are good, bicultural Indian people may attend both Indian and Christian services without personal conflict.

Group activities occupy many Indian people. Some groups, such as veterans' clubs and church auxiliaries, are Indian versions of organizations found throughout the country, and Indian men and women perform much the same fund-raising and support activities as non-Indians. There are also drum groups, and rodeo and powwow committees that are specifically oriented toward Indian activities. Called "clans" by the members, the powwow committees sponsor winter celebrations and activities to raise funds for annual powwows that are held at White Shield, New Town, and Mandaree each summer. The drum groups provide music for the powwows and other traditional Indian activities. These Indian-oriented organizations are based on family relationships and conducted as much as possible according to traditional tribal beliefs. Young children may be made officers of powwow committees so that their parents and other relatives are obligated to work to help them. In that way the children are active participants in the effort and learn at an early age the importance of such undertakings. Weekly bingo games, special dances, and Give-Aways serve to raise funds for powwows.

Some elements of former tribal life-styles, especially those related to the family and kinship, have persisted. Indian families at Fort Berthold, averaging almost five members, are larger than average non-Indian families, and a large percentage of Indian households have other relatives or non-relatives living in them (U.S. Bureau of the Census 1986:178). The more traditional people are likely to maintain their extended family relationships and to depend upon one another more than those individuals who have left the reservation for employment or education opportunities. Any

83

person who has a steady job is expected to help others, especially relatives who may be less fortunate. Those people who refuse to help may be accused of greediness, selfishness, or acting like non-Indians. Other traditional customs that continue to be practiced are name-giving, the Give-Away ceremony, and mourning.

The latter decades of the twentieth century were a time of adjustment for the Three Affiliated Tribes. In the aftermath of Garrison Dam, many people still suffered from isolation and depression, but a new generation born after the

Dam did not experience the old way of life or its disruption, and those people took a greater part in the political and economic development of the reservation.

The experiences of reservation leaders during the Garrison Dam situation taught the Three Affiliated Tribes the necessity of fighting for their rights. In the 1980's the tribe initiated measures that set legal precedents. The tribe was the first in North Dakota to assume jurisdiction over non-Indian fishing rights by announcing that tribal fishing licenses were required to fish in the portion of Lake Sakakawea

inside the reservation boundaries. Another major success was achieved when the federal government returned mineral rights that had been retained during the Garrison Dam negotiations. An important precedent was established when the tribe won a case it took to the U. S. Supreme Court asking for permission to sue non-Indians in state courts. This decision gave the tribe greater opportunities for justice since tribal court decisions could not be imposed outside the reservation (Turosak 1986:2), and extended the possibilities to all the tribes in North Dakota, as well as to many other tribes across the country.

A controversial subject for the tribe was management of natural resources. In the 1980's Fort Berthold Reservation had oil and mineral resources that had not been developed to benefit the tribe, and the tribe moved cautiously to assume control. Earlier, the tribe was pressured by major extractive industrialists to permit development (Ambler 1984:194), but the decline of oil and gas production nationally alleviated the pressure and gave the tribe the chance to regulate their moves into such production. Combining their legal expertise with practice in resources administration provided the Three Tribes with a powerful device for future development.

Even more controversial was the attempt to extend tribal jurisdiction to non-Indians living on the reservation. The issue of tribal jurisdiction arose from federal policies and court decisions that said that non-Indians did not have to abide by tribal laws. Obviously, such limits weaken the tribal justice system. A March 1985 tribal vote to extend tribal jurisdiction to non-Indians was not well received by White residents who viewed it as interference in non-Indian governing systems (Cook 1985:1). Non-Indian residents of New Town and Parshall formed a citizens' group and sought help from the Governor and Congressmen of North Dakota. In the meantime, the tribe followed federal guidelines and submitted its request for jurisdiction to the Department of the Interior, which was expected to approve it. In view of the long history of good relationships between Indians and Whites at Fort Berthold, it is likely that the

issue will be resolved to the satisfaction of both sides.

Contributions to North Dakota History and Culture

Throughout their history the Three Tribes have contributed generously and unselfishly to the development of North Dakota. As agricultural specialists, they provided food and shelter for many early visitors, and later provided seeds that were developed into major North Dakota crops. As traders, their villages became bustling centers of commerce which attracted artists, journalists, and sightseers. The Three Tribes' hospitality has extended to anthropologists and students who lived among them and learned of their ways. Visitors from other countries who are interested in learning about the modern descendants of Prince Maximilian's hosts find themselves warmly received.

Even when they were not considered citizens, these patriotic Indians fought heroically in the wars of the United States. The same heroic spirit appeared during the struggle against Garrison Dam. Although the Three Affiliated Tribes lost the Garrison war, they gained experience in legal battles that serves them today as leaders in establishing tribal rights.

Modern Mandan, Hidatsa, and Arikara educators, artists, clergymen, politicians, businessmen, lawyers, doctors, and architects worked, not just for their tribe, but for all North Dakotans. Others, too, served North Dakota in many ways. Juanita Helphrey, an enrolled member of the Three Affiliated Tribes, served as North Dakota Commissioner of Indian Affairs for more than ten years. Another member, Pemina Yellow Bird, was appointed in 1985 to the North Dakota State Historical Board that oversees the State Historical Society, while Martha Lone Bear served on the North Dakota Arts and Humanities Council. In 1987 the Prairie Rose State Games, an Olympic-style competition open to all North Dakota amateur athletes, took place in Bismarck. Virgil Chase, Sr., a boxing coach, made a successful request to have boxing included in the schedule of games and was named boxing sports commissioner for the Prairie Rose games.

Other members of the tribe have been active participants in programs held at the Knife River Villages National Park. One of the most popular events was a pageant depicting Lewis and Clark's return to the villages after their exploration of the Northwest. Indian people from the reservation acted the roles of the villagers who greeted the expedition.

A century ago, leaders of the Three Tribes complained to the Bureau of Indian Affairs that they were not given as much attention as the hostile Sioux. It is no longer so easy to overlook the contributions of these openhearted people.

Chapter 6

Fort Totten Reservation

Cosily snuggled up to the south shore of Devils Lake, in east-central North Dakota, is Fort Totten Reservation, home of the Sisseton, Wahpeton, Yanktonai, and other Dakota tribes, now known formally as the Devils Lake Sioux Tribe. Except for the Cuthead band of Yanktonai who occupied the area at the time the reservation was designated, the other tribes located themselves on the reservation as refugees from the Dakota Conflict of 1862, and all have close ties with Sioux living on other reservations in the United States and Canada.

The history of the Devils Lake Sioux Reservation, also known as Fort Totten Reservation, reflects a common Federal policy of removal, in which Indians gave up their homelands in exchange for land somewhere else. In the case of the Devils Lake Sioux, the Cuthead and other Yanktonai were already living in central North Dakota, but when the government determined to remove the Dakota from Minnesota and reward some Dakota for not participating in the Conflict, little attention was paid to the Yanktonai presence. The same thing happened in other parts of the country, where tribes with different cultural backgrounds were

given lands already claimed by others. At least the Dakota and Yanktonai recognized a common ancestry and spoke related languages, but they still faced the difficult tasks of getting along together, adjusting to a new environment, and creating a composite identity, that of the Devils Lake Sioux.

Expeditions like the one led by Stephen

Indian agency buildings at Devils Lake, 1881. (UND)

86

These Indian women photographed by Stanley Morrow at Devils Lake Reservation shortly after the reservation was established wore non-Indian style dresses and trade blankets. (SD)

▼ This Cuthead Yanktonai man photographed by Stanley Morrow around 1870 illustrates traditional war dress. (SD)

Long in 1823 (Keating 1824:5-6) met Yanktonai and other Dakota bands west of the Red River, but the extent of Sioux occupation of the region was not recognized until the late 1830's when Joseph N. Nicollet was assigned by the U. S. War Department to survey the area from the Mississippi to the Missouri and to make careful notes on the geography, the plants, and the people he found there (Nicollet 1976). On the basis of his research and map-making, it be-

came generally known that the area between the Mississippi and Missouri rivers was regularly utilized by the four Dakota divisions as well as the Yankton, Yanktonai, Lakota, and Assiniboin (Nicollet 1976). The claim of these Siouan groups to the area was recorded in 1841 in a letter from James Doty, Commissioner appointed to negotiate with the Sioux tribes, to John Bell, Secretary of War (Meyer 1967:383).

Negotiators of treaties, however, generally

87

found it easier to ignore the issue of the western claim until the Treaty of 1867 established the Sisseton-Wahpeton and Devils Lake Reservations. Tacit recognition of the claim was given in the Treaty of 1867 when the Sioux ceded to the United States the right to build roads, railroads, and telegraph lines, and to set up other public utilities in the area. The agreement did not, however, extinguish the claim of the Sioux to more than eight million acres in eastern Dakota Territory. The Treaty establishing the two reservations also provided for allotments of 160 acres to Indians who wished to farm and stated that an agent would be appointed for the Sisseton Reservation; whenever 500 people had located upon the Devils Lake Reservation, an agent would also be appointed for them. Unfortunately the Treaty did not set a figure for appropriations to support the administration and Indians on the reservations, and for many years conditions, especially at Devils Lake, were extremely bad (Meyer 1967:200).

In 1867 emergency provisions were sent from Sisseton to Fort Totten for distribution to starving Indian families (Meyer 1967:220). Even after a permanent agent, William H. Forbes, was appointed, conditions continued to be dismal for many years. One problem was that according to the Treaty of 1867, no food, clothes, goods, or other articles were to be issued to able-bodied Indians except in payment for services (Meyer 1967:226). The aim of the Treaty was to encourage men to become farmers, but agricultural pursuits were limited by the weather and lack of interest, and other work was not available. The extension of the Northern Pacific Railroad to Jamestown in 1872 might have provided wagon-freighting and other employment opportunities for Indian men; instead the railroad turned out to be a focus for Indian protest over the presence of White settlers in the unceded Indian-claimed territory (Meyer 1967:227).

Settling the complaints turned out to be a

▲   Indian woman cleaning a cowhide with a traditional elk antler scraper. (MA)

Indian woman making dried meat. (MA)

lengthy process because the Indian leaders
were definite about their rights, and Congress
was reluctant to accept their demands. An
agreement reached with the Indian leaders in
1872 was eventually confirmed by Congress as
part of the Indian appropriation act of June

1874 (Annual Report of the Commissioner of
Indian Affairs 1905:497). In the agreement, the
Sisseton, Wahpeton, and Yanktonai agreed to
accept $800,000 or 10 cents an acre for the lands
outside the two reservations. At least the
money, paid out over a ten-year period, would

alleviate the poverty for a short time (Meyer
1967:207-208).

One other cession occurred before Devils
Lake Reservation reached its present size and
shape. In 1883 a resurvey of the reservation
boundaries found non-Indians homesteading

The first school at Devils Lake was opened by the Grey Nuns in 1874. (SHSND)

on 64,000 acres of land that belonged to the reservation, but nothing was done to remove the settlers or compensate the Indians until 1891 when the issue became part of the discussions surrounding allotment. Congress agreed to pay the tribe $80,000 for the loss of the 64,000 acres (Annual Report of the Commissioner of Indian Affairs 1891:318), but no payment was made, and the claim was raised again in November 1891, when James McLaughlin, representing the U.S. Government, and the adult males of the Devils Lake Sioux Tribes met to discuss plans for allotting the reservation. They agreed upon the sum of $345,000 to cover the 64,000 acres and other wrongful land uses (Kappler III:83), but when Congress finally approved the agreement as part of the Act which opened the reservation lands for sale to non-Indians in April 1904, it deleted the money and stipulated that the settlers pay for the land at the rate of $3.25 an acre (Kappler III:85).

Immediately upon the passage of the General Allotment Act in 1887, John W. Cramsie, the agent at Fort Totten, began the process of dividing the reservation into parcels but stopped when he learned that a special agent was to be assigned to the task. The resulting two-year delay gave the Indians time to voice their objections and demand compensation for the homestead and railroad lands eventually included in the Act of 1904. Allotment continued during the discussions. Generally, people chose allotments in the area of their camps and near their relatives and this resulted in tribes becoming communities. Yanktonai settled in the Crow Hill area, and Sisseton and Wahpeton established the communities of Wood Lake, Tokio, and St. Michael (Albers 1974:182-183). In 1891 Agent John H. Waugh reported that special agent Joseph R. Gray had managed to divide the lands in such a way that most of the parcels had "some timber, some meadow, and some plow land" (Annual Report of the Commissioner of Indian Affairs 1891:317). The Act of 1904 contained a provision for 61 additional

allotments, reserved 960 acres for Sullys Hill Park, and opened the unallotted lands for sale at $4.50 an acre (Meyer 1967:238,323; Kappler III:86). Land sales were slow, but the proceeds provided a source of income for the tribe, although the loss of lands turned out to be more disastrous than the framers of the General Allotment Act ever conceived.

Before allotment, the reservation consisted of almost 300,000 acres. In 1880 Agent James McLaughlin reported that the reservation was approximately 275,000 acres (Annual Report of the Commissioner of Indian Affairs 1880:28). By 1884 the reservation was considered to be 230,400 acres (Annual Report of the Commissioner of Indian Affairs 1884:74). The Annual Report for 1905 noted that 135,824.33 acres had been allotted to 1,193 Indians; 727.83 acres were reserved for church uses; and 193.61 were reserved for government purposes (Annual Report Commissioner of Indian Affairs 1905:497). Unlike Fort Berthold and some other reservations, no provisions were made for additional allotments to Indians born after 1900, and the inheritance provision by which the original allotments were divided equally

among all the heirs exacerbated the situation. By the third generation there were many claimants to an allotment and, with no provision for settling the individual claims, much land lay idle. The only solution was to sell the land and divide the money among the heirs, but this simply removed more land from Indian control and meant that large numbers of Indian people were without means of subsistence farming.

Following the establishment of the reservation, the Devils Lake Sioux labored faithfully to become farmers. In his annual report for 1880, James McLaughlin described how one of the reservation residents, Sipto, had, in eight years, fenced 80 acres and was raising corn, wheat, potatoes, turnips, beets, and other vegetables. He also owned 18 head of cattle, 14 of which he bought to supplement the cow issued by the agency (Annual Report Commissioner of Indian Affairs 1880:29). Other Indian people were earning money by transporting goods from Jamestown and Grand Forks and by cutting wood and fence-rails. Some men were employed at the agency as interpreters and as Indian police. But, despite these outward signs of successful adjustment, crop failure was common, and the agent found it necessary to issue rations, and men still went hunting to provide food for their families (Annual Report of the Commissioner of Indian Affairs 1880:31).

Although the Devils Lake Sioux were living in difficult conditions, they were able to maintain some of their traditional customs and ceremonies. The people who settled at Devils Lake tended to be more traditional than those who settled at Sisseton, and several aspects of life on the reservation contributed to the continuance of this attitude (Meyer 1967:223). For the first few years after the reservation was established, there was no agent and therefore no pressure to adopt non-Indian ways. Even after an agent was assigned, the people were fortunate enough to have agents who were less interested in "civilizing" and more interested in getting food and other necessities for the reservation. Finally, the agents who were assigned to the reservation viewed the job as a long-term assignment and so were not so concerned about impressing the Washington office with their impact.

In his report for 1880, McLaughlin distinguished between the medicine dance and the medicine feast and noted that the medicine dance had not been performed since 1877 (Annual Report of the Commissioner of Indian Affairs 1880:30). However, special agent Jere Stevens, who visited the reservation in September 1890, reported that the medicine feast was the most important ceremony and that it and other ceremonies were still being held (U.S. Department of the Interior 1894:514). Other evidence for the continuation of traditional patterns comes from reading between the lines written about reservation life by various observers. Walter E. Spokesfield, whose parents homesteaded in Wells County (Spokesfield 1929:209), reported tree burials in the Hawksnest area and recalled that "bits of red cloth, pieces of colored glass, shiny stones and kinnekinnick" were often left on a large rock where a pair of eagles had their nest (Spokesfield 1928:48,81). A continuation of the manner of living in a tipi can be read into Dr. A. Stewart's report on reservation housing conditions, in

▲ Indian girls at the Grey Nuns' school practiced living and dressing like non-Indians. (SHSND)

▼ Music was stressed in all the Indian schools. The Fort Totten Indian School Band performed throughout the lakes region. (SHSND)

91

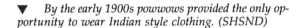

Robert P. High Eagle, Standing Rock Sioux, taught at Waanatan Day School in 1895. He later became a judge at Standing Rock. (SHSND)

▼ By the early 1900s powwows provided the only opportunity to wear Indian style clothing. (SHSND)

▲ Ignatius Court, Tamazakotanka Wiokiya, who helped to translate the Bible into Dakota, was one of the first boys to attend the mission school. He grew up to become a tribal leader. (MA)

which he comments that "over part of the dirt floor they spread a thin mattress, sit around on this during the day and sleep on it at night" (Annual Report of the Commissioner of Indian Affairs 1891:318). Special agent Stevens also noted that tipis were generally used during the summer and that the people preferred to sit and sleep on the floor (U.S. Department of the Interior 1894:513).

One big change was the presence of mission schools and attempts by the agents to encourage children to attend school. Catholic missionaries had been active in the Devils Lake area, and when Agent Forbes determined to begin a school, he and three Sisseton/Wahpeton leaders, Icanajika, Tiyowaste [Good Lodge or Little Fish], and Mato Catka, contacted the Bishop of St. Paul for assistance. In preparation for the day when there would be teachers, a combination residence and school house was built, and in 1874 four Grey Nuns, Sisters of Charity, arrived from Montreal. The first school was a boarding school because, in addition to teaching reading, writing, arithmetic, and other academic subjects, such a school provided experiences in gardening, cooking,

sewing, housekeeping, and other "White" style living. The first teachers spoke little English or Dakota and so classes were conducted with the aid of an interpreter. Although the Sisters had agreed to teach boys up to age twelve, Agents Forbes and McLaughlin wanted to include older boys, and in 1878 a boarding school for older boys, staffed by Benedictine brothers, was established. The agents frequently complained about the difficulties of getting children to attend school, but by 1880 McLaughlin noted a subtle change from strong opposition to the schools to a tone of reconciliation or indifference that permitted children to attend school and church even when the parents would not (Annual Report of the Commissioner of Indian Affairs 1880:30).

Sina Sapa Wocekiye Taeyanpaha.

VOL. XI. NO. 4.   NOVEMBER 15, 1907.   50 cents a year.

Published Monthly, at St. Michaels. Fort Totten, P. O., N. Dakota.
ENTERED AS SECOND CLASS MATTER AT THE POST-OFFICE AT FORT TOTTEN, N. DAK.

HYMN.	otanananhci iwoglakapi kta iyececa ye lo. mitakuyepi.	ye wicaśa wanji kici wowaglaka. Wicaśa kin le wocekiye unkitawapi	na wakanneja wakanś.ca ti el eḣpeya pi kta yuśtanpi enantanś, iye wakan-
DEAR ANGEL EVER AT MY SIDE.	Wic śawaśan unkitawapi wicunk-copi na el nici na owayawa kagapi	el opa śni. ca lecel imunga: "Tuktu-ma w śte nuwo? epe lo. Saḃaun owa-vawa inś tokca." Saḃaun iśnala iyo-	neja atkuku hunku ko iyopewicayapi kta na on etanhan śicewicalakapi kta iyececa kta tka kśto. Ecin. tohanl

St. Michael's Mission began publishing the Catholic Sioux Herald, a Dakota newspaper, in 1890. (MA)

▼ *The Devils Lake Sioux regularly participated in the Chautauqua held annually at Devils Lake. (SHSND)*

Several disastrous fires resulted in changes in the school buildings, but not until 1890 when the buildings at Fort Totten were turned into a government boarding school was there a major change in education. At that time, the Sisters became government employees and taught the curriculum directed by the Office of Indian Affairs. The issue of language continued to be a problem since the course of study demanded that English be the language of instruction, and some of the teachers still spoke poor English. The issue was finally settled in 1927 when the Sisters' government employment ended, and they built a new mission boarding school, the Little Flower School at St. Michael, N.D. (Peterson 1985).

The federal government also opened day schools, but these had little success. Agents Forbes and McLaughlin had found it necessary to attract children to the schools by issuing special rations. In 1891 Agent Waugh complained that "the Indians in general have not

93

shown much alacrity in securing the advantages of even a limited education." He attributed their lack of interest to the emphasis on manual labor, suggesting that such work was still considered woman's work (Annual Report of the Commissioner of Indian Affairs 1891:317). Dr. A. Stewart, the agency physician, however, claimed that most of the school-age children were attending school regularly enough to obtain medical treatment (Annual Report of the Commissioner of Indian Affairs 1891:318).

No one can say whether the nature of instruction or the parental lack of emphasis on education was responsible for the paucity of students who sought higher education, but it is obvious that Devils Lake did not have as many eastern-educated Indians as the other reservations in North Dakota. At a time when other reservations had returning students available as teachers, field matrons, and agency employees, Fort Totten did not. One man, Robert High Eagle, educated at Standing Rock, Devils Lake, and Hampton Institute, began teaching at Waanatan Day School in 1895 (Annual Report of the Commissioner of Indian Affairs 1905:549; Howe 1892). Locally educated Indian people, however, played important roles in tribal history. One such man, Ignatius Court, helped to translate Bible history into Dakota and printed copies of it. Later, Court was one of the tribal leaders involved in allotment proceedings. Court Lake, a small lake on the reservation, was named for him. Josephine Nebraska was one of the first Indian women to take vows as a Grey Nun.

In 1905 the superintendent of schools reported that the large boarding school at Fort Totten had two divisions, one located at the former fort and the other about one mile away. Together, these schools had an enrollment of over 330 students (Annual Report of the Commissioner of Indian Affairs 1905:278). Only one day school, Waanatan, was available, and it was devoted to educating 12- to 20-year-old boys who were too old to attend the boarding school (Annual Report of the Commissioner of Indian Affairs 1905:280).

The early years of the new century were marked by creeping adjustments to White

culture. Agents continued to encourage Indians to be good farmers, but crop failure was common. Frequent droughts made the Indians reluctant to expand or change crops (Meyer 1967:324) and difficulties with the sale and leasing of land contributed to further disenchantment on the part of the Indians.

The city of Devils Lake was established in 1883, but there was little contact between Indians and city residents until a bridge was built across Devils Lake. Before then, it was necessary to travel around the lake to get from the reservation to the city because the Indians would not take canoes onto the lake. Neither would they cross on the steamboat (U.S. Department of the Interior 1894:514). This separation probably helped to maintain Indian traditions because the Indians were not exposed to cultural differences, and the Whites did not attempt to force changes on the Indians. Dakota continued to be the primary language on the reservation (Meyer 1967:326). In a 1976 interview Earl Mann, an early store owner in Devils Lake, told interviewer Robert Carlson that most of the storekeepers in Devils Lake learned enough Dakota so that they could trade with the Indians when they came to town (Mann 1976). In 1908 the Grand Forks Herald published (Cole 1909:274-279) a description of the Devils

▲ *A typical reservation homestead of the 1930's.* (MA)

▼ *Little boys can always find something interesting to do.* (MA)

In 1943, one of the sights of Tokio, then a settlement of about 15 houses, was the dog that carried the mail. When the dog heard the train whistle, he ran to the depot, picked the bag up where it had been thrown from the train and took it back to the post office. (MA)

▼   Who can resist puppies and kittens? (MA)

Lake Sioux reservation which included an interview with "Tiawashti," usually called Little Fish, the leading elder of the Cuthead band. At the time, Little Fish was living on a small farm where he raised enough grain to feed a few head of cattle. A few others were also successful farmers, but most were not.

Lacking buffalo, Indian women treated beef in the ancient manner and continued to dry it and make it into pemmican. Corn was parched and made into corn meal, and prairie turnips were collected and dried (Lambert 1976). Some people had good gardens and put away enough vegetables to get them through the winter, but the tradition of hospitality meant that the reserve would be shared with many others (Cole 1909:271).

Dances also continued to be performed on the reservation. In 1908 a new dance called the "Penny " or "No-Ticket" dance was introduced at Fort Totten and Standing Rock. Although Miss Mary Collins, a missionary at Standing Rock, and James McLaughlin, then special agent for the Indian Service, tried to have the dance prohibited (J. McLaughlin to Sec. of Interior, June 8, 1908, McLaughlin Letters), by 1911 there were four dance halls at Fort Totten, one for each district. The superintendent thought there was no harm in permitting the dances (Meyer 1967:326).

An item worthy of special mention in the

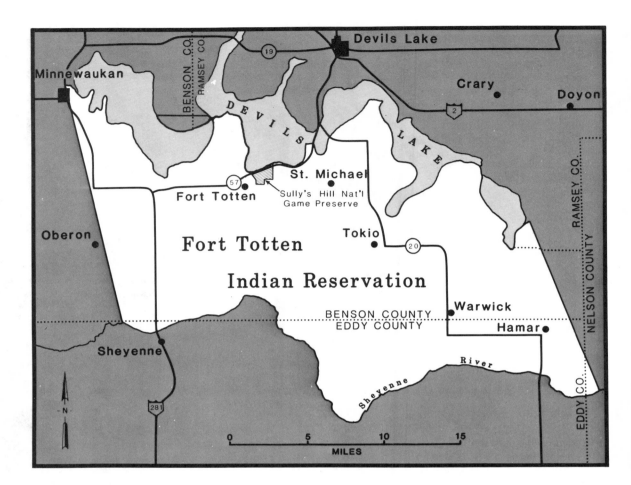

Grand Forks Herald (Herald 1908:8) was Indian attendance at the Chautauqua held annually in Devils Lake. One day was set aside for Indian dance demonstrations and a baseball game between the boys from the Indian school and boys from Devils Lake High School. The reporter noted that the Indian people generally dressed in White-style clothing, with young women from the school dressed all in white. Although Little Fish had been one of the dancers, he posed for his photograph in a blue Prince Albert suit because it was too hot to change into his dance outfit. After the dancing and before the baseball game, the women sold beadwork and other crafts, while the more daring Indian people went roller skating.

The reporter also noted that the Indian people were vitally interested in the state elections. Many of them were wearing buttons supporting Thomas Marshall in his bid for re-election to the Senate.

A committee headed by James McLaughlin visited the reservation in 1916 to investigate applications for fee patents to allotted lands. McLaughlin reported that there were only seventeen applications because five other eligible owners had refused on the basis that they would be required to pay taxes on their land (J. McLaughlin to Sec. of Interior, Sept. 1916, McLaughlin Papers). The investigators found the applicants farming small acreages of approximately 60 acres. The successful applicants generally lived in frame houses, had frame barns, and owned wagons, buggies, and the most necessary farm equipment. One man owned a Cadalac (sic) automobile. It is apparent that if these were the most successful farmers, then the situation for most of the residents was not good.

World War I affected the reservation economically and socially. High prices due to wartime inflation made living more difficult (Meyer 1967:325). A number of men volunteered for military service, but many were rejected because of their poor health (Meyer 1967:325). One man, Robert Bruce, who learned to play the cornet at Carlisle, became a member of the Second Regiment Band, North Dakota National Guard, and was assigned to the 116th Engineers who saw service in France (Spokesfield 1929:333). Other men from the reservation served honorably at home and overseas, and people on the reservation joined in the war effort by buying Liberty Bonds and war stamps and by contributing to the Red Cross.

By 1934, when the Indian Reorganization Act was passed, the Devils Lake Sioux tribe faced a crisis over the lack of land available to its members. The Indian Reorganization Act was designed to ease the land situation by halting the sale of Indian lands and by providing funds to buy reservation lands. In addition, it would provide economic support by establishing an elected government that would enable tribes to conduct business. The Devils Lake Sioux, however, did not vote in favor of the Act and so did not participate in its provisions (Meyer 1967:329). It is doubtful that not accepting the Indian Reorganization Act made any significant differences in the history of the Devils Lake Sioux, because in 1947 Assistant Commissioner of Indian Affairs William F. Zimmerman, Jr., testified that of four criteria used to determine readiness for termination, the Devils Lake Sioux failed on the issue of economic resources (Tyler 1973:163-164). In 1946, however, the tribe adopted a democratic style of government with a constitution and by-laws. The tribal council consists of six

▲ *Devils Lake Sioux Manufacturing provides employment for many Indians and non-Indians.*

The store at St. Michael's is one of the few places to buy groceries and gas on the reservation.

members elected from different districts on the reservation. The tribal chairman and secretary are elected at-large.

Throughout the 30's, 40's and 50's the primary concern of the Devils Lake Sioux was earning a living. The reservation lands were so divided that it was impossible for most people to make a living by farming or cattle ranching. At the same time, rather than providing the assistance necessary to correct the situation, the federal government advocated a policy of leasing land to non-Indians (Albers 1983:195). In 1944, Indians worked only 12,628 acres of trust land, while non-Indians were using 27,879 acres (Fine 1951:39). An economic survey of the reservation in 1949 showed that the average family income for 1948 was $949.00. Leasing contributed an average of $42.70 to each family's income (Fine 1951:40). Most income came from working at whatever jobs were available. During the 1930's, work programs

97

sponsored by the federal government aided some families, but following World War II people had to take advantage of the need for unskilled laborers in the agricultural industry. One irony was that a man sometimes ended up working for the non-Indian farmer who was leasing his land. Women took jobs as domestics and housekeepers. In the fall, whole families moved to the Red River Valley to work in the sugar beet and potato harvests (Albers 1983:201). One side effect of the poor economic situation on the reservation was the relative lack of interest in the tribal council. The few economic assets the council had to manage provided no incentives to develop political machines or other controls. Instead, the coun-

---

Reflecting its history of more than 100 years on the reservation, the Catholic Church remains the most popular denomination on the reservation.

▼ *The new Four Winds School provides education for children from kindergarten through high school.*

FORT TOTTEN SIOUX

The Community Center serves as tribal and federal administrative centers as well as clinic and meeting place.

cilmen were judged on their ability to attract federal funds and, since federal funds were always irregular, there was a frequent turnover in leadership (Albers 1983:205).

The Reservation at the End of the Twentieth Century

Devils Lake Sioux life in the 1980's was a jigsaw puzzle of Indian and non-Indian traditions with shapes cut from the past. The same mixture of Indian and non-Indian that was apparent in Little Fish's appearance at the Chautauqua continued. The reservation population still shopped in Devils Lake, although the shopkeepers no longer had to learn Dakota to transact business. Until the construction of

the Four Winds School, most high school students attended public high schools in Devils Lake or in one of the other non-Indian communities near the reservation, but this did not result in any noticeable assimilation of the Indian population.

The basic four value orientations toward Indian or White life-styles (traditional, transitional, bicultural, and marginal) (Corfman 1979) that were found on other reservations in North Dakota also existed at Devils Lake, but it seemed that more of the Devils Lake Sioux followed the traditional orientation than the bicultural or transitional ones.

Traditional people are those who prefer tribal ways over non-Indian ways. At the Fort Totten Reservation, according to the 1980 cen-

sus, 19.9 percent of the people over five years old usually spoke a language other than English (U.S. Bureau of the Census 1983:36-262). We can assume that the preferred language was Dakota, and that this provides some indication of the size of the traditional population.

In contrast to the traditional orientation, a bicultural point of view finds some positive value in both Indian and non-Indian cultures and attempts to balance both. The small number of college graduates, 1.8 percent in 1980 (U.S. Bureau of the Census 1983:36-262), also suggests a small bicultural population. Although a strong traditional group is necessary for the continuation of Indian language and ideas, the presence of a bicultural population is also a necessity in order for the tribe to com-

99

pete successfully in the political and economic arenas. Until enough Devils Lake Sioux were sufficiently well versed in non-Indian statesmanship to negotiate with the political leaders of Devils Lake city, the state, and the federal government, the tribe continued to struggle.

Transitional people are those who leave Indian culture and move more or less successfully into non-Indian culture. In the early days of White settlement, those Devils Lake Sioux women who married non-Indian men and adopted non-Indian ways encouraged others to do the same. Some individuals with this orientation left the reservation while others pushed their children to obtain an education that would allow them to leave the reservation.

In the face of severe economic difficulties, the problems of marginal people, those who do not identify successfully with either Indian or White values, tend to increase. Without jobs or income sufficient for the necessities, feelings of worthlessness increase and mental health problems become significant. The reservation's annual per capita income of $2,369 in 1980 (U.S. Bureau of the Census 1983:263), the lowest of any in North Dakota, suggests the magnitude of this group's problems.

The economic situation of the Devils Lake Sioux may have been graver than on other reservations in North Dakota, but the opportunities were also greater. The reservation was closer to the largest population areas of North Dakota and nearer to major transportation networks. The city of Devils Lake also provided job opportunities for Indian people although the relationship between Indians and townspeople continued the old model of the Indians as visitors rather than as participants. The rise in the level of the lake increased tourism in the area, and made it possible for the tribe to take advantage of the need for tourist facilities, marinas, motels, shops, and attractions focusing on the reservation population itself. The presence of Fort Totten and Sullys Hill National Game Preserve attracted people to the reservation. As a small step toward economic development that took advantage of the non-Indian population in the area, the tribe opened Dakotah Bingo Palace. The success of this venture not only provided income for tribal projects, but also encouraged others.

Generally, however, prosperity still eluded many of the Devils Lake Sioux. The 1980

▲ Traditional and modern ways came together at the 1967 Centennial celebration. (SHSND)

Singers at the 1967 powwow celebrating the Centennial of the Reservation. (SHSND)

100

census found that 1,228 people over the age of fifteen had an income, but the largest number, 29 percent, earned less than $2,000. Only three percent of the reservation laborers were earning more than $15,000 a year. The average income for employed individuals was $4,495, the lowest for any of the state's reservations, although not significantly lower than Standing Rock's average income (U.S. Bureau of the Census 1986:531).

An analysis of the sources of income showed that most of this reported income came, not from individual earnings, but from leasing land, social security, and pensions. Only 462 individuals were identified as civilian workers. The majority of these workers, 39 percent, were employed by the tribal government while another 32 percent were employed in private or tribal industry (U.S Bureau of the Census 1986:424). Only two percent were engaged in agricultural pursuits because, despite restoration programs, 70 to 80 percent of the land on the reservation was owned and worked by non-Indians. The tribe had purchased some land and started a model farm, but most Indian people continued in the track established by the government and leased their land to non-Indians.

In 1973 the bright spot in reservation economics was the establishment of the Devils Lake Sioux Manufacturing Company, a division of the Brunswick Corporation. Devils Lake Sioux Manufacturing made camouflage nets under contract with the federal government and produced small plastic speciality items. Depending upon the availability of contracts and the success of the plastic products, the company employed from 200 to 300 people, but less than half those employed by Devils Lake Sioux Manufacturing were Indian, and the need for employment was much greater than one company could meet. One attempt to provide more work, Dakota Tribal Industries, a sewing operation owned by the tribe and employing 172 people in 1989, was jeopardized when the Small Business Administration revoked the company's license (*Grand Forks Herald*, 1989:9B).

Life on the reservation was similar to life in other rural communities. There were Indian and non-Indian communities, but the small size of the reservation meant that everyone seemed to know everyone else, and interactions among people occurred frequently and on different levels. Tokio, St. Michael, Crow Hill, and Fort Totten were considered Indian communities while Warwick and Hamar had a majority of non-Indian residents. Unlike larger reservations with satellite centers of administration, Fort Totten was the only administrative center and none of the communities were very far away from the center. Church, school, work, business, and social activities brought people of different ages, sexes, and cultural orientations together.

The major communities, existing since the reservation was established, were composed of newly built modern ranch-style homes that replaced the old log and frame houses. The newer homes were equipped with basic conveniences, but few people had dishwashers or other luxury items. Those individuals at the lowest levels of income could not afford such items as telephones and newer-model cars. These were residential communities with churches, community centers, and a few busi-

▲ *No more log cabins. Modern housing is found throughout the reservation.*

▼ *The Dakotah Bingo Palace provides jobs for tribal members and earns money for tribal expenses.*

nesses, but there was no commercial district on the reservation.

The Catholic Church remained the predominant Christian denomination on the reservation with churches at Fort Totten, St. Michael, Tokio, Warwick, and Crow Hill. Protestant churches were also located on the reservation. Church auxiliaries and associated groups met regularly to sponsor fund raisers for their activities. The Native American Church and some traditional religious practices continued. Although the Sun Dance was no longer held on the reservation, tribespeople participated in Sun Dances in other areas and hoped for a local revival of the ceremony. Since many of the Devils Lake Sioux people had relatives on other Sioux reservations, attending ceremonials at those places had both religious and social significance. The sweat lodge, the use of the pipe, and other religious practices were maintained by dedicated traditionalists.

The schools were also a focus for community involvement, especially in athletic events. The new Four Winds Community School, a joint Bureau of Indian Affairs and tribal operation, educated 200 children from kindergarten through graduation from high school. The majority of children at Warwick public school, a state supported school, were Indian while other Indian children attended state supported schools at Maddock, Oberon, and Devils Lake. It was Four Winds, however, that was the major focus for the reservation because parents were closely involved in all aspects of the academic and social programs.

Major employment opportunities were found at Fort Totten because this was the location of the federal and tribal agencies, the tribal court, the community college, Four Winds School, and Devils Lake Sioux Manufacturing.

Business also brought people together. The agency building in Fort Totten was a central spot for finding out information as people arrived and departed from business appoint-

ments. The Blue Building, as the agency was known, housed both federal and tribal operations, including the health clinic, and so there were always people in and around the building for different reasons. Messages were passed, arrangements made, and social contacts reaffirmed as people came and went from the building.

Social events, however, were the most productive and sustaining uses of people's time and energy. These activities ranged from those that would be found in most rural communities to those that were specifically Indian. Church groups, veteran's clubs, parent-teacher associations, and athletic teams, while employing Indian working methods, duplicated non-Indian organizations. True Indian organizations included drum groups and powwow clubs. Each summer the reservation sponsored a large powwow and rodeo that required continual fund-raising and organizational meetings

throughout the year. Committee members called on family and friends to assist in these activities. Smaller powwow committees sponsored traditional powwows for special occasions such as Veterans Day, Easter, and the Fourth of July.

In addition to the maintenance of language, family and kinship relationships similar to those of tribal days also continued. Devils Lake Sioux families were larger than non-Indian families and twenty percent of the households had other people living with them (U.S. Bureau of the Census 1986:180). Many of these households were multi-generational ones in which grandparents cared for the grandchildren while the parents were occupied elsewhere (Cook 1984; Lang 1985). In such cases the homemaker provided meals for as many as twelve people. The close ties between family members helped to maintain language, oral histories, and tribal traditions. Those families that were oriented toward a White life-style lived much like the non- Indians of the surrounding region. These people were less likely to participate in traditional activities, especially those that conflicted with work and school. They usually attended powwows as observers rather than as participants. Their children were raised speaking English although they probably understood when their grandparents spoke to them in Dakota.

Because the Devils Lake Sioux tribe was relatively small and more highly integrated than some of the other groups in North Dakota, it had more opportunity for self-development than other tribes. The small population meant that the tribe was not given large grants or made the focus of much federal attention, but it slowly created an industrial atmosphere that served as a model for other reservations. Devils Lake and Fort Totten provided ready made opportunities for the tribe to participate in tourist development. Unlike Standing Rock and Fort Berthold reservations, where the federal government's unsuccessful attempt to develop resorts made the tribes wary, Fort Totten had no such negative experience. Instead, the tribe had the examples set by local Devils Lake residents who operated marinas, motels, and restaurants. One tribal member opened a resort on the lake shore. The old fort itself, now operated by the State Historical Society, has always attracted visitors and been a center for summer programs. During the winter, a ski area brought other visitors to the reservation.

The tribe also moved forward in health care. In 1978 the reservation was selected to receive funds for a program to help lower infant mortality. Other programs involved diabetes screening and follow-up programs, alcohol and drug abuse programs, the operation of St. Jude's Elderly Home, and a group-home for juveniles. Without a hospital, many of these programs required the organization and cooperation of health personnel from different agencies throughout the state and region. The tribe frequently had difficulty obtaining sufficient and satisfactory Indian Health Service physicians, and there has been

In 1976 the beadwork skills of Susie Cavanaugh were featured in the Grand Forks Herald. (UND)

more interest in tribal programs that could substitute for the lack of personnel when necessary. The involvement of the local community in determining its own health care programs was a significant step forward for the Devils Lake Sioux.

In the 1980's the Devils Lake Sioux tribe also began to assert its legal rights. One issue concerning water rights and tribal boundaries was the result of the changing shoreline of the lake. As the lake grew, so did the legal questions. Who owned land that disappeared under water? Did the boundaries of the reservation follow the new waterline? In order to safeguard its rights, the tribe monitored and participated in lawsuits that provided some answers to these and similar questions.

Contributions to North Dakota History and Culture

The Devils Lake Sioux tribe has contributed in many ways to the history of North Dakota. The fort is still an important historic site that attracts visitors from all over the world. Men and women from the tribe served in all our country's wars and represented North Dakota with pride. The tribe has given us artists and craftspeople such as Florence White, whose star quilts were included in a national touring exhibition of contemporary Indian women's art. Western-style artists Rex Moore and Ken Greywind have also been recognized and honored locally and nationally. The success of Devils Lake Sioux Manufacturing has made it a model for other tribes and other countries seeking to become economically independent.

One special characteristic of the Devils Lake Sioux deserves recognition. Ever since the days of the Chatauqua, the Devils Lake Sioux people have participated wholeheartedly in local and regional celebrations. A complete list of dates would probably show that tribal groups have presented dance demonstrations in schools for the past fifty years or more. No matter how bad the weather, the students at the University of North Dakota can count on people from the reservation to attend their powwows. In the early years of the Grand Forks County Fair, people from the reservation staged a Wild West show that was a great success. The band from Fort Totten played at the State Fair and numerous Chatauqua meetings. The same spirit of cooperation resulted in Fort Totten Days, Inc., a committee of Indian and Devils Lake residents established to celebrate the centennial of Fort Totten. Working together, the committee raised enough money to support a variety of events. Fort Totten Days is still held on the reservation each July. This sharing of skills, knowledge, time, and energy harks back to buffalo days when survival depended on cooperation and sharing. Modern Devils Lake Sioux remind us that working together means a better life for all of us.

Chapter 7

Standing Rock Reservation

Solidly balanced on the North Dakota-South Dakota border, caught between the badlands and the Missouri, is Standing Rock Reservation, home of the Standing Rock Sioux. Although geographical politics has resulted in the reservation being considered a North Dakota reservation, its history is more closely associated with other Sioux reservations in South Dakota than with any of the other North Dakota reservations.

The tribes making up the Seven Council Fires, more commonly known as the Sioux, claimed lands extending from Minnesota to the Rocky Mountains and from Canada to Kansas. These claims were recognized in numerous treaties, but it was not until 1851, at a major treaty conference at Fort Laramie, that representatives of the different bands of western Sioux (Brules, Minneconju, Oglala, Hunkpapa, Blackfeet, Sans Arc, Oohenonpas) and other northern Plains tribes (Cheyenne, Arapaho, Crow, Assiniboins, Gros Ventres [Hidatsa], Mandan, Arikara) outlined the boundaries of the areas they claimed. In this treaty, the rights of the Sioux tribes to millions of acres were accepted by the government, although no formal reservation boundaries were established, and the treaty was never ratified (Kappler II:440-442).

Between 1851 and 1868, some Oglala, Brule, and other Lakota struggled to prevent the Army, overland travelers, road builders, and other White people from occupying or crossing their territory (Robinson 1904:223-230;350-381). Attempts to create a lasting peace failed until 1867 when the Peace Commission, established by Congress to settle the situation, called all the involved tribes to Fort Laramie to negotiate a new treaty.

The Treaty of Fort Laramie of 1868 outlined the boundaries of a 25 million acre tract encompassing all the land in South Dakota west of the Missouri River, to be known as the Great Sioux Reservation. Other lands in Nebraska, Wyoming, Montana, and North Dakota, part of the area claimed by the Sioux in the Treaty of Fort Laramie of 1851, were identified in the new treaty as unceded hunting

Standing Rock Agency, established in 1873, was named for a rock shaped like a woman with a child on her back.

104

▼ *Sitting Bull, shown here with his mother, wife and granddaughter, did not believe the Indians should sign the treaty agreeing to diminish the Great Sioux Reservation. (SHSND)*

territory which could be used as long as there were buffalo. The 1868 treaty also provided for rations, land allotments, education, an agency, and other assistance in exchange for an agreement by the Lakota that they would no longer harass White officials within their boundaries. The Federal government agreed to remove all military posts in the area and to prevent White settlement on Indian lands. Section XII of the treaty contained a provision that any subsequent treaty for cession of the reservation had to be approved by three fourths of all the adult men of all the tribes who signed the original treaty (Kappler II:770-775).

Some of the Lakota appeared to be satisfied with the treaty, and many kept their word and settled down to try to learn to be farmers and ranchers. Among the settler-Indians were some Hunkpapas, Upper Yanktonais, Blackfeet Sioux, and Lower Yanktonais who moved from Fort Rice, north of the Cannonball River, to the Grand River area where an agency was to be established for them. Under their chief, Two Bears, some Yanktonais who were farming off the reservation on the east side of the Missouri refused to give up their farms, but they maintained a good relationship with the agent (Annual Report of the Commissioner of Indian Affairs 1872:261). In accord with the Treaty of 1868, an

105

agency was established in a central location, which turned out to be Grand River, to serve the tribes living in the northern part of the Great Sioux Reservation. In 1873, however, the Grand River agency was moved 75 miles up the Missouri to a location that became known as Standing Rock, although the agency continued to be called the Grand River agency at Standing Rock until 1875 (Annual Report of the Commissioner of Indian Affairs 1875:244). The move to Standing Rock brought the peaceful Hunkpapa, Blackfeet Sioux, and Yanktonais, except for the farmers on the east side of the Missouri River, under greater control by the agent. Some members of Sitting Bull's band of Hunkpapa, often referred to as the "hostiles," also joined their relatives in the northern part of the Great Sioux Nation, although they chose to settle away from the agency itself (Annual Report of the Commissioner of Indian Affairs 1875:244-245).

Other Lakota, among them most of the Hunkpapas and numerous Oglala, Sans Arc, and Minneconju, did not recognize the Treaty of 1868 and pointed out that Whites were still using Indian lands and that rations and other guarantees of the treaty were not being provided to the tribes. By 1871, when the Northern Pacific Railroad sent out survey crews to locate a route for the proposed tracks across the unceded hunting territory of the Great Sioux Reservation, Lakota opposition was manifested in attacks on White settlements and settlers (Robinson 1904:401). Hostilities increased in 1874 when General George Armstrong Custer, in open violation of the treaty, was sent to survey the Black Hills. Although the Army maintained that the survey was only to gain information, the hostile Lakota were suspicious that the results would be disadvantageous to the Indians (Robinson 1904:415-416).

In many ways, 1875 was a crucial year for the Standing Rock Sioux. In March and again in November 1875, two tracts of land, one on the east side of the Missouri and one extending the northern boundary of the reservation to the Cannonball River, were added to the reservation by executive order of President Ulysses S. Grant (Kappler I:884). In early summer, a peace pact between the Mandan, Arikara,

Two Bears, Yanktonai, convinced his people to follow the agent's advice and become farmers. (SHSND)

▼ *John Grass signed the Treaty of Fort Laramie of 1868 and settled on the reservation. (SHSND)*

▼ *A government boarding school staffed by priests and sisters opened in 1881. (SHSND)*

106

▼ *John Pleets attended Hampton Institute in Virginia from 1878 to 1881. When he returned to Standing Rock he was put in charge of the agency stables. (SHSND)*

Hidatsa, and Standing Rock Sioux was concluded (Annual Report of the Commissioner of Indian Affairs 1875:246). In late summer a military post, originally named Standing Rock, but renamed Fort Yates in 1878, was established two hundred yards south of the agency (Annual Report of the Commissioner of Indian Affairs 1875:247). However, the most significant event of the year occurred in September 1875, when the government called a council of all the tribes and began negotiations to purchase the mining rights in the Black Hills and rights-of-way for roads through the unceded hunting lands (Annual Report of the Commissioner of Indian Affairs 1875:246-247; Robinson 1904:416-421).

The tribes rejected the proposal, but experience had taught them that the government would not accept their decision. Fearing the government would take the land anyway, they determined to fight. The presence of the Army, ostensibly to prevent White incursions into the area, did little to ease the feelings of the Sioux.

The well-known result of the impass was the Battle of the Little Big Horn and a new commission to the Sioux with instructions to obtain a cession of the Black Hills. The commission prepared the treaty in advance and, instead of a large treaty council, traveled from tribe to tribe to present the treaty to small groups. By this method the commission hoped to persuade enough men to sign the agreement to convince Congress to pass it (Robinson 1904:440-442). In September 1876 the commission obtained the signatures of Spotted Tail and Red Cloud and other prominent men of the South Dakota tribes. In October the commission arrived in North Dakota. Forty-eight men, nowhere near the three fourths required by the Treaty of Fort Laramie of 1868, of the Lower Yanktonais, Upper Yanktonais, Hunkpapa, and Blackfeet Sioux tribes signed at Standing Rock on October 11, 1876. In February 1877 Congress passed the act, officially reducing the Great Sioux Reservation and ceding all the hunting territory (Kappler I:168-172).

James McLaughlin was Indian agent at Standing Rock from 1881 to 1895. (SHSND)

▼ Ballots were distributed to Indian men who wanted to vote against the opening of the reservation to White settlement, but Congress approved the opening.

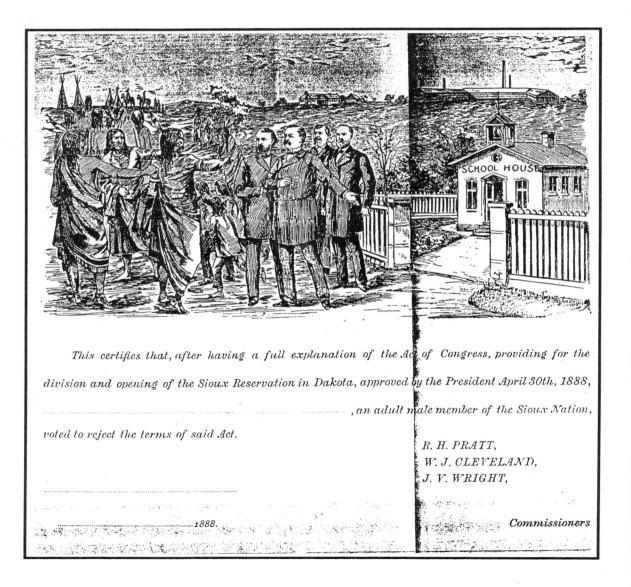

This certifies that, after having a full explanation of the Act of Congress, providing for the division and opening of the Sioux Reservation in Dakota, approved by the President April 30th, 1888, _____, an adult male member of the Sioux Nation, voted to reject the terms of said Act.

R. H. PRATT,
W. J. CLEVELAND,
J. V. WRIGHT,

_____ 1888.

Commissioners

Meanwhile, the Indian people of Standing Rock were trying to adapt to a totally new way of life. Although some had had some success in agriculture, most were dependent on rations and what they could obtain from hunting and wage labor because agriculture was so risky. In 1876 Agent John Burke noted that grasshoppers, drought, and poor soil had contributed to crop failure and that there was little game left on the reservation (Annual Report of the Commissioner of Indian Afairs, 1876:38), although in 1877, Agent W. F. Hughes gave a more positive report (Annual Report of the Commissioner of Indian Affairs, 1877:468). Another sign of Indian acceptance of reservation life was the purchase of two mowing machines by John Grass and Two Bears, the construction of log houses, and the establishment of a school.

The agents had been requesting educational and church facilities for many years, and in 1876 Father Martin Marty, Father Chrysostom Foffa, and Brother Giles arrived to begin a mission school. A day school was opened in 1876, and a school for boys taught by Father Chrysostom was opened in 1877. Education

advanced rapidly, and by 1879 the agent reported in glowing terms on the three schools on the reservation. An industrial farm school, opened in 1878, 15 miles south of the agency, was operated by the Benedictines. A boys' boarding school provided instruction in English, writing, and arithmetic to 45 students, and a girls' boarding school offered English, geography, housework, needlework, and singing to 32 girls (Annual Report of the Commissioner of Indian Affairs 1879:49-50). The boarding schools were combined in 1880 (Annual Report of the Commissioner of Indian Affairs 1880:56). In 1884 a day school operated by the American Board of Foreign Missions of the Congregational Church attracted 25 students from the Antelope area of Grand River while another day school opened by the agent at Cannonball settlement served 60 pupils (Annual Report of the Commissioner of Indian Affairs 1884:99).

Sending their children to school did not mean the Standing Rock Sioux were willing to give up all their traditional customs.   The agents were bewildered by the apparent contradiction between the adoption of White-style clothing and short hair, signs they took for assimilation, and the continuation of Indian dances and give-away ceremonies. A Sun Dance held in the summer of 1880 became a major cause of dissent when Agent J. A. Stephan charged that Captain W. P. Carlin and other officers at Fort

*James McLaughlin and Competency Commissioners at a
ceremony celebrating the Indians receiving the titles to
their allotments and becoming U.S. citizens. (SHSND)*

Yates had encouraged and supported the dance
(National Archives, Record Group 75, Letters
Received by the Office of Indian Affairs, Standing Rock, July 6, 1880). Dances were blamed
for neglect of crops, desire to travel, poor
health, and impoverishment. Agent Stephan
complained that the practice of giving presents
to visitors from other tribes often left the hosts
"in a state of nudity" (Annual Report of the
Commissioner of Indian Affairs 1880:56), and

Agent James A. McLaughlin finally prohibited
all dances except the grass dance which he
allowed to be held only on Saturday after-
noons (Annual Report of the Commissioner of
Indian Affairs 1884:98). The traditional form
of marriage by gift exchange continued although Agent Stephan regarded it as a good
sign that no couples lived together without
some type of ceremony. In 1890 special agent
Gilbert Gaul reported that some residents still

followed traditional religious beliefs (U.S.
Department of the Interior 1894:522), and in
1905 a visitor to the reservation commented
that every log cabin had a tipi and brush arbor
nearby. Sweatlodge frames were also noted
(Wilson 1905:25).

The apparent successful adjustment to reservation living by the Standing Rock Sioux was
threatened by the constant pressure from Whites
for Indian land. The influx of White settlers

110

▲ *To encourage farming and ranching, the government issued wagons, agricultural equipment and cattle to Indian men, but droughts and severe winters brought little success. (SHSND)*

▼ *Before leaving to join the Army, Ben Grayhawk and Ed Lean Elk posed with their friends Albert Grass and Ed Afraid of Hawk. (SHSND)*

that caused the hostilities of earlier years and resulted in the cession of the Black Hills in 1877 continued, and demands to open more reservation lands increased. As early as 1882 a Congressional commission to the Sioux obtained an agreement to establish six smaller, separate reservations and open all other lands of the Great Sioux Reservation to White settlement, but the agreement was never ratified (Annual Report of the Commissioner of Indian Affairs 1904:498). In 1879 and 1884, executive orders signed by Presidents Rutherford B. Hayes and Chester A. Arthur restored lands on the east side of the Missouri to public domain (Kappler I:889,884), and in March 1889 Congress passed an act creating six reservations from the Diminished Great Sioux Reservation (Kappler I:328-339). By this act, nine million acres of reservation lands were opened to White settlement, Standing Rock Reservation received its name, and provisions for allotting the reservation were reaffirmed. The reservation was officially proclaimed on February 10, 1890 (Kappler I:943-945).

One of the more unsettling events at Standing Rock was the return of Sitting Bull from Canada, where he and his followers had fled after the Battle of the Little Big Horn. Life in Canada had not been easy because the United States regarded Sitting Bull as an escaped villain who should be brought back for sentencing and the Canadian government would not support Indians from the United States (Hoover 1980:160-161). Some of the hostiles surrendered in 1880, but it was not until mid-July 1881 that Sitting Bull and several hundred others gave themselves up to the commanding officer of Fort Buford. Following two years' confinement at Fort Randall, Sitting Bull returned to his camp on the Grand River and the administrative control of Agent James McLaughlin. Sitting Bull and his band apparently desired to live quietly and to avoid further trouble, but his presence was a constant reminder that the government was not treating the Indians fairly, and so McLaughlin encouraged Sitting Bull to leave the reservation as often as possible. Between 1883 and 1885 Sitting Bull attended the opening of the North Pacific Railroad in Bismarck, accompanied the

▲ *Albert Grass, Co.I, 2nd.Reg.ND, was killed in action in France in 1918. (SHSND)*

Cannonball Day School was located in one of the Indian district centers. (SHSND)

Alvaren Allen and Buffalo Bill shows through the eastern states and Canada, and visited the Crow Agency in Montana (Hoover 1980:164). Sitting Bull and others from Fort Yates participated in Bismarck's celebration of statehood in 1889 (Heski 1978:46), but when a Congressional commission arrived at Fort Yates to obtain signatures agreeing to the creation of six reservations from the Diminished Great Sioux Reservation, Sitting Bull was not invited. Despite this obvious attempt to avoid Sitting Bull's reaction, he attended anyway and voiced his displeasure with the agreement, which the others signed over his objections.

The failure to prevent the reduction of the reservation and the increasingly obvious presence of non-Indians moving into the newly formed states of North and South Dakota may have encouraged Sitting Bull's interest in the Ghost Dance, a ceremony which promised to make non-Indians disappear so that the buffalo and tribal cultures could return to glory, but the sad result of his participation in the Ghost Dance must be attributed to "bureaucratic blunder" (Hoover 1980:169). Agent McLaughlin regarded the Ghost Dance as a threat to the safety of Whites and Indians in the area, and in December 1890 McLaughlin sent a force of Indian police to arrest Sitting Bull and take him to Fort Yates. There was a scuffle and both Sitting Bull and an Indian policeman were killed. Others were injured. The death of Sitting Bull caused a panic among his followers and they fled south to the Cheyenne River reservation. When they were convinced that they would not be killed, most of the Standing Rock people returned to their reservation, but some stayed with Big Foot's band and went to join others at Pine Ridge. Before the small band of refugees could reach the agency, they were stopped by the cavalry. The tragic outcome of this meeting was the massacre of Big Foot and other refugees at Wounded Knee on December 29, 1890. As Sitting Bull predicted, however, his death did not end his influence, and today his words and actions still inspire Indian people.

For a variety of reasons, allotment was slow in coming to Standing Rock. The General Allotment Act affected Standing Rock Reservation in a different way from the other North Dakota reservations. The idea of alloting land to individual families was contained in the Treaty of Fort Laramie of 1868, and agents were instructed to try to get their charges to settle on farmsteads. In 1879 Agent Stephan convinced 122 Indian families to leave the agency and settle on separate 80-acre tracts. Upper Yanktonai took land north of the agency while the Blackfeet and Hunkpapa settled south of the agency (Annual Report of the Commissioner of Indian Affairs 1880:51). People built houses on their land and grew corn,

squash, potatoes, beans, beets, turnips, carrots, cabbage, and other vegetables for family use. Most of the vegetables were dried, the traditional method of storing food for future use. Hay was grown to feed the cattle and horses (Annual Report of the Commissioner of Indian Affairs 1879:46; Annual Report of the Commissioner of Indian Affairs 1880:51-54).

The allotment process should have been eased by the Standing Rock Sioux' taking 80-acre plots; instead it was made more difficult because the plots had not been taken in accordance with the rules for allotment. First the reservation had to be surveyed. No appropriations for such a survey were made until 1893 (Annual Report of the Commissioner of Indian Affairs 1893:31-32). Then a special agent had to be appointed to make the actual allotments, but this did not occur until 1906 (Annual Report of the Commissioner of Indian Affairs 1906:62). Influential Indian people at Standing Rock were opposed to allotment for many reasons (Johnson 1948:27-28), but once begun, allotment proceeded quickly (Annual Report of the Commissioner of Indian Affairs 1907:62), and in May 1908 the surplus unallotted land was opened for sale to non-Indians (Kappler III:373-377).

▲ *Small frame houses began to replace the old-style log cabins. (MA)*

St. Bernard's Mission School and a government boarding school provided education for children who lived too far away to commute. (MA)

113

The Act of 1908 permitted allotments to anyone who had not previously received one. Recently born children were able to obtain parcels of land. Lands were also reserved for schools and government and religious purposes. Before opening the lands for sale, a commission had to classify and appraise them. Reservation lands were finally opened to White settlement by a Presidential proclamation in August 1909, which set the date of possession as April 1, 1910. The proclamation specified that individuals desiring to acquire lands should register between October 4 and October 23, 1909. Following this date, names would be drawn by lot, and entry numbers assigned. On April 1, 1910, people would be permitted to start the procedure for obtaining their land. After September 1910, any remaining lands would be open for homesteading (Kappler III:657-658). In 1913 Congress approved the sale of all remaining lands at $5.00 an acre (Kappler III:555-558).

As on the other reservations in the Dakotas, allotment created great problems of land

▲   *In 1943 severe flooding of the Missouri affected Standing Rock reservation, but the residents opposed the government's plan to build a dam that would permanently flood the bottomlands. (MA)*

▼   *The waves of Lake Oahe, created in 1958 by damming the Missouri, erode the banks and cause continuing land destruction.*

114

ownership and jurisdiction. Today more than 60 percent of Standing Rock reservation is owned by non-Indians. The process of dividing allotments equally between heirs has meant that many allotments are now shared by so many people that no one can use the land efficiently. Lease payments for shared lands are divided among the owners, but these are often too small to provide any financial benefits.

The opening of the reservation did not make much change in the life-style of the tribespeople. A number of towns were established, but the Indian people continued to live in their kinship-tribally-based localities. In 1914 complaints about the poor conditions of people at Standing Rock were sent to the Secretary of Indian Affairs. One complaining letter was apparently the work of the newly formed governing body of elected officers (A. C. Wells to P. D. Norton, March 10, 1914. McLaughlin Papers), but others were also sent. Some of the letters supported the complaints while others were contradictory, and so McLaughlin, acting in his job as Indian inspector, was sent to the reservation in April to investigate the allegations. His report and the complaint letters provide a picture of life on the reservation. Most of the people were raising small crops and ranching, but three years of drought and neglect of the crops and cattle had resulted in insufficient food to carry people through the winter. McLaughlin reported that one of the reasons people had stopped paying attention to their home gardens and cattle was that loose-ranging cattle owned by White stockmen had destroyed Indian land and crops. He estimated that one of the White cattlemen had 10,000 head ranging freely over the reservation while the number of Indian-owned cattle had dropped from 25,000 head to 6,500 in just a few years. Conditions were severe enough that rations were still being issued once a month, and any elder in need could receive more at any time. McLaughlin noted that

The reservation today. (map)

elders were supplying other family members with food and that there was no real deprivation although no one was doing very well (J. McLaughlin to Secretary of Interior, May 2, 1914. McLaughlin Papers).

World War I found Indian men at Standing Rock ready to serve their country as warriors. Richard Blue Earth of Cannonball, the first North Dakota Indian to enlist (Spokesfield 1928:541), was followed by many others, some of whom such as Albert Grass, nephew of Chief Grass, lost their lives on foreign soil. At home, Standing Rock Sioux supported the war effort through contributions to the Red Cross and by buying bonds (Beede 1942). When the soldiers returned, they were greeted with Victory Dances similar to the ones held for their

grandfathers when they returned victoriously from war.

The experiences of these young men also contributed to the problems perceived by Agent E. Mossman, who complained bitterly to McLaughlin about Indian dances (E. Mossman to Rev. E. Ashley, Aug. 8, 1921. McLaughlin Papers). Mossman identified the returning veterans as the cause of the problems because they claimed they were citizens of the United States and were protected by the Constitution from the agent's prohibitions. These men also brought with them an interest in establishing their citizenship, and the reservation residents became involved with the highly contested state elections of 1922 in which Lynn Frazier defeated Porter McCumber for the Senate seat

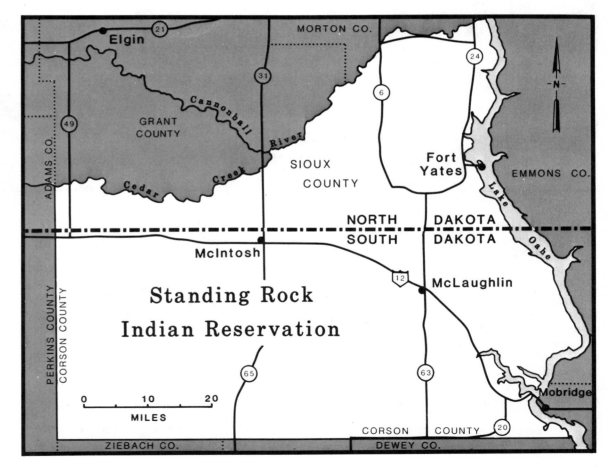

115

Fort Yates is the administrative center for the Standing Rock Sioux tribe.

Fort Yates is the administrative center for the Standing Rock Sioux tribe.

(McLaughlin to Mr. Commissioner, June 22, 1922. McLaughlin Papers). Mossman's letters suggest that the agent made an unsuccessful attempt to control Indian voting.

The Indian Reorganization Act of 1934 was not unrestrictedly accepted at Standing Rock. For one reason, the tribe already had a modern government. In 1914 the tribe adopted a constitutional form of government that melded tribal and Federal characteristics. Shortly after the establishment of the reservation, the Bureau of Indian Affairs had divided the reservation into administrative districts associated with the major camps of the different bands. These districts, Fort Yates, Bullhead, Cannonball, Little Eagle, Porcupine, Wakpala, and Kenel,

were ration distribution sites, school sites, and administrative centers. Under the new tribal government, these administrative units became voting districts that, with the addition of McLaughlin, remain intact today. When tribal members were presented with the opportunity to organize under the Indian Reorganization Act, the tribe chose to remain with their previous constitution (Fay 1967:100), but in 1959 they adopted a new constitution and by-laws. Today the Standing Rock Sioux Tribe is governed by a council elected from eight districts on the reservation.

Like the Three Affiliated Tribes and others living along the Missouri, the Standing Rock Sioux suffered from the construction of dams

that inundated valuable agricultural and range lands. In August 1948 the Army Corps of Engineers began construction of Oahe Dam, which created a reservoir 250 miles long, covering 160,889 acres of Standing Rock and Cheyenne River Sioux land (Lawson 1982:50). Standing Rock was more fortunate than other reservations because the water could not be allowed to threaten Bismarck, and so only 55,994 acres were taken, but even this loss meant relocating 25 percent of the population, destroying the best farm and timber land, and turning Fort Yates into an island (Lawson 1982:51-52). The tribe received slightly more than 12 million dollars as compensation for their loss (U.S. Department of the Interior 1964:4). The money was administered by the tribal council, who divided it between seven programs: relocation, family assistance plan, education, community development, industrial development, cattle improvement, and land management. Even if the psychological impact of the reservoir on the Standing Rock Sioux was less than that felt by the Mandan, Hidatsa, and Arikara, the economic loss and political upheaval were great and the tribe has not yet fully recovered. In 1981 Elizabeth Azure explained her feelings about the changes caused by the dam to a reporter from the *Bismarck Tribune*:

> Life nowadays isn't as good as it used to be....There was a time when people lived near the river. They planted their gardens and stored vegetables in the root cellars for the winter. Most people had a team, some chickens, a milk cow, maybe a pig or two. They didn't depend on the government (Hendrickson 1981:15).

A survey commissioned by the tribe in 1955 to gather facts for use in planning for the impact of Oahe Reservoir showed conditions to be little different from pre-World War I. Incomes were low, and many people, even those with jobs, qualified for welfare. People indicated that they would prefer to earn a living by ranching, but the survey noted lack of land and opportunity to build successful operations. The study concluded that it would be extremely difficult to consolidate Indian lands in sufficient quantity and quality to create

▲   *The grocery store has replaced the buffalo.*

▼   *The Public Health Service provides modern health care to Indian people living on the reservation.*

successful ranching operations (U.S. Department of the Interior 1957:19-21). Other aspects of reservation life were also reported to need improvement. Many of the homes were found to be old and in poor condition and holding too many people. Only seven percent of the homes had indoor toilets. The building of the reservoir opened the possibility of consolidating lands and improving housing, but, as with Fort Berthold, the promised improvements were slow in arriving.

The Reservation at the End of the Twentieth Century

By the middle of the 1980's, the Standing Rock Sioux were enmeshed in a web of Indian and non-Indian life-styles similar to those found on other reservations in the northern Plains. Standing Rock was the largest and most isolated of the North Dakota reservations. Most of the residents lived in the eastern part of the reservation in communities associated with the major rivers, but others lived far from any community. Even the major communities, Fort Yates, McLaughlin, and McIntosh, numbered less than 1,000 people in 1980 (U.S.

117

▲ *Modern multifamily and single family ranch homes have improved living conditions on the reservation.*

A new multimillion dollar school provides modern education to students living near Fort Yates.

Bureau of the Census 1983:10) and were sixty miles or more from an urban area. Many White ranchers and businessmen lived on the reservation, but the large size of the reservation made it possible for Standing Rock Sioux people to maintain their traditional ways by settling away from the agency and populated areas.

The presence of a strong traditional orientation may be a reflection of the continuing influence of Sitting Bull as a promoter of traditional Indian religious beliefs and culture. Religious beliefs and language are closely related. Although all the Standing Rock Sioux spoke some English, more than one third of the Standing Rock Sioux over the age of five - the highest percentage of any North Dakota reservation - reported speaking a language other than English at home (Bureau of the Census 1983:262). In her dissertation research, Karen

Swisher found that 34 percent of the parents in her study spoke Dakota/Lakota as a first language, although English was the language most often used in the home (Swisher 1981:83). Forty-six percent of the parents in Dr. Swisher's study described themselves as traditional. Traditional people attended powwows and participated in other Indian ceremonies. Medicine men were available to those who preferred to follow the Lakota religion. Both the vision quest and sweat lodge were still held. If speaking a language other than English was an adequate measure of traditional orientation, then there were more traditional people living on the South Dakota side of the reservation than on the North Dakota side (U.S. Bureau of the Census 1983:262).

Despite the apparently high concentration of traditional cultural values, four percent of

the Standing Rock Sioux had four or more years of college. These bicultural people supported both Indian and non-Indian ways, but they lived in a life-style more similar to non-Indians because their college education made it possible for them to obtain salaried positions or to become successful ranchers and entrepreneurs, options not generally open to the traditionally oriented people. The importance of the federal and tribal agency as an employer of educated people was suggested by the higher percentage of high school and college graduates living on the North Dakota side of the reservation (U.S. Bureau of the Census 1983:262).

Since settlement, transitional people, those who adopted White ways because they found nothing to value in Indian ways, have been part of the reservation social environment. Some of the transitional people sprang from marriages

Standing Rock Community College educates many adults.

between Indians and Whites in which one partner adopted the non-Indian values of the other. A survey done at Standing Rock in 1955 noted that a few respondents believed that Indians would benefit from marrying non-Indians (U.S. Department of the Interior 1957:33). Transitional people married to non-Indians were more likely to leave the Indian community, but some remained and worked to change Indian ways.

Marginal people, those who were dissatisfied with both Indian and non-Indian cultures, were also found at Standing Rock. Because marginal people lacked positive self-images for either Indian or non-Indian ways, they were more likely to have economic, social, and psychological problems.

These strong differences among orientations, as well as continuing tribal and historic disagreements, were echoed in economic and social problems similar to those faced by other North Dakota reservations. For the Standing Rock Sioux, however, solutions required inno-

vative thinking that integrated the diverse viewpoints and attracted the funds necessary to implement the programs.

The economic difficulties of the Standing Rock Reservation were partly due to its isolated, rural location. Under ideal circumstances, the reservation residents would have been supporting themselves as ranchers, but in 1980 only seven percent of the Indian people were engaged in agricultural pursuits. This figure was only slightly reduced from the 9.7 percent engaged in ranching in 1955 (U.S. Department of the Interior 1957:14). Because allotment broke up the land on the reservation, most of it was owned or leased by non-Indians who could put together a large enough tract to make ranching profitable. The same difficulties with drought, insects, low prices, and insufficent land reported by agents in the late 1800's continued to plague the reservation a century later.

A large percentage of people at Standing

Rock had earned-income from employment, but 30 percent of these had workers an annual income of less than $2,000 (U.S. Bureau of the Census 1986:552). According to the 1980 census only four percent made more than $15,000 a year. As on the other reservations, the majority of the jobs were with the tribal and Federal agencies that provided services to the reservation. Clearly associated with the greater traditionalism and less education was a per capita income slightly higher for the residents on the North Dakota side of the reservation (U.S. Bureau of the Census 1983:263), but the difference amounted to only a few hundred dollars.

Throughout the nation, Indian families tended to be larger than non-Indian, and this trend held true for Standing Rock, where the average family size was nearly five people. Twenty percent of these families also had other relatives or non-relatives living with them (U.S. Bureau of the Census 1986:201). Further substantiating the earlier suggestion that the South

Dakota residents were more traditional were statistics showing that only 16 percent of North Dakota Standing Rock families were extended while 23 percent of South Dakota families were of the extended variety. In areas where income was low, larger families were economically more secure because they obtained more public assistance, and there was an increased chance that some family member would find employment.

The large size of the reservation and the isolation of many of the communities resulted in a diversified school system that educated people from kindergarten through college. Most of the earlier mission schools had been discontinued, but St. Bernard's Mission School for elementary-age children at Fort Yates was still operated by the Catholic Church. The former Bureau of Indian Affairs Boarding School at Fort Yates had been replaced by a new, modern high school. Schools at Fort Yates, Solen/Cannon Ball, Selfridge, McLaughlin, McIntosh, and Wakpala were state supported public schools, while the Bureau of Indian Affairs and the Tribe supported schools at Fort Yates, Bullhead, and Little Eagle. Most of these schools were day schools, and students were bused from their homes to the appropriate school.

Although there was a strong continuing tradition of ancient religious beliefs and practices, the impact of missionaries from different denominations was seen in the large number of Christian churches scattered throughout the reservation. Some of these churches were the successors to earlier mission churches while others, like the Mormon Churches, were more recent additions to the ecumenical preferences of the residents. The churches provided social activities as well as religious opportunities. The Mormons also supported students from the reservation who wished to attend church-supported schools and activities in Utah.

In addition to the social events sponsored by the churches, many powwow committees raised funds for powwows and rodeos held throughout the reservation during the summer months. The numerous powwows necessitated drum groups and dancers. Many of the people who participated in one or more of these activities traveled throughout the northern Plains attending powwows and advertising their own. Good dancers and singers could earn money by competing at powwows; for traditional families, these earnings were im-

Red Tomahawk, said to have shot Sitting Bull, is commemorated on North Dakota State Highway markers. (SHSND)

portant sources of income.

Standing Rock Reservation had many problems, but it also had a rich variety of resources, human and natural, on which to base future developments. Beginning with the council's involvement in planning how the funds received from the lands flooded by Oahe Reservoir were to be used, and continuing in 1970 when the Economic Development Agency provided funds for developmental planning grants, the tribe steadily worked toward economic self- sufficiency. It is important to note that the planning and development were being done by tribal leaders, not by the Federal government. Programs developed internally tended to be more successful than those introduced by outsiders, but they were also slower to show results. A report made in 1972 commented that proposed projects in cattle ranching and irrigated farming appeared to be sound (U.S. Department of Commerce 1972:303). Those projects were not realized for more than a decade. In 1983 the Standing Rock Sioux inaugurated a computer-assisted irrigation program to provide water to a tribally conducted farming operation. In 1985 the program was expanded to irrigate another 1,600 acres. The success of such a program will be not only in demonstrating that farming can be done at Standing Rock but also in claiming and managing the water resource that is a vital necessity in the northern Plains.

The use of a combination of human and natural resources can also be seen in the advances made in resource management. One of the first such moves was the development of a buffalo herd. Oahe Reservoir led the tribe into fish and water management. Just as the Three Affiliated Tribes and the Devils Lake Sioux used different techniques to claim their future rights to water, Standing Rock also established

claims to the water impounded by Oahe Reservoir.

Contributions to North Dakota History and Culture

The Standing Rock Sioux have given us heroic leaders who will forever capture our admiration. The tribe gave us authors such as Marie McLaughlin and Vine Deloria, Jr., musicians and dramatists such as Angela Cournoyer, artists too numerous to name, two Miss Indian Americas, actors, lawyers, educators, politicians, and religious leaders. Sitting Bull is one of the most famous of all American Indians, but it is the profile of Red Tomahawk, who claimed to have shot Sitting Bull, that marks North Dakota highways.

Frank Fiske was so captivated by life at Standing Rock that he spent most of his life there and made a photographic record of Indian life that has not been equaled. His formal portraits depict Sioux people in the classic, studio style of the early twentieth century, but his photographs of activities, scenes, and events record the changing culture of the Standing Rock Sioux.

A more unusual contribution has been reported by Tim Kloberdanz, who learned from German-Russians living in the northern part of the reservation that the immigrants took on so many characteristics of the Sioux that they were sometimes called the German Indians (Kloberdanz 1987:73). Words from Sioux were added to the vocabulary of the German-Russians. Some German-Russian women dried corn and other vegetables in the same manner as their Sioux sisters. It is likely that the immigrants learned to build log cabins from the Sioux. One man reported that his child-rearing methods changed when he saw that the Sioux children grew up well-behaved without physical punishment (Kloberdanz 1987:79). There were intermarriages between the immigrants and the Sioux and the offspring of these marriages exemplify the cultural interchange that took place. Louis Gipp recalled that his mother cooked non-Indian food to please her husband and took the children to their grandmother's to eat Indian food (Hendrickson 1981:54). The name of Solen commemorates another cross-cultural marriage. Maria Louise Picotte, the daughter of Eagle Woman All Look At and Honore Picotte, married George Van Solen. The town of Solen, North Dakota, was named in recognition of their contributions to education (Williams 1966, vol.4:34).

The Standing Rock Sioux well illustrate the traits of courage, adaptation, and perseverance that are associated with North Dakotans.

121

Chapter 8

Turtle Mountain Reservation

Stretching to reach the Canadian border in a landscape dotted with lakes and trees is Turtle Mountain Reservation, home of Chippewa, Cree, and Métis people, now known as the Turtle Mountain Band of Chippewa. Having today the smallest land base and the largest population of any tribe in North Dakota, the Turtle Mountain Band of Chippewa illustrates the difficulties of Indian people whose claims were unheeded by the federal government.

The establishment and subsequent history of the Turtle Mountain Reservation is entirely different from that of Devils Lake, Fort Berthold, and Standing Rock because the complicated issue of whether or not the Métis were American or Canadian resulted in the relatively late recognition of the Chippewa claim (Murray 1984). Even the Chippewa who later became part of the Turtle Mountain Band of Chippewa were not members of a single homogeneous group, and this, too, delayed the reservation process.

According to Chippewa tradition, the tribe was created on the east coast. Historical evidence shows that the Chippewa migration from the East took place in waves. One surge brought Chippewa into the northern Minnesota, southern Canada region around Rainy Lake. These families eventually moved farther west, where they came in contact with Cree and Assiniboin peoples with whom they formed alliances against their common enemy, the Dakota. Because they became buffalo hunters and adopted other characteristics of Plains Indian tribes, these Chippewa became known as the Plains Chippewa. A second wave brought Chippewa into the Leech Lake and Red Lake areas, where they were contacted by fur traders and explorers. Some Leech Lake and Red Lake families were attracted to the Red River Valley by fur traders who guaranteed them profitable occupations as trappers (Hickerson 1959).

One of the earliest European trading posts in the Red River Valley was established at Pembina, and the Chippewa who moved there became known as the Pembina Band of Chippewa (Hickerson 1956). Some of these Chippewa, too, turned their faces to the west and began to use the Turtle Mountains as wintering places. When trapping was no longer profitable in the Red River Valley, these Chippewa moved onto the Plains to hunt buffalo, and adopted various Plains customs such as the tipi and Sun Dance. Some Chippewa remained in the Pembina area, either at Pembina or at St. Joseph, now called Walhalla, where they served as intermediaries between their kinsmen in Minnesota and their relatives on the Plains.

Both the Chippewa in Canada and in North Dakota were closely associated with the fur trade. The majority of the traders were French, but English, Scots, and others entered the area also. A number of Indian women married these men, and the offspring of the European-Indian marriages became known as Métis, or mixed-bloods. Some of the Métis continued to consider themselves Indian and lived with their tribal relatives even though they had French or English surnames. Other Métis formed a distinct group with characteristic dress, language, life-style, and predominantly Catholic religion (Brasser 1976:47). The Métis were also part of the fur trade, and when the trapping was not good, they turned to hunting buffalo to supply the trading posts and settlers with meat.

One of the complicating factors in Turtle Mountain Chippewa history was the determination of the international boundary between the United States and Canada. The Conven-

tion of 1818, between Great Britain and the United States, established the 49th parallel as the boundary from the Lake of the Woods to the Rockies, but the exact location of the boundary line was not established until 1823. Although some Métis and Chippewa lived around Fort Garry and Lake Winnipeg, Pembina was the heart of Chippewa and Métis country and served as the focal point for populations which reached from Minnesota into Montana, from the Lake of the Woods to Woody Mountain, Saskatchewan. As long as Pembina was part of

Rupert's Land or Assiniboia, there was little difficulty, but when the boundary between Canada and the United States was set at the 49th parallel, Pembina was found to be located on the American side of the border. Some people chose to leave Pembina and settle in Canada, while others selected the United States. Relatives made different choices but continued to move back and forth across the border for hunting, visiting, and other purposes. Because neither the Canadian nor the American government understood the close relationship

between the Métis and their Indian relatives, attempts to divide this population mixture into American and Canadian residents caused numerous problems in later years.

By 1850, Chippewa and Métis groups had spread from Minnesota all the way into Montana. Certain areas that had become favorite hunting or wintering spots were associated with specific groups, but it is clear that these groups were not totally independent of each other. Personal histories contained in Laura Law's book, *History of Rolette County, North*

Dakota and Yarns of the Pioneers (1953), and interviews conducted by James McLaughlin in 1917 with members of Rocky Boy's band in Montana (Copies of interviews with members of Rocky Boy's Band, 1917. McLaughlin Papers) show that people born in Pembina, St. Joseph, or the Turtle Mountains spent part of their lives in North Dakota, Montana, Manitoba, and Saskatchewan before settling down on or near a reservation. A slightly different pattern is shown by the early life of Francois Jeannotte, who was born in the early 1800's while his mother, a Turtle Mountain Chippewa, and his father, a French Canadian trapper, were living on the Souris. As a child, Francois lived on Beaver Creek, a tributary of the Assiniboine, on the Pembina River, and on the Salt River before his family returned to settle on the Souris around 1820. Jeannotte eventually moved to the Turtle Mountain Reservation, where he died in 1905 (Jeannotte 1906).

Increasing conflict between buffalo hunting groups, growing White interests in settling the area, and the entrance of Minnesota into statehood necessitated an attempt at some kind of agreement between Indians, Métis, and settlers. One of the earliest attempts was made by Alexander Ramsey in 1851, when he met with Chippewa and Métis to discuss the cession of the Red River area. An agreement between the Red Lake and Pembina Chippewa to cede an area in the northern part of the Red River Valley was never ratified, but Ramsey noted the presence of Chippewa west of the ceded area and recognized that it would be necessary to deal with them separately (U.S. Senate, 55th Congress, 2nd Session, Document No.154:16).

Because the treaty was never ratified, the issues continued unresolved until 1863, when a commission was appointed to treat again with the Red Lake and Pembina Chippewa. The Pembina men who signed the treaty included Red Bear, Little Shell, Summer Wolverine, Joseph Gornon, Joseph Montreuil, and Equal Sky. According to the treaty, the Pembina ceded a strip of land in North Dakota and all their claims to Minnesota land. Adult mixed-blood men of the Pembina and Red Lake bands were given the right to take homesteads in the ceded area, and two 640-acre reservations, one for the Red Lake chief and one for the Pembina chief, Red Bear, were set aside. The reservation for Red Bear was located on the north side of Pembina River (Kappler II:653). This treaty brought the Pembina band under the aegis of the agent at White Earth, but it made little change in the life-style of either the Pembina Chippewa or their relatives to the west. The Pembina Band of Turtle Mountain Chippewa steadfastly maintained that their claim to ten million acres in northern North Dakota had precedence over any treaties with the Sioux or Chippewa.

As long as the northern Plains remained unoccupied by Whites, and the buffalo supply remained steady, the movement of Chippewa and Métis bands around northern North Dakota and Montana continued. In 1868 Agent J.B.Bassett at White Earth noted that the Pembina bands around the Red River were destitute because the buffalo were gone and grasshoppers had destroyed their crops (Annual Report of the Commissioner of Indian Affairs 1868:302). It is not surprising that some of these people moved west to look for better conditions. In 1870 a group of Métis left Walhalla and moved to Montana (Dusenberry 1965), and in 1873 Captain Anderson of the British-

American party surveying the international boundary met a group of eighty families from St. Joseph who were spending the winter at Woody Mountain, Saskatchewan (Parsons 1963:81). Throughout these years of making-do, the Turtle Mountain people continued to seek recognition of their claim and the establishment of a reservation. In 1872 agent Edward Smith at White Earth wrote:

> The Pembina band are in much the same deplorable condition as reported last year. They have no reservation in the vicinity where most of them are trying to subsist. A portion of the band live on Turtle Mountain, in Dakota, and claim that this is a portion of their country which they have never yet ceded; and they say they were living there at the time of the cession in 1864, and that their grounds are west of the line of the ceded territory. They ask that their rights in this unceded country may be recognized... Something should be done to help these Indians out of degradation, and relieve the settlers that are now coming by rail to Pembina from the annoyance of their begging and pilfering. I recommend that the Department either recognize their right to all the territory on Turtle Mountain and give them the means to farm there, or purchase a right on White Earth reservation, and order them to remove. They number, according to the roll this year, about three hundred and fifty Indians and one hundred half-breeds...(Annual Report of the Commissioner of Indian Affairs 1872:209).

Despite repeated requests for recognition, nothing was done until 1882, when President Chester A. Arthur, by executive order, set aside twenty-two townships in what is now Rolette County for "the Turtle Mountain band of Chippewas and such other Indians of the Chippewa tribe as the Secretary of the Interior may see fit to settle thereon" (Kappler I:885). By this simple act, a home for the Turtle Mountain Chippewas was created, but the major issue of cession of the remainder of the claimed area was left open. Also left open was the issue of the Métis and a determination of their status. Further exacerbating the issue was the reduction of the reservation to two townships, 46,080 acres, in March 1884 (Kappler I:885). In June 1884 a third executive agreement amended the designations of the two townships but did not change the size of the reservation. The establishment of Turtle Mountain Reservation brought the Turtle Mountain Band of Chippewa under the administration of the agent at Devils Lake, whose assigned task was to help the tribespeople adjust to reservation life.

It is clear from all accounts that life on the reservation was not easy. In 1884 Agent John Cramsie reported that, while there appeared to be sufficient land for farming, because the people were not practiced in agriculture, it would take a great deal of time and effort to teach them

The Métis adopted both Indian and non-Indian ways. In this dance scene from 1860, everyone is wearing moccasins and dancing to fiddle music. (HM)

125

The Red River cart was developed by Métis trappers working for Alexander Henry in 1801. (HM)

▼ Red Bear signed the Treaty of 1863 and had a small reservation set aside for him near the Pembina River. He later settled at Turtle Mountain. (SHSND)

how to farm (Annual Report of the Commissioner of Indian Affairs 1884:78-79). Laura Law records that the Indians survived by trapping, wood cutting, collecting buffalo bones, and gathering seneca root (Law 1953:79). Conditions were so desperate that in the winter of 1887 150 people starved to death. Special agent Jere Stevens visited Turtle Mountain Reservation in September 1890 and made an extensive report of the conditions there. He found 261 full-blood Chippewa and 1,178 mixed-bloods living on the reservation and another 500 to 600 people living on lands just off the reservation. Stevens reported that only a quarter of the Chippewa wore "White-style" clothing and that only a few lived in permanent houses. "They are here to-day and there tomorrow, on either side of the boundary line, as best suits their fancy, taking good care to be on the reservation, however, when rations are issued" (U.S. Department of the Interior 1894:515).

The Métis, however, wore "White-style" clothing, and many could read (U.S. Department of the Interior 1894:516). Fifteen years later an observer wrote that many of the Chippewa were so traditional that he had been unable to recruit anyone to serve on an Indian police force (Hesketh 1923:128).

Schools accompanied the establishment of the reservation. Catholic priests had been associated with the Chippewa and Métis for many years and they started the first schools (Murray 1953). In 1884 Agent John Cramsie reported that Father John Malo had conducted a day school on the reservation (Annual Report of the Commissioner of Indian Affairs 1884:79). In 1884 the Sisters of Mercy School also opened (Murray 1953:26). All the children enrolled in the schools were Métis, and Sister Mary Joseph told Robert J. Murray, a graduate student at the University of North Dakota, that she could not remember a single Chippewa student

126

Little Shell III argued for a larger reservation for his people. (SHSND)

enrolling in the school during her time there (Murray 1953:27). Children were also sent to schools off the reservation. For many years the majority of students at Fort Totten boarding school were from the Turtle Mountains. In 1884 James McLaughlin was informed by Father J. M. Brouillet that the School of the Good Shepherd in Milwaukee was receiving fifty Turtle Mountain Chippewa girls and that a contingent of boys from the reservation was being sent to another Catholic school in Chicago (J. M. Brouillet to J. McLaughlin Jan. 3, 1884, McLaughlin Papers). Others went to St. Joseph's School in Rensselaer, Indiana, and St. John's in Minnesota (Murray 1953:27-28). By 1891 the reservation had a Catholic boarding school and four day schools, one supported by the Episcopal Church and the others federally supported (Annual Report of the Commissioner of Indian Affairs 1891:319).

The efforts of the agents to force all the children to attend school had little effect on the Turtle Mountain Chippewa people who continued their traditional ways of educating their children. One of the favorite methods of instruction was telling stories in which birds and animals served as examples. In the story of the dancing ducks, Wee-sa-kay-jac lured the ducks and other water birds to a powwow by promising to sing for them if they would dance with their eyes closed. While the birds danced with their eyes shut tight, Wee-sa-kay-jac grabbed them one by one and threw them in a sack for his supper. Finally, one duck opened his eyes and, seeing what was happening, warned the rest. From such stories children learned the characteristics of their environment, learned to be alert and to watch out for each other. Children were also taught the history and traditions of the tribe.

For a number of reasons, not all the eligible people were living on the reservation, and so not all the Turtle Mountain Chippewa were recognized or accepted by the agent. When the reservation was established and by virtue of its

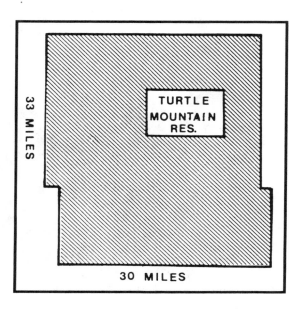

In 1882 an executive order established a 30 by 34 mile reservation for the Turtle Mountain Band of Chippewa. In 1884, the reservation was reduced to two townships, leaving many Chippewa with land and tax problems.

reduction in size, it was impossible for all applicants to settle there. Some of the Chippewa argued that the Métis should be excluded, while government agents wanted to exclude any families who were considered Canadian residents. Other people who had a legitimate right to live on the reservation were still earning their living by trapping and trading, and as long as they were able to continue the way of life they knew best, they refused to make a change that would require them to become farmers (Report of the Commissioner of Indian Affairs 1888:41). In 1890 Little Shell and his group of Chippewa-Métis went to Montana to look for a reservation where they would be permitted to live in a traditional manner, but before they could establish themselves they became embroiled in the ongoing controversy over the settlement of claims (Dusenberry 1965:97-98). Other tribal members recognized the need to acquire land by homesteading on public lands, but experience had taught them that they were often forced off lands they had improved, and so there was reluctance to establish claims. The question of whether or not Indian homestead lands were taxable had not been settled, and without an assurance of their tax-free status, Indian people refused to homestead public lands.

Congress eventually appointed a commission to settle the situation, but the results only caused greater conflicts. One of the tasks of the commission was to determine who was an eligible member of the Turtle Mountain Band of Chippewa and who should be dropped from the tribal rolls. The list that was approved by the commission appeared to most Chippewa and Métis to be arbitrary in its determination of tribal status since members of the same family were treated differently. People who had left the reservation to find subsistence in Montana or other places were dropped,

Poor economic conditions forced many Metis families to travel to distant towns in search of work. (UND)

and people thought to have been born in Canada were excluded. Those whose names were not on the roll were instructed to leave the reservation and were informed that they had no voice in any subsequent proceedings (Dusenberry 1965:98-99).

The people became so concerned about the increasing numbers of non-Indians in the area and White encroachment on Indian claims that in January 1891 they adopted an extensive resolution which they sent to their attorney, John B. Bottineau, for presentation to the Secretary of the Interior. This resolution asked that 446,670 acres be withdrawn from public lands and added to the reservation. Later a delegation was sent to Washington, D.C., to present the tribe's claim to the President.

In 1892 an agreement to cede the Turtle Mountain claim and to recognize the rights of band members who had settled off the reservation was made. Because the Turtle Mountain people were paid one million dollars for the nine million acres of land, the agreement came to be known as the "ten cent treaty." The agreement also provided for the reservation to be surveyed for allotment to individuals and specified that anyone not able to obtain land on the reservation would be permitted to homestead on vacant public land (Kappler III:39-41). Unfortunately, the agreement was not ratified until 1904, and the situation continued to worsen. During the twelve-year wait for ratification, more and more Indians were forced off their homesteads because, believing they already had a legal right to the land, they did not apply for titles. In 1896 another delegation went to Washington, D.C., and in 1898 Little Shell and the councilmen wrote to J. B. Bottineau to see if he could secure funds for them

St. Mary's Indian Mission School, established in 1884 by the Sisters of Mercy, burned in 1907. (SHSND)

By 1900, the Turtle Mountain Band of Chippewa was governed by a council appointed by the Indian Agent. (TM)

▼ In 1901, Kakenowash succeeded Little Shell as leader of the Turtle Mountain Band of Chippewa. For thirty years he worked for his people, but his powers were limited by the agent. (TM)

to make another trip.

When the treaty was finally ratified and allotments were made, there was insufficient land to meet the needs of all band members, and families took public land at Devils Lake and Trenton, North Dakota, and in Montana (Murray 1984:32). Other tribal members living at Rocky Boy and Fort Peck reservations were allowed to take allotments there. Little Shell and his followers refused to sign the agreement and settled on public land off the reservation. Today his descendants still live in the area around Dunseith, North Dakota (Murray 1953:17; Howard 1977:75). This dispersal of the tribe has caused continuing administrative difficulties.

One of the immediate concerns was whether people who had land off the reservation were to be considered citizens with taxable lands or were they to be treated in the same manner as Indians living on the reservation. By determination of the Justice Department and Attorney General's Office, the off-reservation members were to be treated the same as those living on the reservation (Murray 1984:33). A similar issue was raised concerning other rights of those Indians who received public lands. In 1908 James McLaughlin wrote a stern letter responding to the principal of Fort Shaw School in Montana stating that the Chippewa students enrolled in the school were legally entitled to be there (J. McLaughlin to Sec. of Interior, Feb. 10, 1908. McLaughlin Papers). These determinations affected only those Turtle Mountain Chippewa who were enrolled members of the tribe. People who had been dropped from the tribal rolls lost their distinctive Indian rights and were treated as non-Indians. Another difficulty arose concerning the supervision of Indians who lived so far from the tribal administrative center that they were excluded from many decisions affecting them. In recent years the problem has been intensified as enrolled members of the Turtle Mountain Band of Chippewa have grown up without ever seeing the reservation. Other people have inherited shares in lands they have never seen and have had to trust others to administer these lands for them.

Culturally the descendants of the Chippewa and Métis continued to adhere to their distinctive traditions. The Chippewa social structure and religious ceremonies were still in use in 1914 when anthropologist Alanson Skinner made a brief visit to the reservation and included his findings in his reports on Plains Ojibwa culture (Skinner 1914a,1914b,1919,1920). One illustration of the persistence of traditions is found in the continued celebration of the Sun Dance. The Turtle Mountain Band of Chippewa, like the other Indian tribes, were prohibited from holding religious ceremonies, but the Chippewa did not adhere to this provision. In 1887 the self-sacrifice element was ended (Hesketh 1923:98), but the dance continued to be held every year on the sacred grounds north of Dunseith, and in 1952 two dances were held, one near Dunseith and one north of Belcourt (Howard 1952). Anthropologist James Howard reports that in the dances he attended, self-sacrifices were optional (Howard 1977:158). The Midewiwin (Hilger 1959:125) and Shaking Tent (Howard 1977:168) ceremonies also continued to be held during the first half of the twentieth century.

While one segment of the tribe was holding on to traditional ways, another was moving into the White man's world of business and education. When the area was opened to White settlement, some of the Métis opened blacksmith shops, boarding houses, and stores to provide for the needs of the homesteaders. By 1930, members of the tribe were operating many of the businesses in Belcourt. From 1946 to 1949 a cooperative store funded by selling $5.00 shares to tribal members operated in Belcourt. Other Turtle Mountain Chippewa opened shops and other services in their off-reservation communities (St. Ann's Centennial 1985:143-144). Older economic traditions also continued and many people continued to hunt, fish, and trap for a living. Bartering provided goods that could not be obtained through other means. A survey of conditions on the reservation during the 1930's, however, found that most people were destitute and were relying upon rations and commodities for subsistence (Hjerpe 1940). These same reports noted that one of the greatest problems was the lack of sufficient land for either homes or farms (Hook 1936; Hjerpe 1940).

The 1930's saw some changes in the reservation situation. In 1932 the tribe drew up a constitution and by-laws which established the election of an eight-member advisory committee to represent the tribe. This commit-

Rising Sun, his wife Simaquam and other Chippewa continued to follow traditional ways. (SHSND)

tee had no real power, but its presence may have influenced the decision of the tribe not to accept the Indian Reorganization Act (Delorme 1955:29-30). The Turtle Mountain Chippewa did not accept the Indian Reorganization Act, but they benefited from the provision for the Secretary of the Interior to purchase lands to be added to reservations. Based on the Indian Reorganization Act, Congress passed a special bill to purchase lands adjacent to the Turtle Mountain Reservation (Kappler VI:53). Under this action of May 1940, lands could be restored to the reservation, and in 1941, 33,436 acres near the reservation were purchased for the use of landless band members (Murray 1953:16). Even more significant is the inclusion in the enabling act of a statement defining

▲ *Old-style log cabins were gradually replaced by frame houses. (UND)*

Powwows were another expression of Indian beliefs. (SHSND)

the membership of the Turtle Mountain Band of Chippewa because it indicates that the issue of tribal membership had not yet been satisfactorily settled. The purchasing act included unenrolled Indians who were members of the tribe before October 8, 1904, but who were not on the rolls following that date. It was necessary to update the tribal rolls to include those members eligible for lands, but the task of identifying the people with the necessary degree of Indian descent was so difficult that very general criteria were adopted (St. Ann's Centennial 1985:93). The same issue of eligibility for tribal enrollment surfaced in 1964 when the Pembina band received compensation for some land and again in the 1970's when the Turtle Mountain Band of Chippewa's claim against the ten-cent treaty was approved. In both cases it was necessary to draw up a list of people who would receive the money and genealogical searches were conducted to determine degree of descent. Many people were asked to prove they were one-quarter or more Chippewa.

The Turtle Mountain Band of Chippewa was directly affected by House Concurrent Resolution 108, which recommended the tribe's termination from federal supervision at the earliest possible date. In March 1954, hearings were held to determine the readiness of the Turtle Mountain Chippewa for termination (Tyler 1973:173). One outcome of the hearings was the organization of the United Tribes Development Corporation in which the four

North Dakota reservations agreed to work together to benefit all the tribes. The Chippewa escaped the termination process which was so disastrous for so many tribes, but among some members of the tribe the possibility remains a constant fear. Because of the belief that many of the Turtle Mountain Band of Chippewa were educationally sophisticated enough to live off the reservation, the federal relocation program encouraged many families to move to large urban areas, but Delorme's 1955 study of reservation conditions points out that, for a variety of reasons, many of the families returned to the reservation shortly after their relocation (Delorme 1955:180-182). Some families, of course, made successful adjustments to urban living and, like the families living in Montana and western North Dakota, are absentee members of the tribe.

The Reservation at the End of the Twentieth Century

By the end of the twentieth century, the Turtle Mountain Band of Chippewa had the largest tribal membership, more than 22,000, of all the North Dakota tribes, but more than half of the enrolled members lived off the reservation (North Dakota Indian Affairs Commission 1985). Some lived near the reservation in Dunseith and St. John, but others still lived in Montana and western North Dakota. The 1980 census gave some idea of the dispersed

nature of the tribe. The reservation population was reported as 4,234 (U.S. Bureau of the Census 1983:262), but the Indian population of Rolette County, which included both reservation residents and those living near the reservation, was 7,018 (U.S. Bureau of the Census 1983:127). In other words, 40 percent lived off the reservation, but lived close enough to be considered part of the reservation population. More than seven hundred Indians, most of whom were probably enrolled in the Turtle Mountain Band, lived in Williams County (U.S. Bureau of the Census 1983:127). These figures accounted for less than half of the tribal enrollment, indicating that enrolled tribal members lived elsewhere, in the nation's largest cities as well as in the cities of North Dakota.

The Turtle Mountain Chippewa were different in other ways from other tribes. The Chippewa component had, from the beginning, been much smaller than the Métis segment, and so there was a greater divergence between those who placed a positive emphasis only on Indian ways, the traditional orientation, and those who found value in both Indian and non-Indian ways, the bicultural orientation. One almost needs to consider the two groups separately since what was a traditional orientation for a Métis could be quite different from a Chippewa traditional orientation. Once there was a greater distinction between the Métis and the most traditional Chippewa who lived in the more rural areas of the reservation and were more obviously Indian in their looks. Later, however, the major difference was found in the emphasis placed on Indian ways. Traditional Chippewa still gave their children In-

▲ *Although far from their relatives at Turtle Mountain, the people around Trenton, North Dakota lived a similar life-style.*

▼ *In the 1930's powwow dance outfits reflected a new style of dancing. (UND)*

dian names and taught them Indian religious beliefs. For these people the Sun Dance and other Indian ceremonies were still important. The Chippewa who found something of value in both Indian and White cultures not only emphasized the traditional ways but also supported education and Christianity.

Since the Métis, or Michif as they called themselves, originated in the marriage of Indian women and European men, their orientation was always to take the best of both cultures. The combination resulted in a physical type that ranged from the dark hair and eyes of their Indian ancestors to the blond hair and blue eyes of their European fathers, and in the Michif language, a unique combination of French, Chippewa, and Cree. Michif culture also blended Indian religion with Catholicism. Métis once participated in Indian ceremonies, but when the Catholic priests objected, they stopped. The close ties between Indian and Michif, however, resulted in Catholic ceremonies taking on Indian characteristics and being held for four days. Funerals, too, had Indian elements. Later, however, some Catholics strictly followed the teachings of the Church. Some families, too, emphasized their French roots rather than the Métis or Indian heritage.

Music provides another example of the cultural diversity on the reservation. For the traditional Chippewa, dance and sacred songs were sung in Chippewa or one of the other Indian languages. Métis traditional music was dance songs played on the fiddle and sung in French or Michif (Vrooman 1984). But some Chippewa also learned to play the fiddle and dance the jig and reels, and some Michif learned to sing powwow songs. For the most biculturally oriented there was not only the positive attitude toward modern American culture but also the opportunity to engage in both Chippewa and Métis traditions.

Two other statistics from the 1980 census illustrate other ways in which the Turtle Mountain Band of Chippewa differed from the other North Dakota tribes. The 1980 census reported the smallest percentage of people who spoke a language other than English, 17.1, and the highest per capita income, $3,339, for reservation residents (U.S. Bureau of the Census

133

1983:262,263). Another difference was found in Belcourt, the reservation administrative center, which, because it was the largest town in the area, had become a regional shopping center with a mall and other services.

The Chippewa continued to be more oriented toward their traditional means of subsistence from hunting and gardening, while the Métis, who had engaged in trade before the reservation was established, continued this commercial enterprise by establishing shops and stores. Because the land was needed for other purposes, few of the residents on or near the reservation were engaged in agriculture. A slightly higher percentage of those living off the reservation in Rolette County made their living by farming. As on other reservations, the largest percentage was employed by the federal, state, and tribal governments, but unlike the other reservations in North Dakota, the next highest percentage was employed in private industry (U.S. Bureau of the Census

---

The reservation today. (map)

▼ *The reservation has gently rolling hills, lakes and trees.*

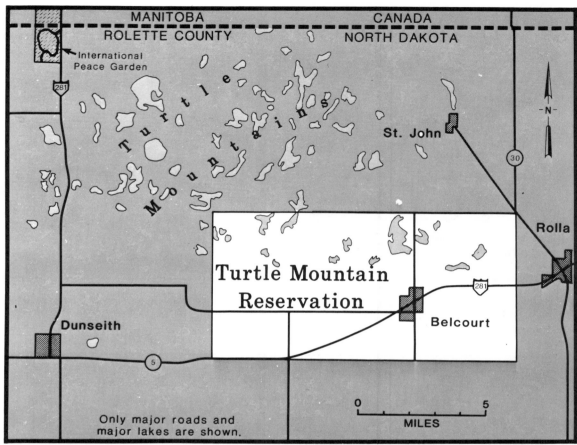

MANITOBA   CANADA
ROLETTE COUNTY   NORTH DAKOTA
International Peace Garden
281
Turtle Mountains
St. John
30
Rolla
Turtle Mountain Reservation
281
Belcourt
Dunseith
5
Only major roads and major lakes are shown.
0   5
MILES
-N-

1986:472). The situation was completely different for those tribal members living in Williams County because there the major source of income was from private employment rather than from government. One of the differences between those living on the reservation and those living off the reservation, but in the area, was seen in the fact that a slightly higher percentage of those living off the reservation were employed in private business, while a higher percentage of those living on the reservation were employed in government jobs. Meanwhile, the per capita income for Indians living in Rolette County was slightly less than the per capita income of Indians living on the reservation, an indication that employment may have been more seasonal or lower-paying than government jobs.

One large advantage the tribe had over other reservations was the size of Belcourt and its local population. Belcourt was the largest community in the region and attracted people

▲ *St. Ann's Catholic Church, Belcourt, North Dakota, is the center of religious life for most Turtle Mountain residents.*

▼ *Modern housing is found at Belcourt and throughout the reservation.*

from a wide area. The presence of a significant number of consumers encouraged the development of individually owned businesses, as well as a tribally owned and operated shopping mall. Tourist attractions in the area, the International Peace Garden and many lakes, also provided opportunities for the Chippewa to draw on populations beyond the local area. Taking advantage of this, the tribe established a heritage center and a buffalo park. Churches also attracted visitors to the reservation. St. Paul's Ojibwa Church developed the Anishnabeg resource center, and the St. Ann's Day annual celebration in July brought people from all over the country. A recently established, tribally-run bingo operation took advantage of the transient population.

The statistical data for Indian people living in Williams County, most of whom were enrolled members of the Turtle Mountain Band of Chippewa, showed a different economic pattern. The per capita income of $3,864 was higher than that of Indians living in Rolette County or on the reservation (U.S. Bureau of the Census 1983:238). Even more distinctive was the employment of many of the Indian residents of Williams County in private industry, while only 24 percent worked for federal, state, and tribal governments (U.S. Bureau of the Census 1983:232). The census also showed that the value of Indian housing in Williams County was almost twice as high as housing in Rolette County, suggesting that off-reservation residents lived better than those on the reservation (U.S. Bureau of the Census 1983:136).

Whether they lived on or off the reservation, for most people of Turtle Mountain Chippewa descent, life was much like that of other rural North Dakotans. Family, work, school, church, and social activities occupied most people's time. Even though the average family size of Turtle Mountain people was larger than that of most North Dakotans, the families were slightly smaller than those on other reservations. This marked a real change from earlier times when families were very large (Murray 1953:17; Delorme 1955:41) and may have reflected changing attitudes towards the role of children and slightly improved economic conditions on the reservation. That this was the reason for the trend at Turtle Mountain was substantiated by the presence of smaller families in Williams County, where economic conditions were better (U.S. Bureau of the Census 1983:127).

Schools on and off the reservation provided education for students from kindergarten through college. Joint Bureau of Indian Affairs and tribal schools were found at Belcourt and Dunseith. The Ojibway Indian School at Belcourt, formerly a Catholic mission school, was turned over to the tribe and became one of the earliest tribally operated schools in North Dakota. Indian children also attended public schools at St. John, Rolette, Dunseith, and Rolla. A tribally supported community college at Belcourt, incorporated by tribal charter in 1971, provided educational opportunities for several hundred people. The tribe, especially the Metis, had had a long interest in education, but in 1980 the reservation ranked third among the four North Dakota reservations in its percentages of high school and college graduates (U.S. Bureau of the Census 1983:262). One reason for the small number of college graduates may have been that people who graduated from college did not return to the reservation to live. Such was the case in 1952 when Robert Murray found that most of the men and women who had left the reservation for schooling had not returned (Murray 1953:28). The continuing scarcity of jobs and housing on the reservation forced people to find employment off the reservation. Some waited a number of years before return-

▲ The Turtle Mountain Mart is a tribally owned and operated shopping mall.

▼ The Turtle Mountains provide many opportunities for winter sports.

136

ing. Others viewed education as a way to better the situation for others by working in off-reservation jobs that directly affected Indian people. Some, of course, simply preferred to live off the reservation. In the mid-1980's more people from Turtle Mountain than any other reservation attended state colleges and universities.

The predominant religious denomination in the area was Roman Catholic, and a number of churches served the reservation environs. Beginning with the assignment of Catholic priests to Pembina and continuing with the long service of Father George Belcourt, for whom the city of Belcourt was named, the Métis and Chippewa followed the teachings of Catholic priests in church and school. The opening of the contested area to White settlement saw the establishment of Catholic churches in Dunseith, Belcourt, and Rolla. At the same time, an Episcopal Church was built at Belcourt with a small chapel near Dunseith (Law 1953:195-197). Lutheran churches were also located near the reservation and other Protestant denominations soon arrived.

Because of the presence of large numbers of Métis who dressed and lived similarly to non-Indians, the Turtle Mountain Band of Chippewa was long assumed to be the most acculturated of the North Dakota tribes (Hjerpe 1940:44), but surface appearances did not necessarily reflect the inner reality. People who identified with their Chippewa ancestors maintained some ancient social and ceremonial traditions.

The use of kinship terms that classified cousins and other close relatives as mothers, fathers, brothers, and sisters was not so common, but the extended family remained important. Even the Métis who adopted French kinship terms still used the Cree or Chippewa

137

words for grandmother and classified a grandfather's sister as a grandmother (Laverdure and Allard 1983:115). Chippewa beliefs about the universe, humans, and animals still existed. The Sun Dance continued to be an important ceremony for the most traditionally oriented. People more often attended Canadian Sun Dances while they attempted to revive the one formerly held at Turtle Mountain.

The Michif language of the Métis was still spoken by some of the elders, but most spoke English. An attempt was made to teach the Michif language to the children, and the publication of a Michif dictionary (Laverdure and Allard 1983) aided in the preservation of the language. For more than a century, St. Ann's Day was an important celebration for the less-traditional people. For the Métis, their culture was preserved in the performing arts, music, and story-telling. Fiddle players were still considered important components of traditional celebrations, and skilled dancers performed the jig and other dances. Many of the Métis still told stories about rugarous, werewolf-like creatures who roam the reservation, during Lent and recounted the adventures of Che Jean (Petite Jean). Both Métis and Chippewa enjoyed telling stories about Nanaboshu and Weesa-kay-jac.

Two major issues concerned the Turtle Mountain Band of Chippewa: establishing the list of those who should share in the land claims settlement and developing an economically self-sufficient population. For obvious reasons, determining who was legally entitled to share in the claims money was difficult. Ancestry was not clearly definable and those who were declared not eligible did not accept the decision without an argument. Many of the

Young dancers prepare for the grand entry.

(left) Patrick Gourneau (Aun nish e naubay), tribal chairperson from 1953 to 1959, published a brief history of the Turtle Mountain Band. (SHSND)

(right)   Charles Gourneau, following in his father's footsteps, has also written a book.

▼   *In 1988, Twila Martin Kekahbah was elected chairperson of the tribal council. Other members are: Patrick Marcellais, Alfred Lafountain, Melvin Lenoir (behind), Raphael Decoteau, Jimmy Baker, David "Sandy" Morin, Fred "Fritz" Monette, and Ronald J. Peltier. (TM)*

OLD WILD RICE
"The Great Chief"

Forerunner of the Pembina/Turtle Mountain
Ojibway/Chippewa in the State of North Dakota

(migrated to Red River country in 1789-1790)

Historical excerpts on some of the earliest
chiefs and leaders of note who made major
contributions to the history of the region.

by
Charles J. Gourneau

Chippewa worried that the claims money would cause deep resentments and divisions that would destroy tribal unity.

Working toward self-sufficiency was slow because it involved education, creation of employment opportunities, and changing attitudes. At first, the emphasis was on education and employment. Changing attitudes came about later. People who recalled the threat of termination also feared the idea of self-sufficiency because they thought it could mean a withdrawal of federal obligations, but many Turtle Mountain people believed individual economic independence was the only way to deal effectively with the social problems. Education, employment, and self-image were closely related, and the tribe worked to improve all three in order to achieve a better life for all its members.

139

Willow baskets woven by Turtle Mountain residents are modern examples of an ancient art.

Contributions to North Dakota

The ancestors and present members of the Turtle Mountain Band of Chippewa have contributed significantly to the growth of North Dakota, particularly in the fields of economics, politics, and education. These interests continue, and a number of Turtle Mountain Chippewa have been recognized during Minority Enterprise Week for their contributions to the state's economic development. In 1982 the tribe sold its stock in a formerly joint venture with Northern Plains Industry of Minot and reopened the Turtle Mountain Manufacturing Company. In 1985 the company employed from 130 to 160 people in the manufacture of small cargo trailers for military uses, and the operators were planning for expansion (Henderson 1986:6-7).

Beginning with the involvement of traders from Pembina in the establishment of Minnesota and continuing with the Pembina representatives to the Dakota Territorial Legislature, the "moccasin democrats," members of the Turtle Mountain Chippewa were politically active. With statehood, the interest shifted to local politics. Men and women from the tribe served as local and county elected officials. Students at the University of North Dakota successfully appealed to the legislature to establish Indian Studies at the University. The first Indian to occupy the "Indian desk" in the Department of Public Instruction was from Turtle Mountain, as was his successor.

The strong interest in education that began with the first school at Pembina has contributed to North Dakota in many ways. There are too many highly educated Turtle Mountain Chippewa to list them all, but educators, social workers, doctors, and lawyers have been graduated from colleges all over the United States.

Turtle Mountain Chippewa men and women have also contributed to the arts and literature. Award-winning author Louise Erdrich is an enrolled member of the tribe. Other tribal members have written about the history of the reservation. One of the most recent publications is the massive volume of family and tribal histories compiled in commemoration of the centennial of St. Ann's Church. A welded sculpture of a buffalo by Ben Brien was recently added to the grounds in front of the state capitol building in Bismarck. Leo Wilkie travels around the state giving demonstrations of carving, basketmaking, and story-telling. Older art styles continue, too. The willow baskets woven by the descendants of Selina Cree family are modern examples of an old art form. Fiddle-players and jig dancers from the reservation still perform in North Dakota and at national events.

Throughout their history, the Turtle Mountain Band of Chippewa have been noted for their love of freedom and zest for living. These traits continue to add to North Dakota's unique heritage.

Chapter 9

A Long and Difficult Path

North Dakota's Indian heritage is more than feathered warriors that flicker across a movie screen and disappear before the movie ends; it is a continuing epic of hardship and adaptation, survival and vitality that, because it happened only in North Dakota, helped to develop the state's unique character. Unquestionably, some parts of the story, especially those concerning treaty-making, reservations, and assimilation, echo the experiences of other tribes and other states, but those other states lacked either the geographic or the cultural diversity that characterized North Dakota.

The dramatic extremes of temperature, the short growing season, the varied but not very high landforms, and the presence of two major rivers provided prehistoric peoples with challenges and opportunities not found in other states. For some tribes, the difficulties and possibilities were included in the origin traditions and provided spiritual support for the struggle to survive. The origin traditions of the Mandan describe the different contours of the land on each side of the Missouri and explain the uses that may be made of each. The Arikara told Melvin Gilmore (1987:173):

In ancient time God sent Mother Corn to our people to be their friend and helper, to give them support and health and strength. Mother Corn has come to us out of the ancient time. She has walked with our people the long and difficult path which they have traveled from the far-away past; and now she marches with us toward the future.

The archaeological record provides another story of adaptation. Ten thousand years ago the Paleo-Indians, the first people to enter North Dakota, found a region inhabited by large game animals that thrived in the colder, wetter climate. Those early Indian people may not have stayed long. Archaeologists have found ample evidence of their presence in the form of projectile points, but no traces of their camping or hunting activities. The projectile points match those found in other places and indicate that these original North Dakotans were either visitors or in close communication with other people in the region. If visitors, they stayed long enough to recognize the superb flint-knapping qualities of Knife River flint and initiate North Dakota's first commercial enterprise. If residents, they adapted to the hostile climate and

their descendants are still here on the land they settled.

Shortly after the arrival of the Paleo-Indians, the environment changed and forced people to make a new adjustment. The new way of life is called the Archaic. Except for the buffalo, the big game animals died out and tribes were forced to make greater use of the local resources. Much of the technology of later Plains Indians, the buffalo drive over a cliff, the use of plant foods, and the tipi, probably developed during the Archaic. Some archaeologists believe that the Archaic people became the nomadic tribes of historic times.

The Woodland period marks the introduction of the bow and arrow, pottery-making, agriculture, and other new technologies, and identifies the second prehistoric adaptation to the northern Plains. As happened in later times, the technologies appeared much earlier in the eastern United States and spread slowly into the West. The life-style of the historic Arikara, Mandan, and Hidatsa seems to derive from the Woodland.

The two basic life-styles, nomadic buffalo-hunting and agriculture, that originated prehistorically were well established when the first Europeans entered the region. Unfortunately the tribes associated with these lifestyles cannot be identified with much certainty, but, in addition to the villages assumed to be Arikara, Mandan, and Hidatsa, some of the tipi rings and other archaeological manifestations must relate to the Dakota, Cree, Assiniboin, and Yanktonai tribes who were also in the area. The movement of the Cheyenne, Chippewa, and Lakota into the region between the Red River and the Missouri is better known because there are historic reports of the migrations. It is important to note, however, that the tribes that moved into the northern Plains adapted to their new home by adopting the technology, social organization, and religious practices of the resident tribes.

The tribes living in North Dakota at the time of European exploration had different technologies, social organization, religion, and languages. Four tribes, Arikara, Mandan, Hidatsa, and Yanktonai, were earthlodge builders and agriculturalists who spent part of the year as nomadic buffalo hunters. The Dakota, Lakota, and Chippewa were tipi-dwelling buffalo hunters who procured their corn, squash, and beans through trade with the village people. The tribes were divided into villages and bands that were autonomous units, coming together only for major religious ceremonies or for mutual protection. Each of these tribes not only spoke a distinct language, but there was enough variation within the tribes that communication between residents of different villages or bands was sometimes difficult.

All American Indian tribes gave a similar emphasis to kinship and, by extending kinship terms for close family members to more distant relatives, created a large network of kinfolk to care for orphans, elderly, and the disabled. The Arikara, Hidatsa, and Mandan organized these relatives into clans. The Dakota thought in terms of villages of kinfolk and required people to take mates from other villages. Other tribes simply worked with the basic network of relatives indicated by the terminology.

Religious beliefs and practices varied from tribe to tribe, although there were some basic similarities. All the tribes believed in a uni-

verse filled with unseen powers that could aid or injure. A human who properly humbled or sacrificed himself during a vision could obtain some of the power in the form of a spiritual protector. Having spiritual protection meant that the man could become a warrior and participate in important religious ceremonies. All the tribes had ceremonies to thank the buffalo for providing food and other needs. The agricultural tribes also had ceremonies to help the crops grow.

Sometimes the differences between tribes resulted in hostilities. Disagreements over hunting territory, failure of crops or buffalo, revenge for enemy action, and the effects of disease made warfare a common problem. Men were encouraged to become good warriors in order to gain status so they could participate in ceremonies. But even in the face of warfare and pressure to kill, the tribes worked out methods of accommodating to the needs of trade and social interaction. Even when the Arikara and Mandan were having periods of hostility, young Arikara men moved into the Mandan villages (Nasatir 1952, vol.II:303), and marriages often took place between men and women of warring tribes. Because of inter-marriage and other close contacts, most tribes had people who spoke other languages, but for times when the interpreters were not available, sign-language aided communication.

The first Europeans entered the northern Plains more than a century after they arrived on the east coast, but the impact on tribal cultures was similar. As on the coast, well-developed trade networks distributed guns, metal tools, beads, and disease many years before the actual visitation by Europeans. Like the Pilgrims landing at Plymouth Rock and finding that an epidemic had killed off most of the Cape Cod Indians, Tabeau in 1803 reported that an epidemic had reduced the number of Arikara villages from eighteen to three (Abel 1939:123-124).

Another devastating smallpox epidemic occurred in 1837 and threatened the survival of the Mandan and Hidatsa. It took almost a decade for the tribes to regroup, but realizing that there were too few survivors to defend their villages on the Knife River, they moved

up-river and established Like-a-Fishhook Village, where the Arikara joined them in 1862. The new earthlodge village became a center of commerce and government on the Upper Missouri.

Tribes not devastated by epidemics had other problems with which to contend. The early relationships between Indians and non-Indians were generally harmonious and based on accommodation rather than hostility, but when the time came to deal with Indian claims to the land, the government followed the same procedures of treaty-making used elsewhere. At this point, the various tribal stories take on veneers of federal policy and assimilationist attitudes that mask tribal differences. The creation of reservations, prohibition of traditional customs, allotment, bureaucratization, and other procedures resulted in tribal histories becoming similar to each other and North Dakota's Indian history being more like other states.

The first treaty dealing with land in what is now North Dakota was made between Lord Selkirk and the Cree and Chippewa of the Red River Valley in 1817. Under the agreement, the Indians ceded a strip of land along the Red River for Lord Selkirk's colonists in exchange for a yearly payment of one hundred pounds of tobacco.

The first major peace treaty, the Treaty of Fort Laramie of 1851, established the various tribes' claims to land in the northern Plains. The Mandan, Hidata, Arikara, and Lakota were recognized as having land in North Dakota. The treaty was never approved by Congress, but the government followed its provisions and that was later considered to indicate approval.

In 1867 the first treaty to create a reservation in North Dakota set aside a large portion of land for Dakota and Yanktonai. The treaty rewarded the Dakota for not participating in the Dakota Conflict of 1862 and recognized the claims of the Cuthead Band of Yanktonai to the region around Devils Lake. Later, a cession agreed to by the various tribes reduced the land base to two smaller reservations, Devils Lake and Sisseton-Wahpeton.

Later treaties established the Fort Berthold

and Standing Rock reservations. Turtle Mountain Reservation was created after treaty-making ended and so it was formed by a direct order of the President of the United States. Another executive order reduced the size of the Turtle Mountain Reservation and changed its location. Because the Turtle Mountain Band of Chippewa were not completely involved in the reservation-making process, the land base was much too small for the tribe's population and many Chippewa settled on other reservations or homesteaded on public lands.

Following the establishment of the reservations, tribes struggled to adapt to increasing government interference in their tribal cultures. The government, through agents, missionaries, and educators, attempted to turn the Indians into White people, but the tribes adopted various ways of frustrating assimilation. Some tribespeople gave in to the assimilation process and became educated and went to the work for the government or church. Other people, however, fought overtly and covertly against giving up traditional ways.

One example of this struggle can be seen in the ways in which the tribes protected their traditional religious practices. The Office of Indian Affairs instructed the agents to punish people for participating in religious ceremonies; therefore, those who continued the practices did so in secret. Ceremonies that had once been held openly now became secret. The Turtle Mountain Chippewa moved their Sun Dance ceremony off the reservation where the agent had no authority to arrest participants.

Agents' attempts to change tribal customs by educating the children also failed when some parents told children they had to attend school until they were old enough to drop out, but they did not have to listen to the teachers. Some parents told their children to go to school and learn to read and write so that they could deal more effectively with White people, but that did not necessarily require abandonment of traditional ways.

Another way in which government bureaucrats tried to change tribal cultures was through employment. Indian men were required to work in order to get the food and supplies guaranteed in the treaties. Work was considered anything for which the person received pay. Indian men became interpreters, blacksmiths, wood-cutters, wagoneers, and farmers and ranchers. But some men refused to spend all their time engaged in activities that were not an integral part of the old ways. Agriculture was woman's work. Hunting was more interesting than ranching. Farming and ranching were not particularly successful in North Dakota and many men gave up after years of crop and stock loss.

During the later years of the nineteenth century Congress passed the Allotment Act that divided the reservations into individually owned tracts of land and sold any tracts not needed by Indians. This policy resulted in a large number of non-Indians owning land on Fort Berthold, Standing Rock, and Devils Lake Sioux reservations and the division of the reservations into units too small to work successfully. In addition, the Allotment Act stated that allotments were to be divided equally among an allottee's heirs, and this divided the plots even further. The problem of fractionated heirship plagues all the reservations in North Dakota.

The Indian Reorganization Act of 1934 was designed to correct the problems caused by Allotment and shift attitudes away from assimilation. Under the Act, land sales were stopped, tribes were encouraged to revive their languages and religious practices, and constitutional governments that would give tribes more decision-making powers were created. The Mandan, Hidatsa, and Arikara people were the only ones in North Dakota to form a government under the conditions of the Indian Reorganization Act, but the other tribes have since adopted constitutional tribal governments.

The 1950's saw another shift in federal Indian policy, this time to termination and relocation. Congress became convinced that tribes did not need the services guaranteed in the treaties and voted to end federal obligations to as many tribes as possible. Relocation would serve the same purpose, ending federal obligations for individuals and families. None of the North Dakota tribes was terminated, but many North Dakota Indian people moved to large urban areas. Some people returned immediately to their reservation, but others who found jobs and spent twenty-five or thirty years in the city are only now retiring and returning home.

In 1975 Congress passed a new Indian policy known as Self-Determination. Under this policy, tribes contract with the Bureau of Indian Affairs to administer programs normally directed by the Bureau. The tribe determines how the program should run and receives the money that the Bureau would spend to do the job. Tribes have contracted to run schools, to build houses, to maintain roads, to provide police, and to administer many other programs; in the process, they have learned valuable lessons in administration, planning, and negotiation.

In the 1980's the four North Dakota reservations were alike in their isolation from urban areas, their rural economies, their reliance on federal and tribal governments for employment, their modern housing and education systems, and their mix of traditional and modern religions. Generally, the Indian people lived much like other rural North Dakotans, and many of the reservations' problems were those of rural life, not Indian culture. The 1980 census showed that each reservation had a large percentage of employed Indian people, but the statistics also revealed that incomes were so low that families required additional help. Adding to the economic difficulties were the larger families with many young children.

The isolation that created the economic difficulties also made it possible for traditional ceremonies to survive the federal attempts to crush them. Some Indian people adapted to assimilationist policy by giving up some of their tribal customs, but others risked punishment and protected the tribe's sacred objects and continued to perform the ceremonies. After a century of unsuccessful attempts to turn Indians into Whites, the federal government finally abandoned the idea and encouraged the revival of traditional languages, customs, and religions. Utilizing the contracting right of self-determination and taking advantage of the new attitude toward Indian culture, the tribes initiated programs to educate their children and promote native arts; people moved away from a generalized or "pan-Indian" culture and began to revive specific tribal customs; the number of powwows and sacred ceremonies increased, and a new pride and assertiveness appeared throughout Indian country.

The ancient story that began in the shadows of the glaciers has not yet come to a conclusion. In April 1989, Governor George Sinner proclaimed Native American Week in recognition of the many contributions of North Dakota Indians and in July, Indians performed at the Centennial Celebration in Bismarck. An event of particular significance, the distribution of a Native American curriculum to every school in North Dakota, was timed to coincide with Native American Week. Written by Sandra Fox, an Indian woman from Fort Berthold, and university educators, the curriculum aimed to educate North Dakota school children about the special place of Indians in the state's history. Tribal people hope that such education will help to eliminate the stereotypes and other misunderstandings that exist between Indian and White. They look forward to the day that Indian contributions are known, Indian rights are recognized, and Indian values are accepted; a day when the struggle will no longer be against the ignorant, unthinking actions of other people and Indians are again walking the good red road of peace and prosperity.

References Cited

Abel, Annie Heloise, editor
1939 *Tabeau's Narrative of Loisel's Expedition to the Upper Missouri*. Norman: University of Oklahoma Press.

Albers, Patricia
1974 *The Regional System of the Devils Lake Sioux: Its Structure, Composition, Development and Functions*. Dissertation, Department of Anthropology, University of Wisconsin-Madison.

1983 Sioux Women in Transition. In *The Hidden Half*, edited by Patricia Albers and Beatrice Medicine. Washington, D.C.: University Press of America, Inc.

Albers, Patricia and Beatrice Medicine
1983 *The Hidden Half: Studies of Plains Indian Women*. Washington, D.C: University Press of America, Inc.

Ambler, Marjane
1984 The Three Affiliated Tribes at Fort Berthold - Mandan, Hidatsa, Arikara - Seek to Control their Energy Resources. In *Native Americans and Energy Development II*, edited by Joseph G. Jorgenson. Boston, Mass: Anthropology Resource Center.

Annual Reports of the Commissioner of Indian Affairs for the years
1868,1872,1875,1876,1877,1879,1880,1882,1884,1888,1891, 1893,1895,1904,1905,1906,1907

Beede, Aaron McGaffey
1942 The Dakota Indian Victory Dance. *North Dakota Historical Quarterly* 9:167-178.

Black Elk
1971 *The Sacred Pipe*. Norman: University of Oklahoma. (Reprint Penguin Books 1971).

Boller, Henry A.
1972 *Among the Indians: Four Years on the Upper Missouri, 1858- 1862*. Lincoln, Nebraska: University of Nebraska Bison Books.

Bowers, Alfred W.
1950 *Mandan Social and Ceremonial Organization*. Chicago: University of Chicago Press. (Reprint Midway Reprints 1973).

1965 Hidatsa Social and Ceremonial Organization. *Bureau of American Ethnology Bulletin* 194. Washington, D.C.: Smithsonian Institution and U.S. Government Printing Office.

Brackenridge, Henry M.
1906 Journal of a Voyage up the River Missouri Performed in Eighteen Hundred and Eleven. In *Early Western Travels* edited by Reuben G. Thwaites, vol.6.

Bradbury, John
1904 Travels in the Interior of America in the Years, 1809, 1810, and 1817. In *Early Western Travels*, edited by Reuben G. Thwaites, vol. 5.

Brasser, Ted. J.
1976 *"Bou'jou, Neejee!"* Ottawa: National Museum of Man.

Bruner, Edward
1956 Primary Group Experience and the Processes of Acculturation. *American Anthropologist*, vol.58:605-623.

Buechel, Rev. Eugene, S.J.
1970 *A Dictionary of the Teton Dakota Sioux Language*. Vermillion, S.D.: University of South Dakota.

Canby, Thomas Y.
1979 The Search for the First Americans. *National Geographic*, vol. 156, no.3:330-363.

Canfield, Sarah
1953 An Army Wife on the Upper Missouri. *North Dakota History* 20:191-220.

Case, Rev. Harold
1976 *100 Years at Fort Berthold*. Bismarck: Bismarck Tribune.

Catlin, George
1973 *Letters and Notes on the Manners, Customs and Condition of the North American Indians*. New York: Dover Books.

Claiborne, Robert
1973 *The First Americans*. New York: Time-Life Books.

Cohen, Felix S.
1952 Americanizing the White Man. *The American Scholar*, vol.XXI, no.2,177-91.

Cole, J.R.
1909 The Indians. In *History of the Red River Valley Past and Present*. vol.I, 259-279.

Collections of the State Historical Society of North Dakota
1908 Expeditions of Capt. Jas.L.Fisk to the Gold Mines of Idaho and Montana, 1864-1866. vol.II,pp.421-461.

Cook, Michelle
1984 Relatives Take Active Role in Child Rearing. *Grand Forks Herald*, March 5:1A-8A.

1985 Who Runs the Reservation? *Grand Forks Herald*, May 19:1A,6A.

Corfman, Eunice, editor
1979 Families Today: A Research Sampler on Families and Children. Vol. 1. *Science Monographs* No. 1. Washington, D.C.: U.S. Department of Health, Education and Welfare; Public Health Service, Alcohol, Drug Abuse, Mental Health Administration.

Coues, Elliot editor
1965 *New Light on the Early History of the Greater Northwest: Manuscript Journals of Alexander Henry and David Thompson, 1799-1814.* Vol.1. Minneapolis: Ross and Haines, Inc.

Delorme, David P.
1955 *A Socio-Economic Study of the Turtle Mountain Band of Chippewa Indians and a Critical Evaluation of Proposals Designed to Terminate their Federal Wardship Status*. Dissertation, University of Texas.

Demallie, Raymond
1983 Male and Female in Traditional Lakota Culture. In *The Hidden Half* edited by Patricia Albers and Beatrice Medicine. Washington, D.C.: University Press of America, Inc.

Denig, Edwin T.
1961 *Five Indian Tribes of the Upper Missouri: Sioux, Arikaras, Assiniboines, Crees and Crows*. Edited by John C. Ewers. Norman: University of Oklahoma Press.

Densmore, Frances
1929 Chippewa Customs. *Bureau of American Ethnology Bulletin* 86. Washington, D.C.: U.S. Government Printing Office. (Reprint Minnesota Historical Society 1979).

Dorris, Michael
1987 Indians on the Shelf. In *The American Indian and The Problem of History*, edited by Calvin Martin. New York: Oxford University Press. pp.98-105.

Dorsey, George
1904 Traditions of the Arikara. *Carnegie Institution of Washington Publication* 17. Washington, D.C.: Carnegie Institution.

Dorsey, James O.
1897 Siouan Sociology: A Posthumous Paper. *Bureau of American Ethnology Annual Report* 15:218-222. Washington, D.C.: U.S. Government Printing Office.

Dusenberry, Verne L.
   1965 The Métis of Montana. In *The Red Man's West*, edited by Michael Kennedy. New York: Hastings House, Publishers.

Ewers, John C.
   1975 Intertribal Warfare as the Precursor of Indian-White Warfare on the Northern Plains. *Western Historical Quarterly*, October, pp.397-410.

   1979 Images of the White Man in Nineteenth-Century Plains Indian Art. In *The Visual Arts: Plastic and Graphic* edited by Justine Cordwell. The Hague: Mouton Publishers.

Fay, George E.
   1967 *Charters, Constitutions and By-Laws of the Indian Tribes of North America: Part IIa: The Northern Plains*. Greeley, Colorado: Museum of Anthropology, Colorado State College.

Federal Writer's Project
   1950 *North Dakota: A Guide to the Northern Prairie State*. New York: Oxford press.

Fine, James O.
   1951 *An Analysis of Factors Affecting Agricultural Development on the Fort Totten Indian Reservation*. Thesis, University of North Dakota.

Fitzgerald, Frances
   1979 *America Revised*. New York: Vantage Press.

Gillette, John M.
   1906 The Medicine Society of the Dakota Indians. *Collections of the State Historical Society of North Dakota* 1,no.5:459-474.

Gilmore, Melvin R.
   1919 Uses of Plants by the Indians of Missouri River Region. *Thirty-third Annual Report of the Bureau of American Ethnology*. Washington, D.C.: Government Printing Office.

   1987 *Prairie Smoke*. St. Paul: Minnesota Historical Society.

Giraud, Marcel
   1947 *Le Métis Canadien*. Paris: Institut d'ethnologie.

Good, Kent N., et al.
   1977 *Archaeological Investigations of the Hendrickson III Site - 32SN403*. Department of Anthropology and Archaeology, University of North Dakota, Grand Forks.

Grand Forks Herald
   1908 *Chatauqua Notes*. July 15:8.
   1989 *Tribal company sues SBA, Abdnor*. March 15:9B.

Gregg, Michael
   1985 *An Overview of the Prehistory of Western and Central North Dakota*. Billings, Montana: Bureau of Land Management.

Hagan, William T.
   1966 *Indian Police and Judges*. New Haven: Yale University Press.

Hanna, Paul Shelley
   1953 *An Analysis of the Assimilation of White Culture by Hidatsa Indians of North Dakota*. Master's thesis, University of North Dakota.

Hassrick, Royal
   1944 Teton Dakota Kinship System. *American Anthropologist* 46:338-348.

   1964 *The Sioux: Life and Customs of a Warrior Society*. Norman: University of Oklahoma Press.

   1977 *The George Catlin Book of American Indians*. New York: Watson-Guptill Publications, Inc.

Henderson, Julie editor
   1986 *North Dakota Minority Business Today*. Bismarck, N.D.: North Dakota State Highway Department.

Hendrickson, Lucille
   1981 Lifestyle. North Dakota Indians. *Bismarck Tribune*, October 23:15.

Hesketh, John
   1923 History of the Turtle Mountain Chippewa. *Collections of the State Historical Society of North Dakota* 5:85-154.

Heski, Thomas M.
   1978 *Icastinyanka Cikala Hanzi: The Little Shadow Catcher, D.F. Barry*. Seattle: Superior Publishing Company.

Hickerson, Harold
   1956 The Genesis of a Trading Post Band: The Pembina Chippewa. *Ethnohistory* 3:289-345.

   1959 The Journal of Charles Jean Baptiste Chaboillez, 1797-1798. *Ethnohistory* 6:265-316; 363-427.

Hilger, Sister M. Inez
1959 Some Customs of the Chippewa on the Turtle Mountain Reservation of North Dakota. *North Dakota History* 26, no.3:123-125.

Hjerpe, Clara C.
1940 *Report of the Governor's Survey of the North Dakota Rolette County Indian Situation*. Bismarck, North Dakota.

Hook, A. L.
1936 *Analytical Report Relating to Land and Allied Problems on the Turtle Mountain Indian Reservation*.

Hoover, Herbert T.
1980 Sitting Bull. In *American Indian Leaders: Studies in Diversity* edited by David R. Edmunds. Lincoln: University of Nebraska Press.

Howard, James H.
1952 The Sun Dance of the Turtle Mountain Ojibwa. North Dakota History 19, no.4:249-264.

1976 The John K. Bear Winter Count. *Plains Anthropologist Memoir* 11.

1977 *The Plains Ojibwa or Bungi*. Lincoln, Nebraska: J. & L. Reprint Co.

Howard, James H. and Alan Woolworth
1954 An Arikara Bear Society Initiation Ceremony. *North Dakota History*, 21, no.4:169-179.

Howe, Albert
1892 *Report on Returned Hampton Institute Students*. Washington, D.C.: Government Printing Office.

Huddleston, Lee E.
1967 *The Origins of the American Indians*. Austin, University of Texas Press.

Jackson, Donald, editor
1962 *Letters of the Lewis and Clark Expedition*. Urbana, Illinois: University of Illinois Press.

Jacobson, Clair
1980 A History of the Yanktonai and Hunkpatina Sioux. *North Dakota History* 47, no. 1:4-24.

Jeannotte, Francois
1906 Biography of Old Settlers. *Collections of the State Historical Society of North Dakota*, vol.I:339-340.

Johnson, Sister Mary Antonio
1948 *Federal Relations with the Great Sioux Indians of South Dakota, 1887-1933*. Ann Arbor, Michigan: University Microfilms International.

Kappler, Charles J.
1904 *Indian Affairs, Laws and Treaties*. Washington, D.C.: U.S. Government Printing Office.

Keating, William H.
1959 *Narrative of an Expedition to the Source of St. Peter's River, Lake Winnipeek, Lake of the Woods, etc. Performed in the Year 1823*. St. Paul: Ross & Haines Inc.

Kloberdanz, Timothy J.
1987 In the Land of Inyan Woslata. *Great Plains Quarterly*, vol.7,no.2: 69-82.

Lambert, Grace
1976 Oral History. North Dakota Oral History Project, State Historical Society of North Dakota Archives.

Lang, Gretchen
1985 *Food, Diet, and Diabetes in a Dakota Sioux Community*. Unpublished manuscript.

Laverdure, Patline and Ida Rose Allard
1983 *The Michif Dictionary*. Winnipeg, Manitoba: Pemmican Publications.

La Vérendrye, Pierre Gaultier de Varennes Sieur de
1927 *Journals and Letters of Pierre Gaultier de Varennes Sieur de la Vérendrye and his Sons*. Edited by Lawrence J.Burpee. Toronto: The Champlain Society.

Law, Laura
1953 *History of Rolette County, North Dakota and Yarns of the Pioneers*. Minneapolis: Lund Press, Inc.

Lawson, Michael
1982 *Dammed Indians*. Norman: University of Oklahoma Press.

Leakey, Richard and Roger Levin
1977 *Origins*. New York: E.P. Dutton Co.

Lehmer, Donald J.
1971 Introduction to Middle Missouri Archaeology. *National Park Service Anthropological Papers* 1. Washington, D.C.: U.S. Department of the Interior.

Lowie, Robert H.
1913 Societies of the Hidatsa and Mandan. *Anthropological Papers of the American Museum of Natural History* 11:294-358.

1954 *Indians of the Plains*. New York: American Museum of Natural History.

Lynd, James W.
1864 The Religion of the Dakotas. *Minnesota Historical Society Collections*, vol.II, pp.150-174.

MacGregor, Gordon
1949 Attitudes of the Fort Berthold Indians Regarding Removal from the Garrison Reservoir Site and Future Administration of their Reservation. *North Dakota History*, vol. XVI, no.1:31-60.

Malouf, Carling
1963 Crow-Flies-High (32MZ1), A Historic Hidatsa Village in the Garrison Reservoir Area, North Dakota. *Bureau of American Ethnology Bulletin* 185:133-166. Washington, D.C.: Government Printing Office.

Mann, Earl
1976 Oral History. North Dakota Oral History project, State Historical Society of North Dakota Archives.

Martin, Calvin, editor
1987 *The American Indian and the Problem of History*. New York: Oxford University Press.

Matthews, Washington
1873 *Grammar and Dictionary of the Language of the Hidatsa*. New York: Cramoisy Press.

Mattison, Ray H.
1954 The Army Post of the Northern Plains, 1865-1885. *Nebraska History* 35:17-43.

McLaughlin, James
Papers. Microfilm Edition. Special Collections, University of North Dakota, Grand Forks.

Meyer, Roy
1967 *History of the Santee Sioux*. Lincoln: University of Nebraska Press.

1977 *The Village Indians of the Upper Missouri*. Lincoln: University of Nebraska Press.

Miller, David Humphreys
1965 Sitting Bull's White Squaw. In *The Red Man's West* edited by Michael S. Kennedy. New York: Hastings House, Publishers.

Murray, Stanley N.
1984 The Turtle Mountain Chippewa, 1882-1905. *North Dakota History,* 51 (1):14-37.

Murray, Robert J.
1953 *History of Education in the Turtle Mountain Indian Reservation in North Dakota*. Thesis, University of North Dakota.

Nasatir, A. P.
1952 *Before Lewis and Clark*. vol.II. St. Louis: St. Louis Historical Documents Foundation.

National Archives. Office of Indian Affairs, Letters Received, Fort Berthold Agency.

Office of Indian Affairs, Letters Received, Standing Rock Agency.

Nichols, Roger L.
1986 Backdrop for Disaster: Causes of the Arikara War of 1823. In *The American Indian*, edited by Roger L. Nichols. pp.166-178.

Nichols, Roger L., editor
1986 *The American Indian*. Tucson, Arizona: University of Arizona Press.

Nicollet, Joseph N.
1976 *Joseph N. Nicollet on the Plains and Prairies*. Edited by Edmund C. Bray and Martha C. Bray. St. Paul: Minnesota Historical Press.

North Dakota Indian Affairs Commission
1985 *Fact Sheet: Fort Totten, Fort Berthold, Standing Rock, Turtle Mountain*. Bismarck: North Dakota Indian Affairs Commission Office.

Parsons, John E.
1963 *West on the 49th Parallel: Red River to the Rockies, 1872-1876*. New York: William Morrow and Company.

Peterson, Susan
1985 Doing "Women's Work": The Grey Nuns at Fort Totten Indian Reservation, 1874-1900. *North Dakota History* 52 (2):18-25.

Pond, Samuel W.
1986 *The Dakotas or Sioux in Minnesota as they were in 1834*. St. Paul: Minnesota Historical Society.

Prucha, Francis
1971 *Indian Peace Medals*. Madison: Wisconsin State Historical Society.

1975 *Documents of United States Indian Policy*. Lincoln: University of Nebraska Press.

Reid, Russell, editor
1947-48 *The Journals of Lewis and Clark in North Dakota*. Bismarck: North Dakota State Historical Society.

Robinson, Doane
1904 History of Dakota or Sioux Indians. *Collections of the South Dakota State Historical Society* 2. (Reprint Ross and Haines 1956).

Robinson, Elwyn B.
1966 *History of North Dakota*. Lincoln: University of Nebraska Press.

St. Ann's Centennial
1985 *100 Years of Faith*. Rolla, North Dakota: Star Printing.

Schell, Herbert S.
1975 *History of South Dakota*. Lincoln, Nebraska: University of Nebraska Press.

Schier, Sister M. Angela
1938 *A History of Indian Missions in North Dakota*. Thesis, Catholic University of America.

Skinner, Alanson
1914a The Cultural Position of the Plains Ojibway. *American Anthropologist* 16:314-318.

1914b Notes on the Plains Cree. *American Anthropologist* 16: 68-87.

1919a The Sun Dance of the Plains Ojibway. *Anthropological Papers of the American Museum of Natural History* 16:311-315.

1920 Medicine Ceremony of the Menomini, Iowa, and Wahpeton Dakota. *Indian Notes* 4:262-302.

Smith, G. Hubert
1972 Like-a-Fishhook Village and Fort Berthold, Garrison Reservoir, North Dakota. *Anthropological Papers* 2, National Park Service. Washington, D.C.: U.S. Department of Interior.

Sneve, Virginia Driving Hawk
1973 *The Dakota's Heritage*. Sioux Falls, S. Dakota: Brevet Press.

Spokesfield, Walter E.
1929 *The History of Wells County and Its Pioneers*. Jamestown, North Dakota.

Standing Bear, Luther
1975 *My People, The Sioux*. Nebraska: University of Nebraska Press.

Stewart, Frank H.
1974 Mandan and Hidatsa Villages in the Eighteenth and Nineteenth Centuries. *Plains Anthropologist* 19:287-302.

Superintendent's Day Book. Fort Berthold Agency, National Archives, Kansas City, Record Group 75.

Swisher, Karen Gayton
1981 *A Study of the Attitudes of Parents and Teachers at Standing Rock Community Elementary School Toward Multicultural Education*. Dissertation, University of North Dakota.

Syms, E. Leigh
1970 The McKean Complex in Manitoba. In *Ten Thousand Years: Archaeology in Manitoba* edited by Walter Hlady. Winnipeg: Manitoba Archaeological Society. 123-139.

Thompson, David
1962 *David Thompson's Narrative: 1784-1812*. Edited by Richard Glover. Toronto: The Champlain Society.

Thwaites, Reuben Gold, editor
1904-06 *Original Journals of the Lewis and Clark Expedition, 1804-1808*. New York: Dodd, Mead and Company.

1906 *Travels in the Interior of North America, 1832-1834*. vols.22-24 of Early Western Travels. Cleveland: Arthur H. Clark Co.

Turosak, Greg
1986 High Court Rules in North Dakota Indian Case. *Grand Forks Herald*, June 17:2.

Tyler, S. Lyman
1973 *A History of Indian Policy*. Washington, D.C.: U.S. Department of the Interior, Bureau of Indian Affairs.

U.S. Bureau of the Census
1983 *1980 Census of the Population, Characteristics of the Population: North Dakota, General Social and Economic Characteristics*. Washington, D.C. : U.S. Government Printing Office.

1985 *1980 Census of the Population. U.S. Summary: American Indians.* Washington, D.C.: U.S. Government Printing Office.

1986 *1980 Census of the Population: American Indians, Eskimos, and Aleuts on Identified Reservations and in the Historic Areas of Oklahoma* (PC80-2-1d,pt.2). Washington D.C.: U.S. Government Printing Office.

U.S. Department of Commerce
1972 *Indian Economic Development: An Evaluation of EDA's Selected Indian Reservation Program.* Prepared by Boise Cascade Center for Community Development. vol.II. Washington, D.C.: Government Printing Office.

U.S. Department of Interior
1894 *Report on Indians Taxed and Indians Not Taxed at the Eleventh Census: 1890.* Wasington D.C. Government Printing Office.

1912 *Executive Orders Relating to Indian Reservations from May 14, 1855 to July 1, 1912.* Washington, D.C.: U.S. Government Printing Office.

1922 *Executive Orders Relating to Indian Reservations from July 1, 1912 to July 1, 1922.* Washington, D.C.: U.S. Government Printing Office.

1957 Cultural and economic Status of the Sioux People, 1955, Standing Rock Reservation, North and South Dakota. *Missouri River Basin Investigations Project 151.*

1964 Family Plan and Rehabilitation Programs, Standing Rock Reservation. *Missouri River Basin Investigations Project Report* No. 177. Billings, Montana.

U.S. Senate, 55th Congress, 2nd Session, Document No.154.
1898 *Turtle Mountain Band of Pembina Chippewa.*

Vogel, Virgil
1972 *This Country Was Ours.* New York: Harper & Row.

Vrooman, Nicholas Curchin
1984 *Turtle Mountain Music.* New York: Folkways Records.

Walker, Francis
1872 *A Compendium of the Ninth Census.* Washington, D.C.: Government Printing Office.

Walker, James R.
1914 Oglala Kinship Terms. *American Anthropologist* 16:96-109.

1980 *Lakota Belief and Ritual.* Edited by Raymond J. DeMallie and Elaine A. Jahner. Lincoln: University of Nebraska Press.

1982 *Lakota Society.* Edited by Raymond J. DeMallie. Lincoln: University of Nebraska Press.

1983 *Lakota Myth.* Edited by Elaine A. Jahner. Lincoln: University of Nebraska Press.

Warren, William
1974 *History of the Ojibways.* St. Paul: Ross & Haines.

Wied-Neuwied, Prince Alexander Philip Maximilian of
1906 *Travels in the Interior of North America,* 1832-1834. In Early Western Travels, vols. 22-25. Edited by Reuben Gold Thwaites.

Wilkins, Robert and Wynona Wilkins
1977 *North Dakota: A Bicentennial History.* New York: W. W. Norton and Company, Inc.

Williams, Mary Anne Barnes
1966 *Origins of North Dakota Place Names.* Washburn, N.D.

Wilson, Gilbert L.
1905 Diary. Wilson Papers, Minnesota Historical Society Archives.

1985 *Goodbird the Indian.* St. Paul: Minnesota Historical Society.

1917 Agriculture of the Hidatsa Indians: An Indian Interpretation. *Bulletin of the University of Minnesota. Studies in Social Sciences* No.9. Minneapolis: University of Minnesota. (Reprint J. & L. Reprints 1977).

1971 *Waheenee.* North Dakota Historical Society.

1934 The Hidatsa Earthlodge. *Anthropological Papers of the American Museum of Natural History* 33:341-420. (Reprint J & L Reprint 1978).

1979 Notes on the Hidatsa Indians based on data recorded by the Late Gilbert L. Wilson. *Anthropological Papers of the American Museum of Natural History* 56,2:183-322.

Woods, Samuel
1850 Pembina Settlement. House of Representatives, 31st Congress, Ist Session, Ex.Doc. No.51.

Wood, W. Raymond
1971 Biesterfeldt: A Post-Contact Coalescent Site on the Northeastern Plains. *Smithsonian Contributions to Anthropology* No. 15. Washington, D.C.: Smithsonain Institutioon press.

Wood, W. Raymond and Tom Thiessen
1985 *Early Fur Trade on the Northern Plains.* Norman; University of Oklahoma Press.

Word Carrier
1925 November-December. Santee, Nebraska.

Index

Africa, 16, 17
Agency, 59, 65, 73, 74, 75, 77, 91, 102, 105, 106, 111, 112, 118, 125
    (see also Fort Yates, Fort Totten, New Town, Belcourt)
Agents, 7, 45, 46, 59, 62, 63, 65, 66, 67, 72, 73, 88, 90, 91, 92, 93, 94, 95, 106, 109, 112, 113, 124, 125, 126, 127, 142, 143,
    J. B. Bassett, 125
    John Burke, 108
    H. L. Clifford, 73
    John W. Cramsie, 90, 125, 126
    William H. Forbes, 88, 92
    Abram J. Gifford, 73
    W. F. Hughes, 108
    James McLaughlin, 90, 92, 93, 95, 96, 110, 111, 112
    E. Mossman, 115, 116
    Edward Smith, 125
    Lyman B. Sperry, 73
    J. A. Stephan, 109, 112
    John H. Waugh, 90, 93.
Agricultural tribes, see Arikara, Hidatsa, Dakota, Mandan, Yanktonai
Agriculture, 10, 30, 25, 42, 44, 50, 51, 52, 55, 74, 77, 79-81, 141, 142, 143
Alaska, 16, 17
Albany Plan of Union, 1754, 3
Aleuts, 8
Allen, Alvaren, 162
Allotment, 9, 10, 72, 74, 79, 89, 90, 94, 105, 112, 113, 119, 128, 129, 143 (see also Land)
American Fur Company, 56
Anderson, Captain, 125
Anishnabeg Resource Center, 135

Antelope, 30
Arapaho, 104
Archaeology, 15-21, 23, 30, 141
Archaic, 18-19, 141
Arikara, 5, 6, 9, 13-14, 20, 21, 23, 25, 26-27, 31, 34, 38, 44, 45, 49, 56, 59, 64, 66, 67, 71, 72, 74, 75, 79, 104, 106, 117, 141, 142 (see also Three Affiliated Tribes)
Armstrong, North Dakota 73
Army, 58, 59, 62, 64, 66, 104, 106, 107
Army Corps of Engineers, 116
Arthur, President Chester A, 6, 11, 125
Articles of Confederation, 3
Artists, non-Indian, 4, Indian, 10, 103, 140
Asia, 16, 17
Assimilation, 7-8, 62-63, 64, 79, 99, 109, 141, 142, 143
Assiniboins, 21, 22, 31, 47, 48, 50, 87, 104, 122, 142
Assiniboin River, 22, 123
Awatixa, 13
Awaxawi, 13

Bad Gun, 67
Bassett, J. B., 125
Battle of the Little Big Horn, 107, 111
Bear Den Hill, 23
Beauchamp, Peter, 74
Belcourt, North Dakota, 45, 130, 134, 135, 136, 137
Belcourt, Father George Antoine, 54, 137
Beliefs, 42
Bell, John, 87
Benedictine Brothers, 92, 109
Bering Strait, 16
Beringia, 17
Bible, 11, 94
Biesterfeldt Site, 20

Big Foot, 112
Big White, 12, 49
Billings, Frederick, 66
Bishop of St. Paul, 92
Bismarck, North Dakota, 7, 57, 85, 111, 116
Bison (See Buffalo)
Black Hills, 7, 106, 111
Blackfeet Sioux tribe, 6, 104, 105, 106, 107, 112
Black Mouth Society, 36
Blue Earth, Richard, 115
Boarding schools, 73-74, 79, 92, 94, 109, 120, 127 (see also Education)
Bodmer, Karl, 45
Boller, Henry, 56
Bottineau County, 64
Bottineau, John B., 128
Bottineau, Pierre, 65
Bow and arrows, 20, 32, 141
Boy Scouts 1, 2
Brackenridge, Henry, 49
Bradbury, John, 49
Brien, Ben, 140
British, 6, 47, 49, 51
Browning, boarding school 73
Bruce, Robert, 96
Brule tribe, 51, 154
Bruner, Edward S., 76
Buffalo, 11, 16, 18, 19, 20, 29, 30-31, 42, 44, 51, 52, 56, 58, 105, 141
    Buffalo hunting, 51, 52, 58, 122, 141
    Buffalo drive, 20
    Buffalo societies, 36
    Giant bison, 10
Buffalo Bill, 112
Buffalo Bird Woman, 56

Bullhead, South Dakota, 116, 120
Burdick, Usher L., 45
Bureau of Indian Affairs, 62, 63, 66, 82, 85, 102, 116, 120, 136, 143
Burial Mounds, 19
Burke, John, 108

Cabins, 30, 54, 66, 67, 76, 110, 121,
California, 10, 17
Camps and campsites, 11, 16, 20, 29, 32, 35, 51, 11, 116, 141,
Canada, 50, 58, 86, 104, 11, 122-123, 128
    Canadians, 49
Canfield, Sarah, 62
Cannonball, North Dakota, 115, 116
Cannonball River, 105, 106
Carlin, Captain W. P., 109
Carlisle Institute, Pennsylvania, 73, 96
Carlson, Robert, 94
Catlin, George, 11, 12, 22, 45, 49, 52, 64
Cattle, 90, 95, 115
    Cattle ranching, 97, 115
Cemetery, 36
Census, 8-10,
Ceremonies, 11, 12, 13, 14, 15, 24, 25, 30, 32, 34, 36, 38, 41, 42, 44, 49, 56, 63, 67, 72, 77, 79, 82, 91, 129, 130, 133, 138, 142, 143, (see also Ghost Keeping, Give-Away ceremony, Making of Relatives, Medicine Dance, Midewiwin, Sun Dance, Vision Quest)
Chaboillez, Charles Jean Baptiste, 22, 49, 50
Charbonneau, Toussaint, 49
Charges Alone, 75
Charred Body, culture hero, 13
Chase, Virgil, Sr., 85
Chautauqua, 96, 99, 103
Cheyenne Indians, 20, 48, 104, 142
Cheyenne River, see Sheyenne River
Cheyenne River Reservation, 112, 116
Cheyenne Women Society, 38
Chief, 3, 38-39, 52, 59, 124
Children, 7, 32-33, 63, 72, 73, 83, 92, 93, 94, 100, 102, 126, 133, 136
Chippewa, 5, 6, 14, 22, 31, 32, 36, 42, 45, 50, 51, 52, 62, 122-140 (see also Turtle Mountain Band of Chippewa)
Christmas, 72
Church, 65, 82, 137
Cities, 132
Civilize, 7
Clan, 32, 83, 142 (see also Kinship)
Clark, William, 12, 49, 51 (see also Lewis and Clark)
Clifford, H. L., 65
Clovis, projectile points, 18
College, 79, 81, 99, 118, 120, 136, 137

Collier, John, 63
Collins, Mary, 95
Colonists, 3
Columbia Fur Company, 51
Commissioner of Indian Affairs, 63, 96
Congress, 6, 58, 62, 72, 89, 90, 104, 107, 127, 143
Congressmen, Indian, 4,
Corn, 3, 4, 14, 19, 21, 30, 31, 45, 76, 90, 95,
Counties, 64
Cournoyer, Angela, 121
Court, Ignatius, 94
Court Lake, North Dakota, 94
Cramsie, John, 125, 126, 127
Cree Indians, 6, 22, 30, 47, 49, 50, 51, 122, 133, 141, 142
Cree, Selina, 140
Crops, 3, 27, 31, 44, 54, 67, 85
Crow Agency, Montana, 112
Crow Creek Reservation, 58-59
Crow-Flies-High, 65, 66, 67, 72,
Crow Hill, North Dakota, 90, 101, 102
Crow Indians 13, 21, 104
Crows Heart, 67
Cultural pluralism, 62
Custer, General George Armstrong, 64, 106
Cuthead band of Yanktonai, 6, 58, 86, 142

Dakota Indians, 5, 6, 10, 20, 21, 22, 23, 27, 30, 31, 36, 42, 44, 45, 47, 57-59, 86, 87, 94, 122, 141, 142
Dakota Conflict of 1862, 6, 58, 86, 142
Dakota Territorial Legislature, 56, 140
Dakota Territory, 51, 56-57, 58, 59, 88
Dakota Tribal Industries, 101
Dakotah Bingo Palace, 100
Dams, 116
Dances, 1, 51, 63, 72, 83, 95, 96, 109-110, 115, 130, 138, (See also Powwows)
Dating, archaeological, 16
Dawson, Annie, 74
Death, 36
Declaration of Independence, 4
Deer, 30
Deloria, Vine, Jr., 121
Department of Public Instruction, 140
Department of the Interior, 85
Devils Heart, named, 23
Devils Lake, 6, 13, 21, 23, 59, 142,
Devils Lake, North Dakota, 4, 94, 96, 99, 100, 102
Devils Lake Sioux Manufacturing, 101, 102, 103
Devils Lake Sioux Reservation, 7, 58-59, 86-103, 122, 125, 129, 142, 143
Devils Lake Sioux Tribe, 7, 9, 10, 86, 90, 91, 96, 99, 100, 102, 103, 121
Dickson, Robert, 51
Diminished Great Sioux reservation, 111
Dipauch, Mandan, 11

Diseases, 5, 10, 20, 24, 36, 142
    Smallpox, 5, 12, 21, 47, 56, 142
Divorce, 35
Dogden Butte, named, 23
Dorion, 51
Dorris, Michael, 1
Doty, James, 87
Drying stages, 27
Dumoulin, Father Sévére, 51, 65
Dunseith, North Dakota, 129, 130, 131, 136, 137

Eagle Woman All Look At, 121
Easter, 102
Eastman, Seth, 45
Earthlodge, 6, 19, 20, 23, 26, 27, 66, 142
Economy, 7, 12, 56
Economic development, 100, 139, 140
Economic Development Agency, 121
Education, 32, 63, 71, 73, 79, 92-94, 104, 121, 132, 136, 140, 143
Educators, 4, 45, 62, 142
Elbowoods, North Dakota, 67, 77
Employment, 7, 8, 90, 97-98, 100, 101, 102, 117, 118, 119, 120, 135, 136, 139, 142, 143
End of the Current, 52
Enemy Women Society, 38
English, 122, 123
Enrollment, see Tribal enrollment
Equal Sky, 124
Erdrich, Louise, 140
Ernst, Max, 4
Eskimos, 8
Europe, 16
Europeans, 3, 11, 15, 20, 21, 47, 55, 62, 122, 141, 142,
Executive orders, 66, 72, 106, 125, 142
Expedition, 51, 52-54, 58,
Explorers, 11, 49, 65, 122, 142

Family, 3, 24, 26, 30, 32-36, 38, 41, 67, 72, 76, 79, 83, 91, 102, 112, 119, 122, 127, 136, 143,
    Family relationships, 32
    (see also Kinship)
Farming, 79-81, 90, 96, 97, 101, 105, 106, 125, 143
    Farm tools, 71
    Farmers, 94, 105, 127, 143
    (see also Agriculture)
Fargo, North Dakota, 57
Federal government, 7
Federal Indian policy, 6, 10 (see also Assimilation, Allotment)
First Creator, culture hero, 11, 13, 42
First Man, culture hero, 11, 12
Fishing, 30
Fishing rights, 84
Fisk, Captain James L., 59

Fiske, Frank, 121
Foffa, Father Chrysostom, 108
Folsom, projectile points, 33
Forbes, William H. 88
Food, 3, 16, 18, 30-32, 36, 47, 48, 49, 71, 76, 85, 113
Foolish society, 61
Forts (See also Trading posts), 49, 58, 59, 62, 64, 66
    Fort Atkinson, 56
    Fort Buford, 66, 11
    Fort Clark, 56
    Fort Garry, 51, 123
    Fort Laramie, 104, 142
    Fort Randall, 118
    Fort Rice, 59, 105
    Fort Stevenson, 59, 66
    Fort Totten, 10, 88, 94, 100, 101, 103,
    Fort Union, 22, 52, 64
Fort Berthold Reservation, 6, 7, 8, 9, 11, 17, 45, 56,
    62, 63, 65, 66-85, 72, 73, 90, 103, 117, 122, 142
Fort Peck Reservation, 59, 129
Fort Shaw School, 129
Fort Stevenson Boarding School, 73
Fort Totten Reservation (See also Devils Lake Sioux
    Reservation), 6, 8, 9, 10, 45, 58-59, 86-103
    Fort Totten Boarding School, 94
Fort Yates, North Dakota, 23, 45, 59, 107, 109, 112,
    116, 117, 120
Four Winds School, 99, 102
Fourth of July celebrations, 72, 102
France, 96
Frazier, Lynn, 115
Franklin, Benjamin, 3
French, 6, 47, 49, 122, 133
Fur trade, 21, 51, 52,
    Fur traders, 22, 30, 39, 50-51, 64, 122
    Fur trading posts, 64

Gall, 65
Galpin, Mrs., 65
Gardens, 31, 32, 76, 95, 113, 115
Garreau, Joseph, 49
Gaul, Gilbert, 110
Garrison Dam, 20, 75-77, 82, 84, 85
General Allotment Act, 63, 71-72, 90, 112, 143
Genoa Boarding School, Nebraska, 73
Geologists, 15,17
German-Russians, 121
Ghost Dance, 112
Ghost Keeping, 36, 44, (See also Ceremonies)
Gingras, Antoine, 65
Gipp, Louis, 121
Gitche Manitou, 42
Give-Away ceremony, 72, 83, 109, (see also Ceremo-
    nies)
Glaciers, 17, 141

God, 3, 42
Gornon, Joseph, 124
Good Furred Robe, culture hero, 12
Goose Society, 38
Government, 26
Grand Forks, North Dakota, 7, 45, 51
Grand River, 105, 106, 111
Grant, Cuthbert, 65
Grant, President Ulysses S., 106
Grass, Albert, 115
Grass, John, 65, 108
Gray, Joseph R., 90
Great Britain, 122
Great Northern Bean, 4, 45
Great Sioux Nation, 6
Great Sioux Reservation, 6, 104, 106, 107, 111
Green Feather, 52
Grey Nuns, 98, 92, 94
Greywind, Ken, 103
Gros Ventres, 104, (See also Hidatsa)
Gun Society, 38

Hall, Charles L., 73
Hamar, North Dakota, 101
Hampton Institute, Virginia, 73, 74, 94
Hanna, Paul, 71
Hat-wearers, see also Europeans, 42, 49, 51, 62
Hawksnest Hill, named, 23, 91
Hayes, President Rutherford B., 111
Health, 32, 42, 44, 79, 63, 102, 103
Heart Butte, named, 23
Heart River, 21, 23
Heinemeyer, Edward, 45
Helphrey, Juanita, 85
Henry, Alexander, 47-48, 49, 50
Hickerson, Harold, 21
Hidatsa, 5, 6, 9, 10, 12-13, 15, 20, 21, 23, 25, 26, 27, 31,
    32, 33, 34, 36, 38, 42, 44, 45, 47-48, 49, 56, 59, 64,
    66, 67, 71, 72, 74, 75, 79, 104, 107, 117, 141, 142,
    (see also Three Affiliated Tribes)
High Eagle, Robert, 94
Historic period, 20
Hoffman, Charles, W., 74
Hospitality, 48-49, 51, 64, 65, 85, 95
House Concurrent Resolution 108, 63, 131, 139, 143
Houses and housing, 6, 19-20, 26-30, 32, 82, 101, 108,
    112, 117, 125, 135, 136
Hudson's Bay Company, 50, 51, 55
Hughes, W. F., 108
Hunkpatina tribe, 58
Hunkpapa tribe, 6, 104, 105, 106, 107, (see also
    Lakota)
Hunters, 34, 38, 53-54, 66
Hunting, 16, 18, 19, 25, 27, 29, 30-31, 36, 39, 41, 42, 44,
    52, 66, 67, 91, 104, 106, 108, 141, 143, (see also

Buffalo, Deer)
Huskies, 66 (see also Crow-Flies-High)

Icanajika, 92
Identity, 8
Ikce, culture hero, 15
Iktomi, culture hero, 15
Images, 1-2
Income, 79-81, 82, 90, 98, 100, 101, 117, 119, 120, 133-
    135, 143
Independence, North Dakota, 67, 73, 76, 77
Indian police, 90
Indian princesses, 3
Indian Reorganization Act, 63, 75, 96, 116, 131, 143
Industrial development, 57, 81, 134, 135
International Peace Garden, 135
Interpreters, 90
Inyan, 15
Iroquois, League of the, 3
Irrigation, 121

James River, 23, 51, 59
James River Valley, 20
Jamestown, North Dakota, 88
Jeannotte, Francois, 123
Jusseaume, Rene, 49

Kane, Paul, 45
Kansas, 104
Keating, William H., 53
Kenel, South Dakota, 116
Killdeer Mountains, 23, 59
Kinship, 72, 77, 102, 137-138, 142
Knife River, 21, 56, 142
Knife River flint, 141
Knife River Villages National Park, 10, 23, 46, 85,
Korean Conflict, 3

La Vérendrye, Pierre Gaultier de Varennes, Sieur de,
    49, 64
Lake of the Woods, 123
Lake Traverse, 51
Lake Sakakawea, 20, 66, 77, 84
Lake Winnipeg, 21, 23, 182
Lakota tribe, 5, 6, 10, 15, 21, 23, 27, 29, 30, 31, 32, 35,
    36, 38, 39, 42, 44, 47-48, 51, 59, 62, 87, 104-121,
    141
Land, 7, 47, 56, 63, 64, 67, 71-72, 75, 77, 79-81, 89-90,
    94, 96, 101, 106, 111, 126, 127
Language, 3, 10, 23, 45, 47, 62, 63, 64, 66, 72, 76, 77,
    79, 92, 94, 99, 102, 118, 122, 133, 137-138, 142,
    143
Law, Laura, 123, 126
League of the Iroquois, 3
Leakey, Louis S. B., 17

Leech Lake, Minnesota, 122
Legal system, 41
Lewis, Meriwether, 49, 51 (see also Lewis and Clark)
Lewis and Clark, 12,20,21,39, 51, 64, 65
Liberty, 3
Liberty Bonds, 96
Libby, Orin G., 45
Like-a-Fishhook Village, 6, 56, 59, 66, 67, 75, 76, 77, 142
Liquor, 51
Little Eagle, South Dakota, 116, 120
Little Fish, 96, 99
Little Flower School, 93
Little Shell, 124, 127, 128-129
Locke, John, 3
Lone Bear, Martha, 85
Lone Man, culture hero, 11-13, 15
Long, Stephen, 51, 53, 86-87
    Long expedition, 52
Long Legs, 52
Lord Selkirk, see Selkirk, Lord,
Los Angeles, 10
Lower Yanktonais, 105, 107, (See also Yanktonai)

Macgregor, Gordon, 76
Maddock, North Dakota, 102
Mail order catalogues, 74
Making of Relatives, 44, (see also Ceremonies)
Malo, Father John
Mammoths, 17,18
Mandan tribe, 5, 6, 9, 10, 11-13, 15, 20, 21, 23, 25, 26, 27, 31, 34, 38, 42, 44, 45, 46, 47-48, 49, 55-56, 59, 64, 66, 67, 71, 72, 74, 75, 79,104, 106, 117, 141, 142, (see also Three Affiliated Tribes)
Mandan, North Dakota, 4
Mandaree, North Dakota, 79, 82, 83
Manitaries, 12
Manitoba, 123
Mann, Earl, 94
Marriage, 34-35, 49, 50, 51, 100, 118, 119, 121, 122, 133, 142
Marshall, Thomas, 96
Marty, Father Martin, 108
Massachusetts, 74
Mato Catka, 93
Matta, Echaurren, 4
Maximilian (See Wied-Neuwied)
McCumber, Porter, 117
McIntosh, South Dakota, 117, 120
McLaughlin, James, 72, 74, 90, 91, 92, 95, 95, 110, 11, 112, 115, 123, 127, 129
McLaughlin, Marie Louise 121
McLaughlin, South Dakota, 116, 117, 120
Mdewakanton, 27, 29, 58
Medicine, 62, 63

Medicine Dance, 91 (see also Ceremonies)
Medicine Feast, 91
Medicine Lodge, 44
Medicine Lodge Spring, 23
Medicine men, 118
Medicine pipes, 11
Megis, 14
Menitarras, 12
Menard, 49
Men's military societies, 36
Metal tools, see Trade goods
Métis, 6, 30, 50, 51, 52-55, 64, 122-140, (see also Turtle Mountain Band of Chippewa)
Midewiwin, 45, 130, (see also Ceremonies)
Migrations, 11, 21, 122, 141
Military, 25, 45, 58-59, 62, 64, 66, 75, 96,
    Military societies, 36, 41
    Military police, 30
    Military posts, 105, 106, 107 (see also Forts)
Milwaukee, Wisconsin, 127
Minneconju tribe, 104, 106
Minnesota, 27, 29, 30, 34, 51, 57, 58, 86, 104, 122, 123, 124, 127, 140
Minot, North Dakota, 7
Missionaries, 25, 45, 51, 52, 62, 65, 66, 73, 92, 95, 108-109, 120, 142
    Missionizing, 56
    Missions, 65, 73, 120, 136
Missouri River, 5, 12-13, 14, 15, 19, 21, 23, 39, 49, 50, 51, 52, 55, 56, 58, 59, 64, 66, 67, 75, 77, 87, 104, 105, 106, 11, 116, 142
Mississippi River, 58
"Moccasin Democrats", 56, 140
Montaigne, Michel de, 3
Montana, 10, 59, 66, 104, 111, 123, 124, 125, 127, 129, 131
Montgomery Ward, 74
Montreal, 92
Montreuil, Joseph, 124
Moore, Rex, 103
Mossman, E., 115, 116
Mother Corn, culture hero, 14, 141
Murray, Robert J., 126
Music, 133, 138

Names and naming, 4, 32, 36, 42, 47, 66, 84, 133
National Park Service, 64
Native Hawaiians, 8
Native American, 8, 10
Native American Church, 83, 102
Navajo, 4, code talkers, 4, sand painters, 4
Nebraska, 21, 74, 104
Nebraska, Josephine, 94
New Mexico, 18
New Town, North Dakota, 45, 77, 82, 83, 85

Nicollet, Joseph N., 87
Nishu, North Dakota, 67
North Dakota, 4, 104
North Dakota Arts and Humanities Council, 85
North Dakota Commissioner of Indian Affairs, 85
North Dakota Indian Affairs Commission, 9-10
North Dakota National Guard, 96
North Dakota State Historical Board, 85
Northern Pacific Railroad, 66, 88, 106, 111
Northern Plains Industry, 140

Oahe Dam, 116, 117
    Oahe Reservoir, 117, 121
Oberon, North Dakota, 102
Office of Indian Affairs, 66, 71, 72, 93, 143 (See also Bureau of Indian Affairs)
Oglala tribe, 15, 51, 104, 106, (see also Lakota)
Ojibbeway, 22 (See also Chippewa)
Ojibway Indian School, 136
Okipa, 12
Old age, 35
Old Women Society, 38
Oohenonpa tribe, 104
Opposition, 56
Oral histories, 11-15, 21, 45, 141
    Origins, 11-23, 141
Otter, 14

Pacific Ocean, 65
Paleo-Indians, 18, 141
Parshall, North Dakota, 74, 77, 85
Peace Commission, 104
Pembina, North Dakota, 22, 45, 50, 51, 52, 54-55, 56, 65, 122, 123, 124, 137, 140
Pembina Chippewa, 62, 124, 125
    Pembina band, 125
Pembina County, 56
Pembina River, 124
Pemmican, 55, 65, 95,
Philosophers, influenced by Indians, 3
Picotte, Honore, 121
Picotte, Maria Louise, 121
Pine Ridge Reservation, 15, 112
Plains Chippewa tribe, 22, 31, 52, 64
Plains Cree tribe, 31
Plains Village, 20
Plains Ojibwa tribe, 22, 129
Plano, 18
Plants, 30-31,
Plaza, North Dakota, 74
Pocahontas, 2
Police, 36
Policy, 62-63, 64, 85, 86
Political organization, 38-41, 56
Pollock, Jackson, 4

156

Pond, Samuel William, 29
Poor Wolf, 65
Population, 8-10, 99, 132
Porcupine, North Dakota, 116
Pottery, 19, 141
Powwows, 1, 4, 65, 83, 103, 118, 121, 127, 133, 143,
       Powwow committees, 83
       (see also Dances)
Prairie Rose State Games, 85
Prairie Sioux, 21
Prairie turnips, 95
Presidents,
       Arthur, Chester A, 6, 11, 125
       Grant, Ulysses, 66, 106
       Harrison, Benjamin, 72
       Hayes, Rutherford B., 111
Pryor-Chouteau trading party, 49
Public assistance, 81, 117, 120

Radisson, Pierre Esprit, 21
Railroad, see also Northern Pacific Railroad, 52, 66,
       90
Rainy Lake, Minnesota, 122
Ramsey, Alexander, 124
Ranching, 79, 105, 117, 119, 121, 143, (see also Farm-
       ing)
Raven Societies, 36
Red Bear, 124
Red Cloud, 107
Red Cross, 96, 115
Red Fox Site, 19
Red Lake, Minnesota, 122
Red River, 21, 22, 23, 49, 50, 51, 52, 56, 57, 59, 62, 87,
       124, 125, 142
       Red River carts, 64
       Red River Valley, 51, 55, 98, 122, 124, 142
Red Thunder, 51
Red Tomahawk, 121
Religion, 7, 24, 26, 29, 41, 42, 77, 82, 110, 118, 122, 132-
       133, 142
       Religious practices, 102, 143
       (See also Ceremonies)
Relocation, 131, 143
Renville County, 97
Renville, Gabriel, 87
Reservations, 4, 6, 7, 8-10, 24, 45, 56, 58, 59, 62, 63, 65,
       66-85, 86-103, 104-121, 122-140
Riel, Louis, 65
Rindisbacher, Peter, 45
River Crow, 13
River Women Society, 38
Robinson, Doane, 59
Robinson, Elwyn B., 2
Rocky Boy's Band, 124
Rocky Boy's Reservation, 129

Rocky Mountains, 22, 29, 104, 123
Rodeos, 65, 83, 102, 120
Rogers, Tom, Jr., 75
Rolette County, 64, 125, 132, 134, 135
Rolette, North Dakota, 136
Rolette, Joseph, 4
Rolla, North Dakota, 136, 137
Rousseau, Jean Jacques, 3
Rupert's Land, 123

Sacajawea, 4 (See also Sakakawea)
Sacred Bundles, 11, 32, 77, 83
Sacred cedar, 12
Salt River, 123
Sand painters, 4
Sanish, North Dakota, 74
Sakakawea, 65
Salaries, 118
Sanish, North Dakota, 74
Sans Arc tribe, 104, 106, (see also Lakota)
Santee tribe, 27, 58
Santee, Nebraska, 73
Saskatchewan, 123
Sault Ste. Marie, 52
School of the Good Shepherd, 127
Schools, 8, 51, 62, 63, 64, 65,66, 73-74, 81, 82, 92-94,
       99, 102, 108-109, 116, 126, 127, 129, 136-137
Scientists, 11, 15-16 (see also archaeologists and
       geologists)
Scottish, 6, 51, 122
Sears, Roebuck Company, 74
Second Regiment Band, 96
Secretary of the Interior, 7, 128, 131
Self-Determination and Education Act, 63, 143
Seligmann, Kurt, 4
Selkirk, Lord, 51, 64, 142
Seven Council Fires, 10 (See also Dakota, Lakota,
       Sioux)
Shacopay, 22
Shaking Tent, 130
Shell Creek, North Dakota, 74
Sheyenne River, 20, 22,23, 51,
Siberia, 16
Sibley, General Henry Hastings, 86
Sign language, 47, 142
Sioux, 3, 5, 10, 51, 52, 56, 58, 59, 66, 85, 86, 87, 88, 104,
       107
Sioux Falls, South Dakota, 56
Sipto, 90
Sisseton tribe, 27, 58, 86, 89-90
Sisseton Reservation, 8, 88, 91
Sisseton-Wahpeton Reservation, 88, 92, 142
Sisters of Mercy School, 126
Sitting Bull, 4, 5, 65, 106, 111, 112, 118, 121
Skinner, Alanson, 129

Skunk Women Society, 38
Slant Village, 23
Small Ankle, 67
Small Business Administration, 101
Smith, Edward, 125
Smith, Tom, 74
Solen, North Dakota, 120, 121
Son of a Star, 45, 65
Souris River, 52
South America, 17, 18
South Dakota, 8, 10, 20, 21, 56, 58, 104, 107, 118, 119
       Sioux Falls, 56
       Yankton, 21
Sovereignty, 62, 63
Spanish, 47, 49 (see also Europeans, Traders)
Spokesfield, Walter E., 91
Spotted Tail, 107
Sports, Indian influence on, 4, team names, 4
St. Ann's Day, 135, 138
St. Bernard's Mission School, 120
St. John, North Dakota, 127, 131, 136
St. Joseph, North Dakota, 122, 124, 125
St. Joseph's School, Rennsselaer, Indiana, 127
St. Michael, North Dakota, 90, 93, 101, 102
St. Joseph, 55
St. Jude's Elderly Home, 103
St. Paul, 55, 57, 64
Standing Bear, Luther, 35
Standing Rock, Ransom County, 23, Sioux County,
       23
Standing Rock Sioux Reservation, 6, 7, 8, 9, 23, 94,
       103, 104-121, 122
       Standing Rock Sioux Tribe, 2, 7, 104, 107
State Historical Society, 45, 85, 103
Steamboats, 56, 63, 65, 94
Stephan, J. A. 109, 112
Stereotypes, 2
Stevens, Jere, 91, 125
Stewart, Dr. A., 91, 94
Stock grazing, 79
Stories, 138
Subsistence, 23, 26, 30-32, 79, 90, 127, 130, 134
Sully, General Alfred, 58, 59
Sullys Hill National Game Preserve, 90, 100
Summer Wolverine, 124
Sun Dance, 24, 30, 41, 44, 71, 82, 102, 109, 122, 129,
       133, 138, 143, (see also Ceremonies)
Superintendent, 74, 75
Sweat Lodge, 44, 83, 102, 110, 118 (see also Ceremo-
       nies)
Swisher, Karen, 118
Swiss, 51
Symbols, 2, 4, 27, 33

Tanguy, Yves, influenced by Indians, 4
Ten Cent Treaty, 128, (see also Treaties)
Termination, see House Concurrent Resolution 108
Teton tribe, 51
Thompson, David, 50
Three Affiliated Tribes, 7, 9, 10, 63, 66-85, 116, 121
    Three Affiliated Tribes Business Council, 75
    (see also Fort Berthold Reservation)
Throwing the Ball, 44
Tiawashti, see Tiyowaste
Tiospaye, 29
Tipis, 19, 20, 26, 27, 29-30, 54, 92, 110, 122, 141, 142
    Tipi rings, 23
Tiyowashte, 59, 92, 95
Tobacco, 3, 11
Tokio, North Dakota, 90, 101, 102
Tools, 20, 30
Tourism, 10
Trade, 26, 31, 45, 47,   211
    Trade goods, 20, 25, 47, 56, 142
    Traders, 25, 31, 34, 47, 49, 50-51, 52, 55, 56, 65, 85
    Trading, 56, 127
    Trading post, 50, 51, 84, 122
Travois, 35
Treaties, 6, 56, 58, 59, 62, 63, 71, 88, 104, 105, 107, 124, 128, 131, 142, 143
    Treaty of Fort Laramie, 1851, 6, 10, 66, 105, 142
    Treaty of 1867, 88
    Treaty of 1868, 6, 11, 59, 105, 106, 107, 112
    Ten Cent Treaty, 128
    Treaty-making, 47, 57, 66
    Treaty council, 107
Trenton-Williston, 10, 129
Tribal council, 38, 51, 54, 63, 74, 75, 96, 98, 107, 116, 117
Tribal enrollment, 9, 127, 129, 131
Turtle Mountain Band of Chippewa, 5, 9, 10, 30, 63, 122-140, 142
    (see also Chippewa, Métis)
Turtle Mountain Manufacturing Company, 140
Turtle Mountain Reservation, 6, 7, 8, 10, 122-140, 142
Turtle Mountains, 22, 52, 122, 124
Twin Buttes, North Dakota, 77, 79, 82
Two Bears, 105, 108

Unemployment, 79
United Tribes Development Corporation, 131
University of North Dakota, 71, 103, 126, 140
Upper Yanktonai tribe, 105, 107, 112, (see also Yanktonai)
Urbanization, 8, 131, 143

Values, 77, 82, 99, 100
Van Hook, North Dakota, 74

Van Solen, George, 121
Veterans Day, 102
Vice-President, Indian, 4
Victory dances, 75, 115
Villages, 6, 12, 19, 21, 23, 25, 26-30, 32, 36, 45, 48, 49, 50, 56, 59, 66, 67, 71, 75, 76, 77, 85, 141, 142
    Village organization, 26, 32
    (see also Like-a-Fishhook Village)
Vision quest, 33-34, 44, 83, 118, (see also Ceremonies)

Waanatan Day School, 94
Wahpakoota tribe, 58
Wahpeton, North Dakota 4,
Wahpeton tribe, 27, 58, 86, 90
Wakan Tanka, 42
Wakpala, South Dakota, 116, 120
Walhalla, North Dakota, 45, 122, 125
Walker, James, 15
Wanatan, 51, 59,
Warfare, 6, 24, 36, 142
Warren, William, 14, 15
Warriors, 38, 56, 59, 142
Wars, 6
    World War I, 2, 74-75, 96
    World War II, 3, 4, 98
    War of 1812, 51
    (see also Dakota Conflict, Korean Conflict)
Warwick, North Dakota, 101, 102
Warwick Public School, 102
Washington, D.C., 7, 63, 91, 128
Water resources, 7, 103, 121
Waugh, John H., 90
Wee-sa-kay-jac, 127, 138
Welfare, see Public assistance
Wells County, 91
White Buffalo Calf Society, 38
White people, 5, 32, 49, 51, 52, 55, 56, 59, 63, 64, 65, 66, 72, 74, 75, 77, 79, 81, 85, 88, 100, 104, 105, 107, 110, 124, 142
    White officials, 105
    White settlers, 7, 106, 111, 114, 130, 137
    (see also Agents, Europeans, Traders)
White Shield, North Dakota, 77, 79, 82, 83
White, Florence, 103
Whitestone Hill, 58
Wied-Neuwied, Prince Maximilian, 11, 12, 25, 49, 52, 64
Wigwam, 30
Wild rice, 31
Wild turnip, 31
Wilkie, Jean Baptiste, [Wilky], 54, 65
Wilkie, Leo, 140
Williams County, 132, 135
Williston, North Dakota, 23 (see also Trenton-Williston)

Wills, Oscar H., 45
Windy Grass, 75
Winnipeg, 51, 55, 64
Wolf Chief, 15
Wood Lake, North Dakota, 90
Woodland period, 19-29, 141
Woods, Brevet Major Samuel, 52, 54
Woody Mountain, Saskatchewan, 123, 125
Work (see Employment)
Wounded Knee, South Dakota, 112
Writers, Indian, 10, non-Indian, 2
Wyoming, 104

Yankton, South Dakota, 21
Yankton tribe, 5, 6, 10, 51, 56, 87,
Yankton Reservation, 56
Yanktonai tribe, 5, 6, 10, 21, 23, 26, 27, 31, 44, 48, 51, 56, 86, 87, 89, 90, 68, 73, 77, 78, 106, 142, (see also Cuthead band of Yanktonai)
Yellowstone River, 23, 66, 77

Zimmerman, William F., Jr., 96